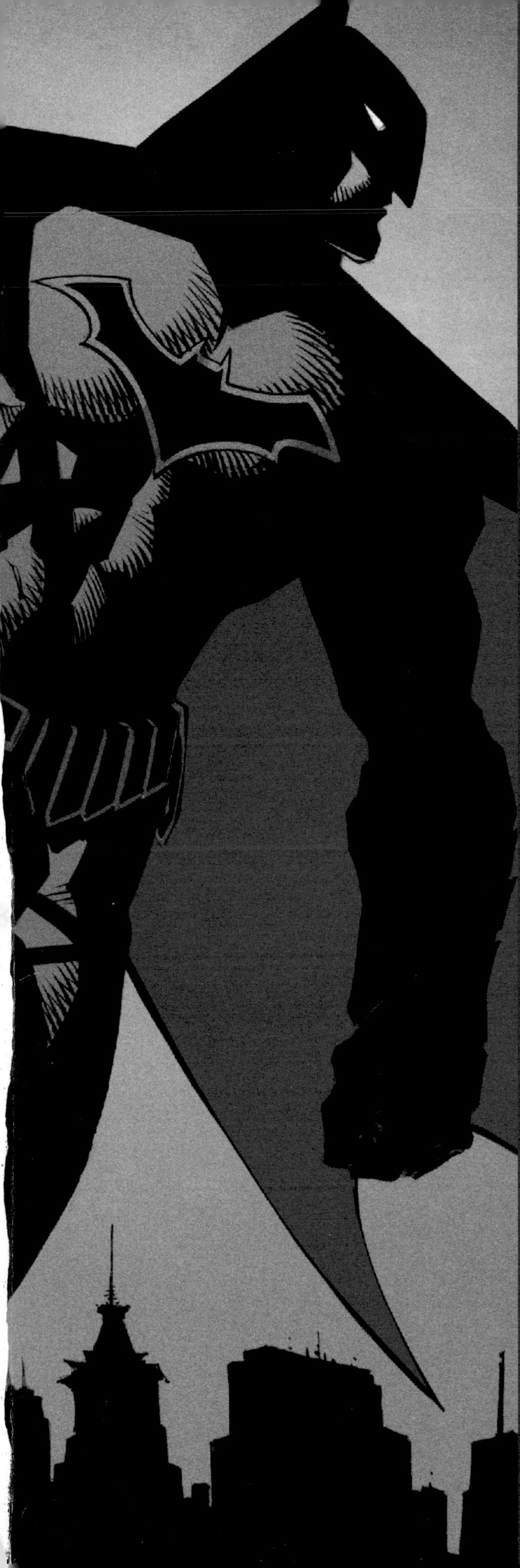

BATMAN

VOLUME 10

EPILOGUE

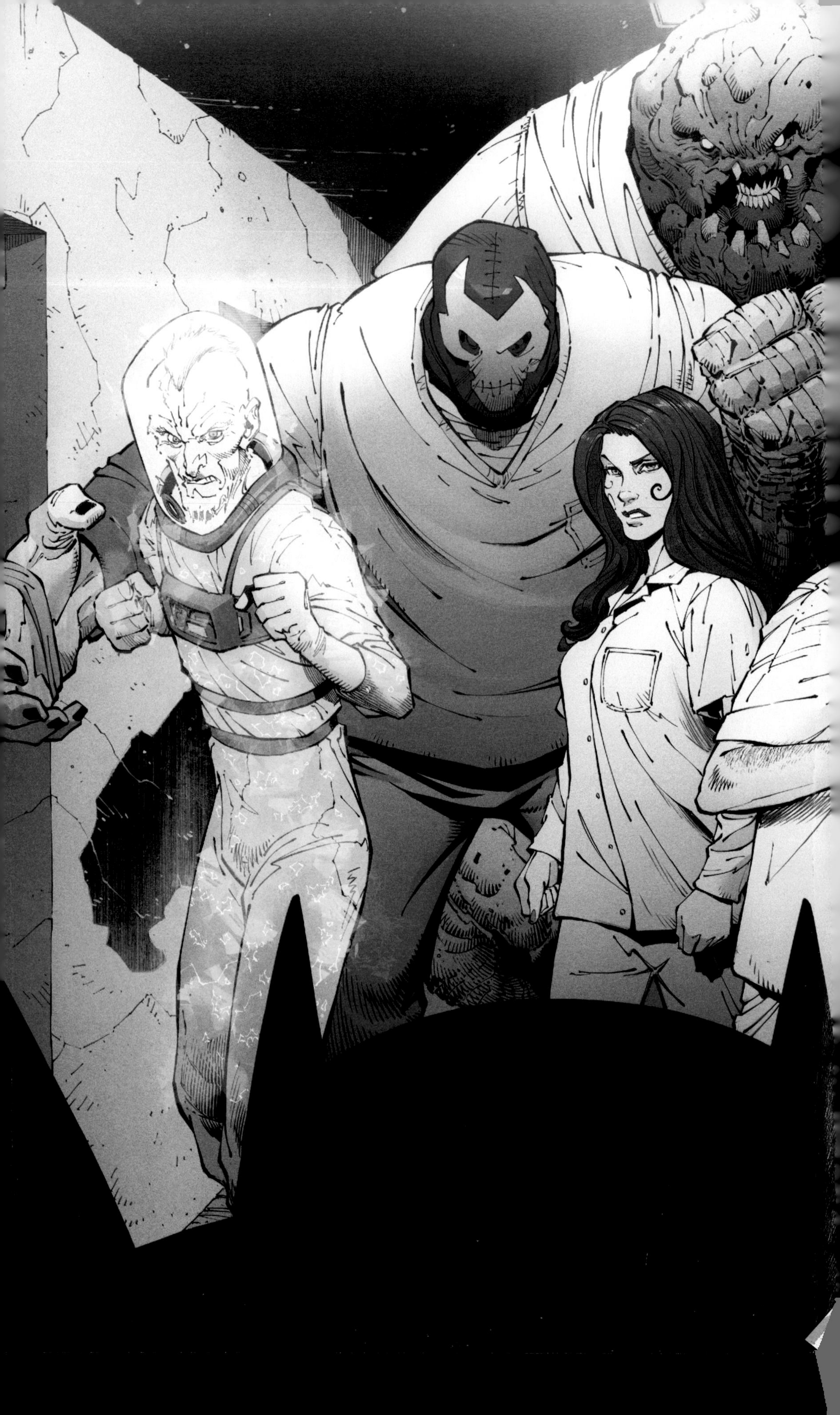

VOLUME 10
EPILOGUE

BATMAN

WRITTEN BY
SCOTT SNYDER
JAMES TYNION IV
RAY FAWKES

ART BY
GREG CAPULLO
ROGE ANTONIO
ACO
RILEY ROSSMO
DANNY MIKI
BRIAN LEVEL

COLOR BY
FCO PLASCENCIA
DAVE McCAIG
IVAN PLASCENCIA
JORDAN BOYD

LETTERS BY
STEVE WANDS
DEZI SIENTY
CARLOS M. MANGUAL

COLLECTION COVER ART BY
GREG CAPULLO,
DANNY MIKI &
FCO PLASCENCIA

BATMAN CREATED BY
BOB KANE with **BILL FINGER**

MARK DOYLE Editor – Original Series
REBECCA TAYLOR Associate Editor – Original Series
MATT HUMPHREYS Assistant Editor – Original Series
JEB WOODARD Group Editor – Collected Editions
ROBIN WILDMAN Editor – Collected Edition
STEVE COOK Design Director – Books
DAMIAN RYLAND Publication Design

BOB HARRAS Senior VP – Editor-in-Chief, DC Comics

DIANE NELSON President
DAN DiDIO Publisher
JIM LEE Publisher
GEOFF JOHNS President & Chief Creative Officer
AMIT DESAI Executive VP – Business & Marketing Strategy, Direct to
Consumer & Global Franchise Management
SAM ADES Senior VP – Direct to Consumer
BOBBIE CHASE VP – Talent Development
MARK CHIARELLO Senior VP – Art, Design & Collected Editions
JOHN CUNNINGHAM Senior VP – Sales & Trade Marketing
ANNE DePIES Senior VP – Business Strategy, Finance & Administration
DON FALLETTI VP – Manufacturing Operations
LAWRENCE GANEM VP – Editorial Administration & Talent Relations
ALISON GILL Senior VP – Manufacturing & Operations
HANK KANALZ Senior VP – Editorial Strategy & Administration
JAY KOGAN VP – Legal Affairs
THOMAS LOFTUS VP – Business Affairs
JACK MAHAN VP – Business Affairs
NICK J. NAPOLITANO VP – Manufacturing Administration
EDDIE SCANNELL VP – Consumer Marketing
COURTNEY SIMMONS Senior VP – Publicity & Communications
JIM (SKI) SOKOLOWSKI VP – Comic Book Specialty Sales & Trade Marketing
NANCY SPEARS VP – Mass, Book, Digital Sales & Trade Marketing

BATMAN VOLUME 10: EPILOGUE

Published by DC Comics. Compilation and all new material Copyright © 2016 DC Comics. All Rights Reserved. Originally
published in single magazine form in BATMAN 51-52, BATMAN ANNUAL 4, BATMAN: FUTURES END 1, BATMAN: REBIRTH 1.
Copyright © 2014, 2015, 2016 DC Comics. All Rights Reserved. All characters, their distinctive likenesses and related elements
featured in this publication are trademarks of DC Comics. The stories, characters and incidents featured in this publication are
entirely fictional. DC Comics does not read or accept unsolicited submissions of ideas, stories or artwork.

DC Comics, 2900 West Alameda Ave., Burbank, CA 91505
Printed by LSC Communications, Salem, VA, USA. 11/11/16. First Printing.
ISBN: 978-1-4012-6773-5

Library of Congress Cataloging-in-Publication Data is available.

PEFC Certified

Printed on paper from
sustainably managed
forests, controlled
sources

PEFC

PEFC/29-31-337   www.pefc.org

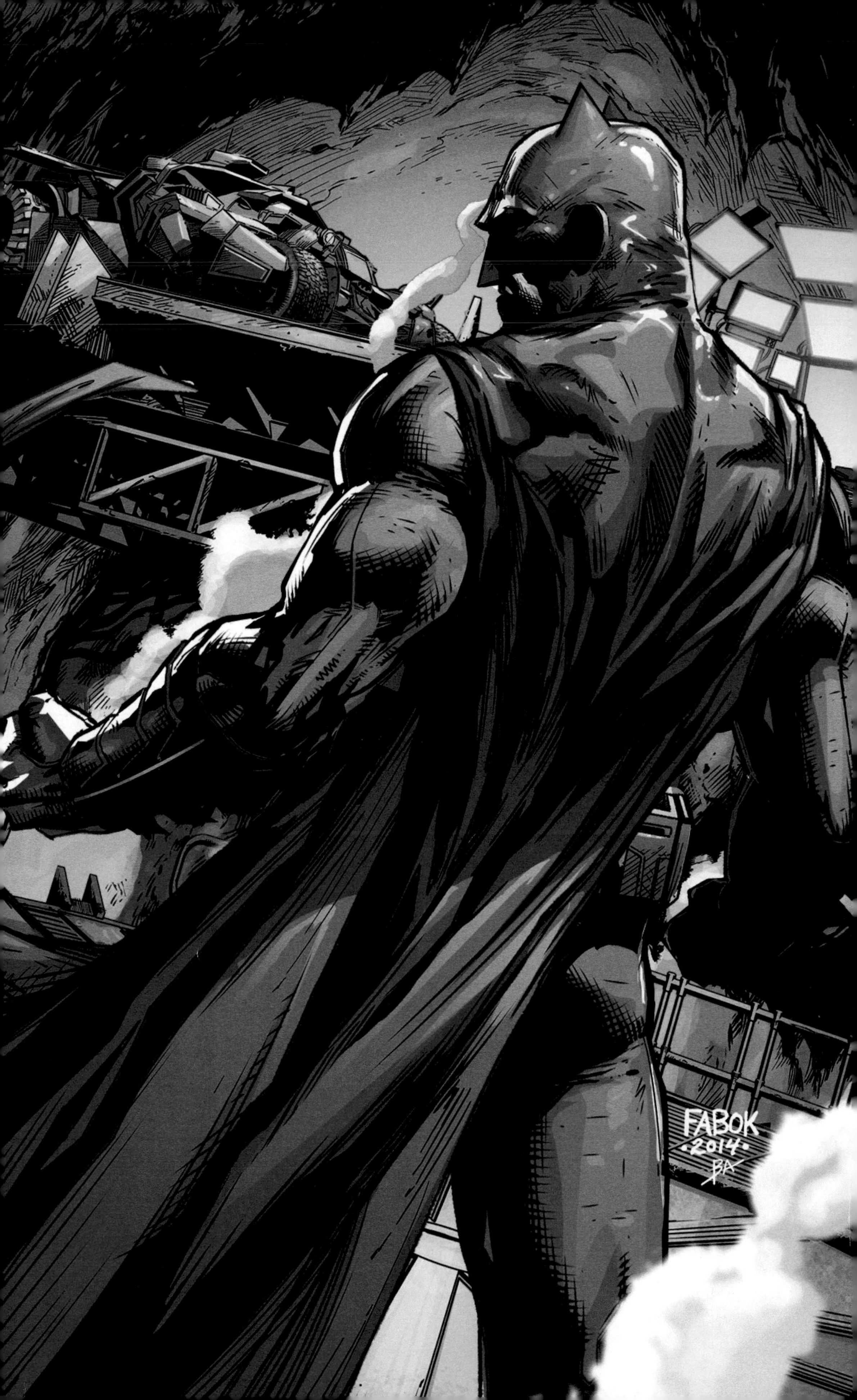
FABOK
·2014·
BA

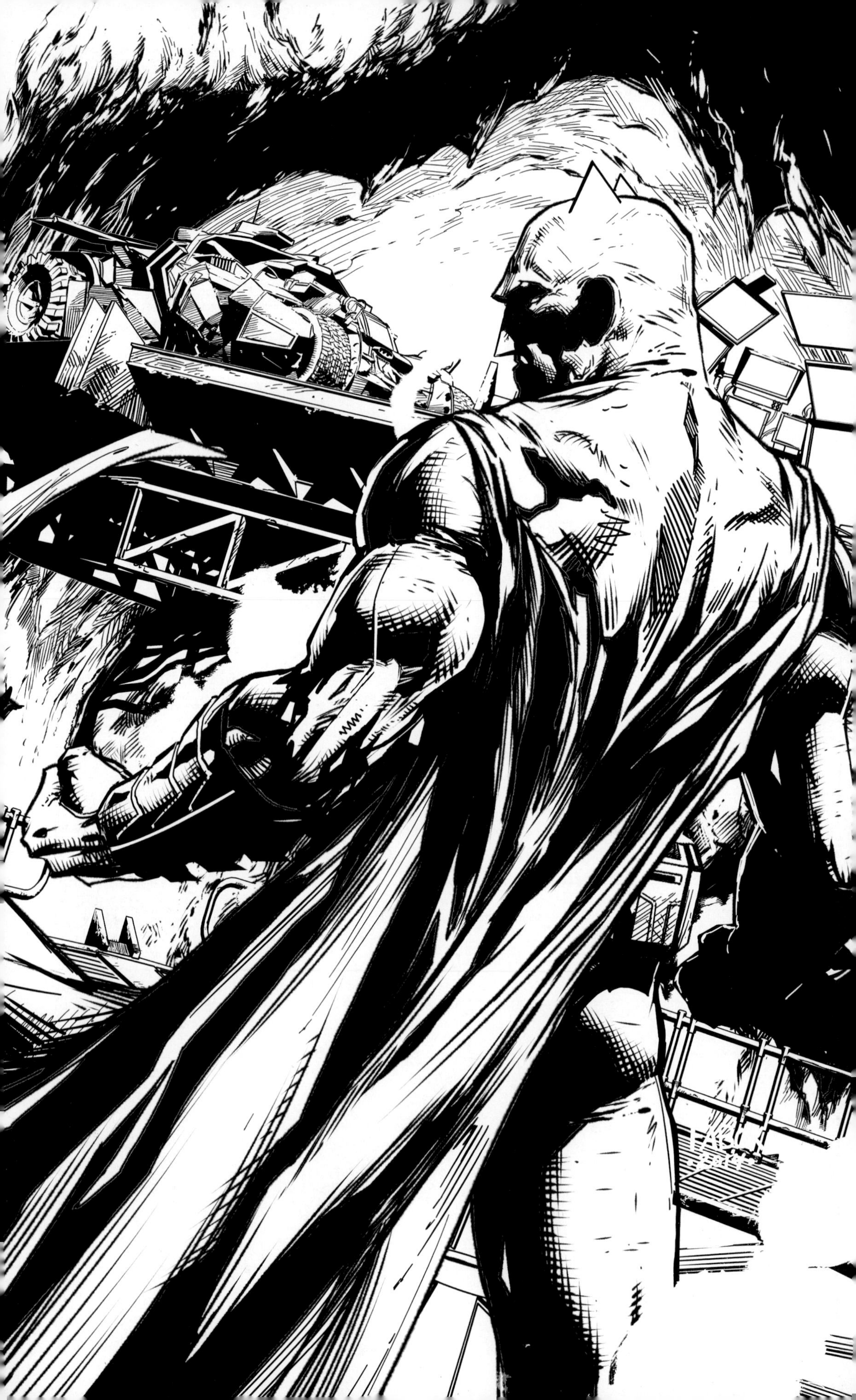

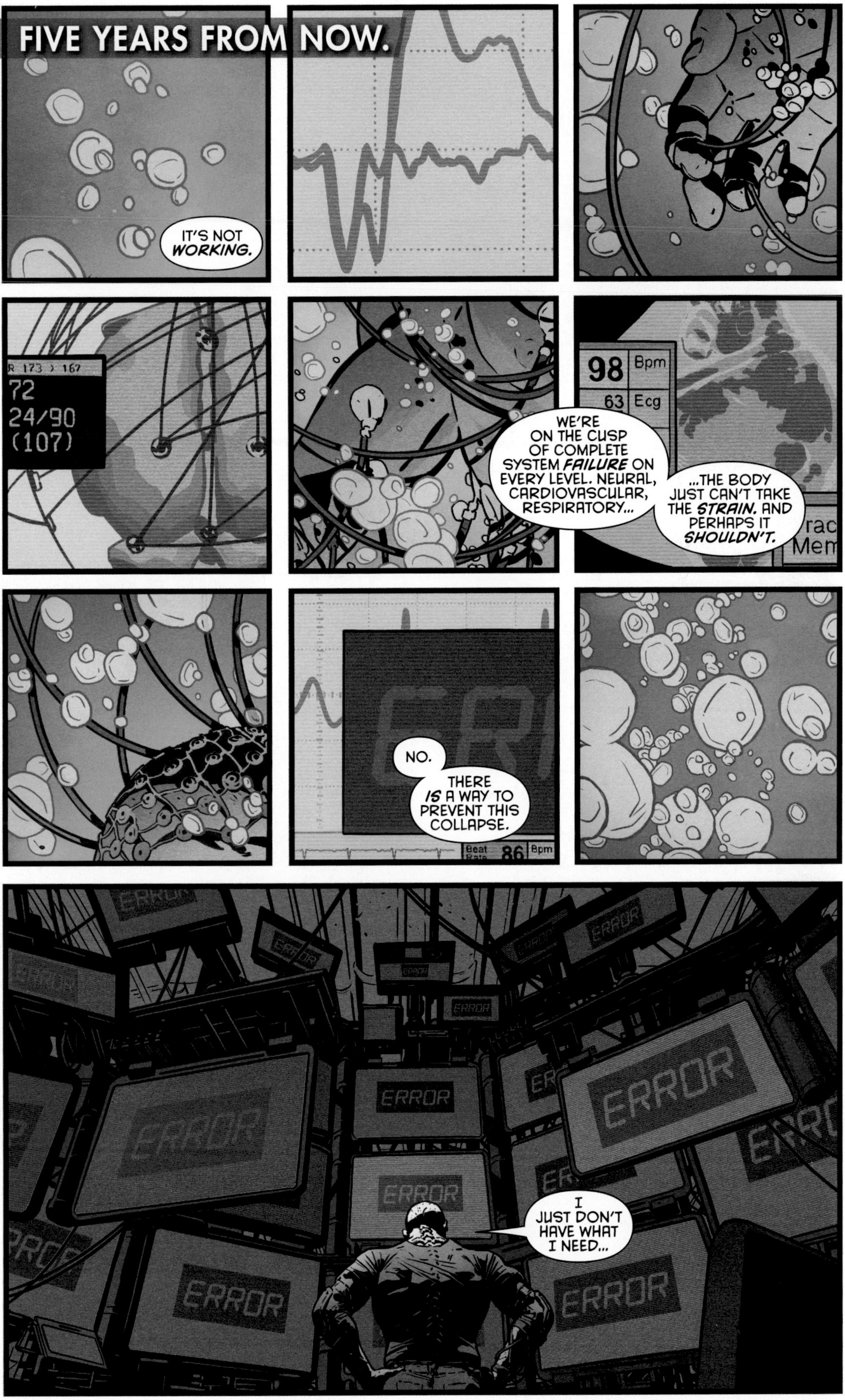
FIVE YEARS FROM NOW.
IT'S NOT WORKING.
72
24/90
(107)
98 Bpm
63 Ecg
WE'RE ON THE CUSP OF COMPLETE SYSTEM FAILURE ON EVERY LEVEL. NEURAL, CARDIOVASCULAR, RESPIRATORY...
...THE BODY JUST CAN'T TAKE THE STRAIN. AND PERHAPS IT SHOULDN'T.
NO.
THERE IS A WAY TO PREVENT THIS COLLAPSE.
Beat Rate 86 Bpm
ERROR
I JUST DON'T HAVE WHAT I NEED...

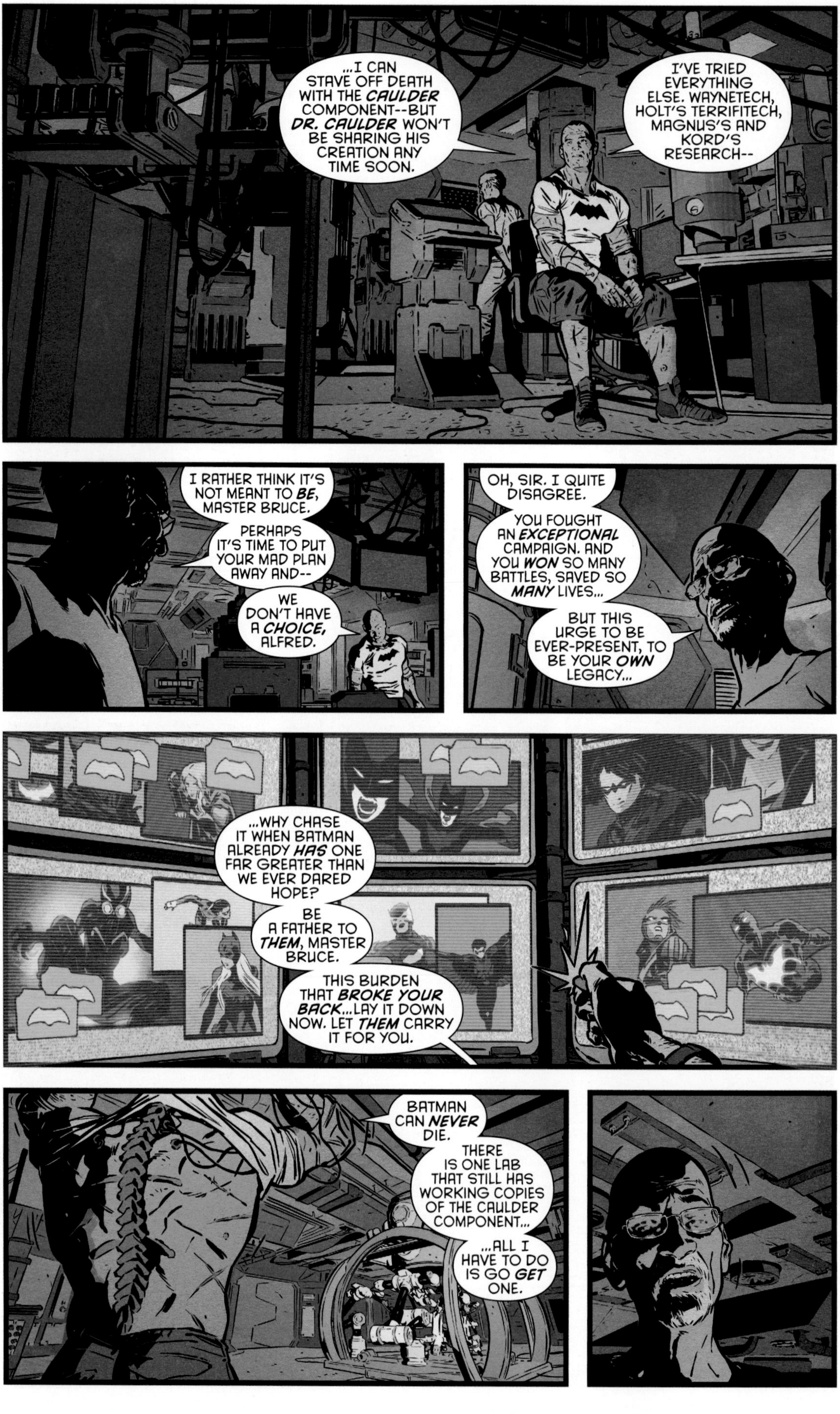
...I CAN STAVE OFF DEATH WITH THE CAULDER COMPONENT--BUT DR. CAULDER WON'T BE SHARING HIS CREATION ANY TIME SOON.
I'VE TRIED EVERYTHING ELSE. WAYNETECH, HOLT'S TERRIFITECH, MAGNUS'S AND KORD'S RESEARCH--
I RATHER THINK IT'S NOT MEANT TO BE, MASTER BRUCE.
PERHAPS IT'S TIME TO PUT YOUR MAD PLAN AWAY AND--
WE DON'T HAVE A CHOICE, ALFRED.
OH, SIR. I QUITE DISAGREE.
YOU FOUGHT AN EXCEPTIONAL CAMPAIGN. AND YOU WON SO MANY BATTLES, SAVED SO MANY LIVES...
BUT THIS URGE TO BE EVER-PRESENT, TO BE YOUR OWN LEGACY...
...WHY CHASE IT WHEN BATMAN ALREADY HAS ONE FAR GREATER THAN WE EVER DARED HOPE?
BE A FATHER TO THEM, MASTER BRUCE.
THIS BURDEN THAT BROKE YOUR BACK...LAY IT DOWN NOW. LET THEM CARRY IT FOR YOU.
BATMAN CAN NEVER DIE.
THERE IS ONE LAB THAT STILL HAS WORKING COPIES OF THE CAULDER COMPONENT...
...ALL I HAVE TO DO IS GO GET ONE.

SIR, NO! YOU CAN'T BE SERIOUS! THE SECURITY ON THAT PLACE IS *LETHAL.* YOU'VE DECLARED IT *OFF-LIMITS* TO ALL OF YOUR PEOPLE...

YOUR BACK, YOUR LEGS...EVEN AT YOUR *BEST* YOU CAN'T POSSIBLY--

INITIATE.

SUIT ME UP.

INITIATING.

EMERGENCY PROTOCOL.

FZZT

THE PAINKILLERS AND STIMULANTS WILL GIVE ME ABOUT *FORTY MINUTES* FROM TOUCHDOWN.

KSSH

NANOMESH WILL HOLD ME TOGETHER WHILE I GET THE JOB DONE.

WHIRR

YES, MASTER BRUCE, LIKE ELASTIC BANDS ON A *PUPPET.* AND WHEN THE TIME RUNS OUT, THEY'LL *SNAP...*

...YOU'LL FALL TO *PIECES.*

CLINK

NOT IF I DO THIS *RIGHT.*

AND WHEN I'M DONE, I'LL MAKE SURE TO GET BACK HERE SO YOU CAN PUT ME BACK TOGETHER.

WILL YOU MAN THE SYSTEMS FOR ME, OLD FRIEND?

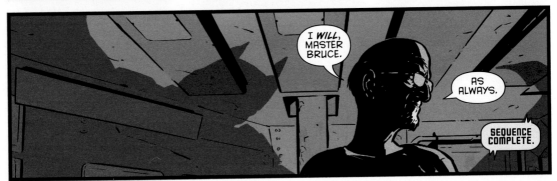

I *WILL,* MASTER BRUCE.

AS ALWAYS.

SEQUENCE COMPLETE.

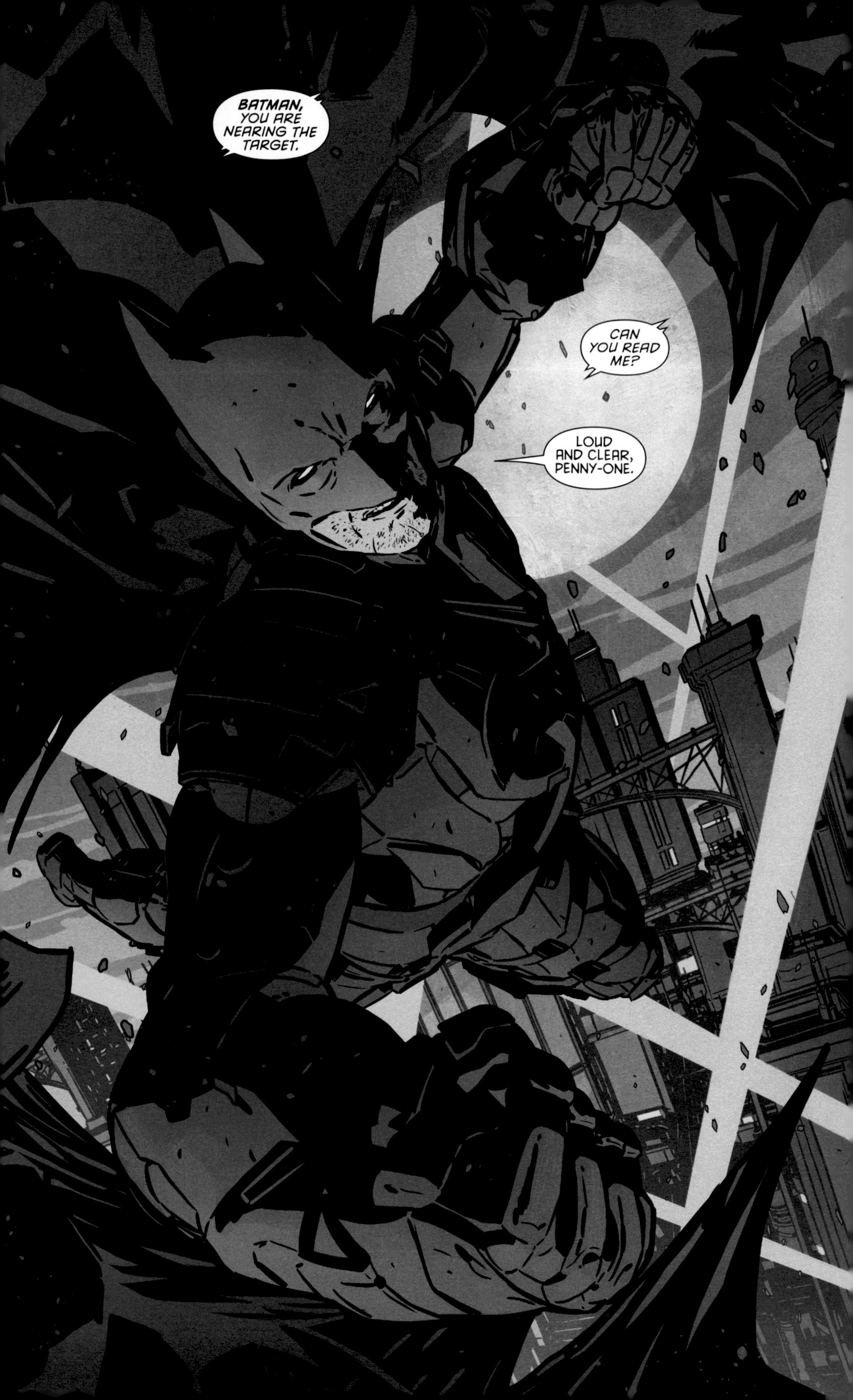
BATMAN, YOU ARE NEARING THE TARGET.
CAN YOU READ ME?
LOUD AND CLEAR, PENNY-ONE.

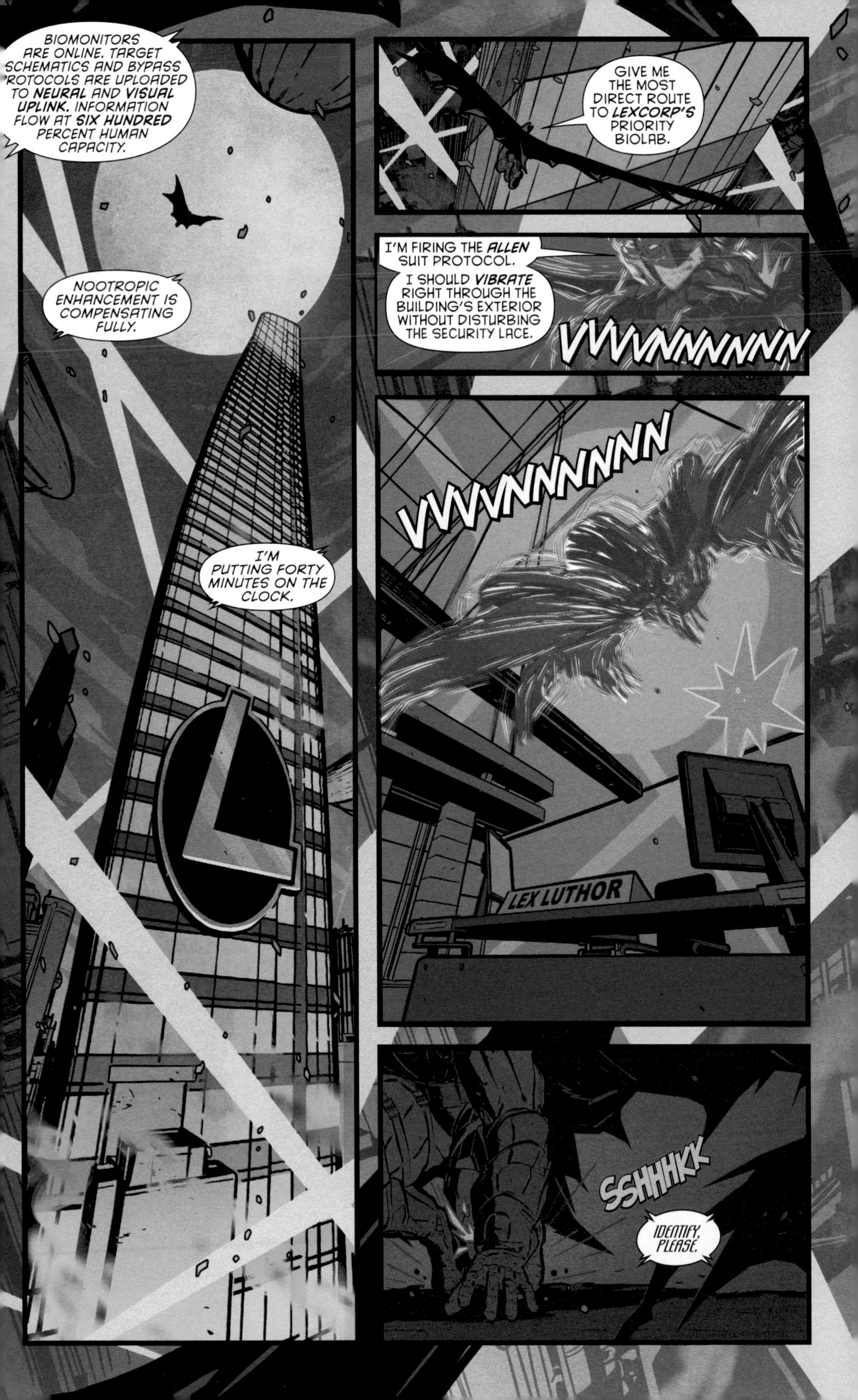
BIOMONITORS ARE ONLINE. TARGET SCHEMATICS AND BYPASS PROTOCOLS ARE UPLOADED TO NEURAL AND VISUAL UPLINK. INFORMATION FLOW AT SIX HUNDRED PERCENT HUMAN CAPACITY.
NOOTROPIC ENHANCEMENT IS COMPENSATING FULLY.
I'M PUTTING FORTY MINUTES ON THE CLOCK.
GIVE ME THE MOST DIRECT ROUTE TO LEXCORP'S PRIORITY BIOLAB.
I'M FIRING THE ALLEN SUIT PROTOCOL.
I SHOULD VIBRATE RIGHT THROUGH THE BUILDING'S EXTERIOR WITHOUT DISTURBING THE SECURITY LACE.
VVVVNNNNNNN
VVVVNNNNNNN
LEX LUTHOR
SSHHHKK
IDENTIFY, PLEASE.

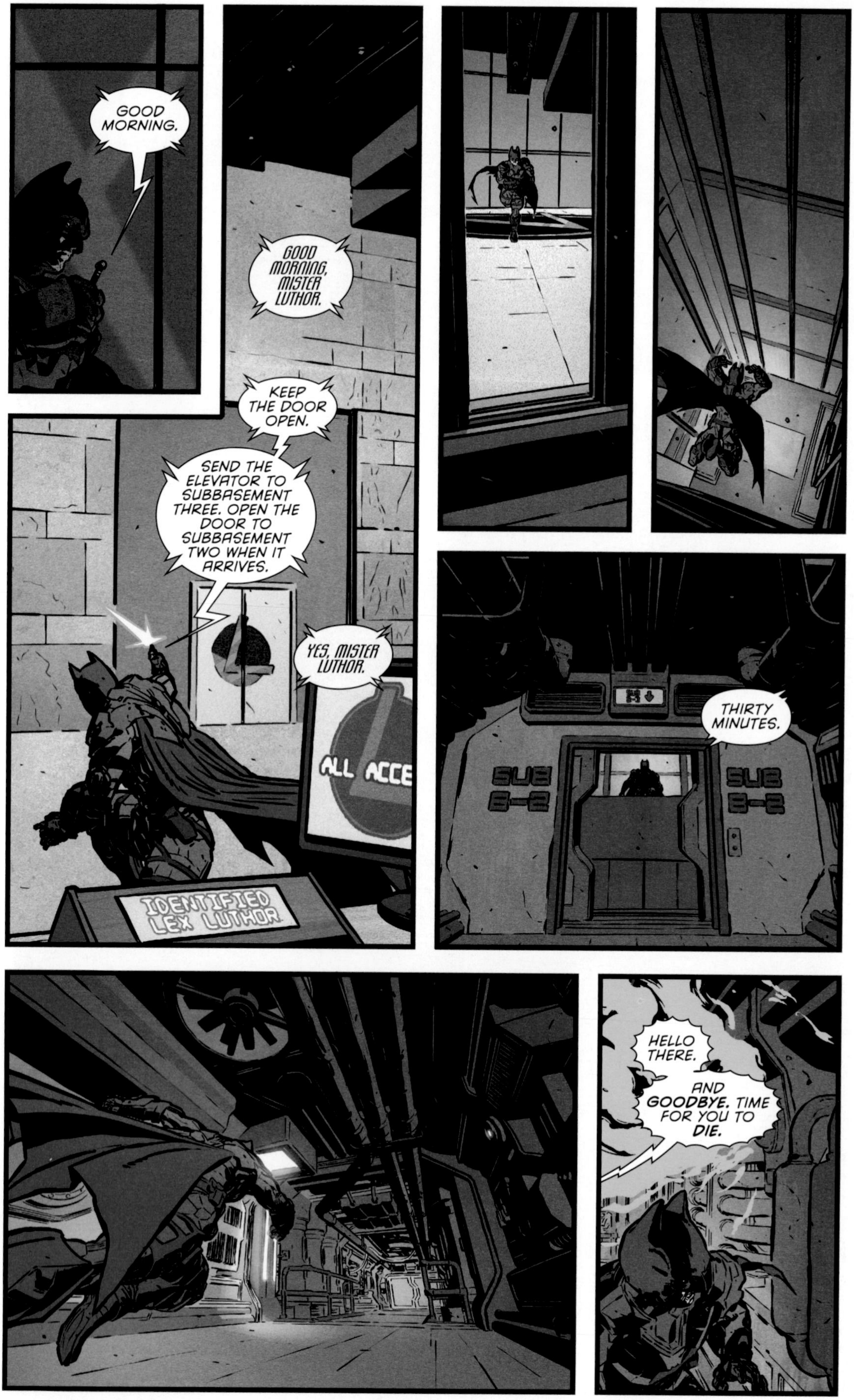
GOOD MORNING.
GOOD MORNING, MISTER LUTHOR.
KEEP THE DOOR OPEN.
SEND THE ELEVATOR TO SUBBASEMENT THREE. OPEN THE DOOR TO SUBBASEMENT TWO WHEN IT ARRIVES.
YES, MISTER LUTHOR.
ALL ACCE
IDENTIFIED LEX LUTHOR
SUB B-2
SUB B-2
THIRTY MINUTES.
HELLO THERE.
AND GOODBYE. TIME FOR YOU TO DIE.

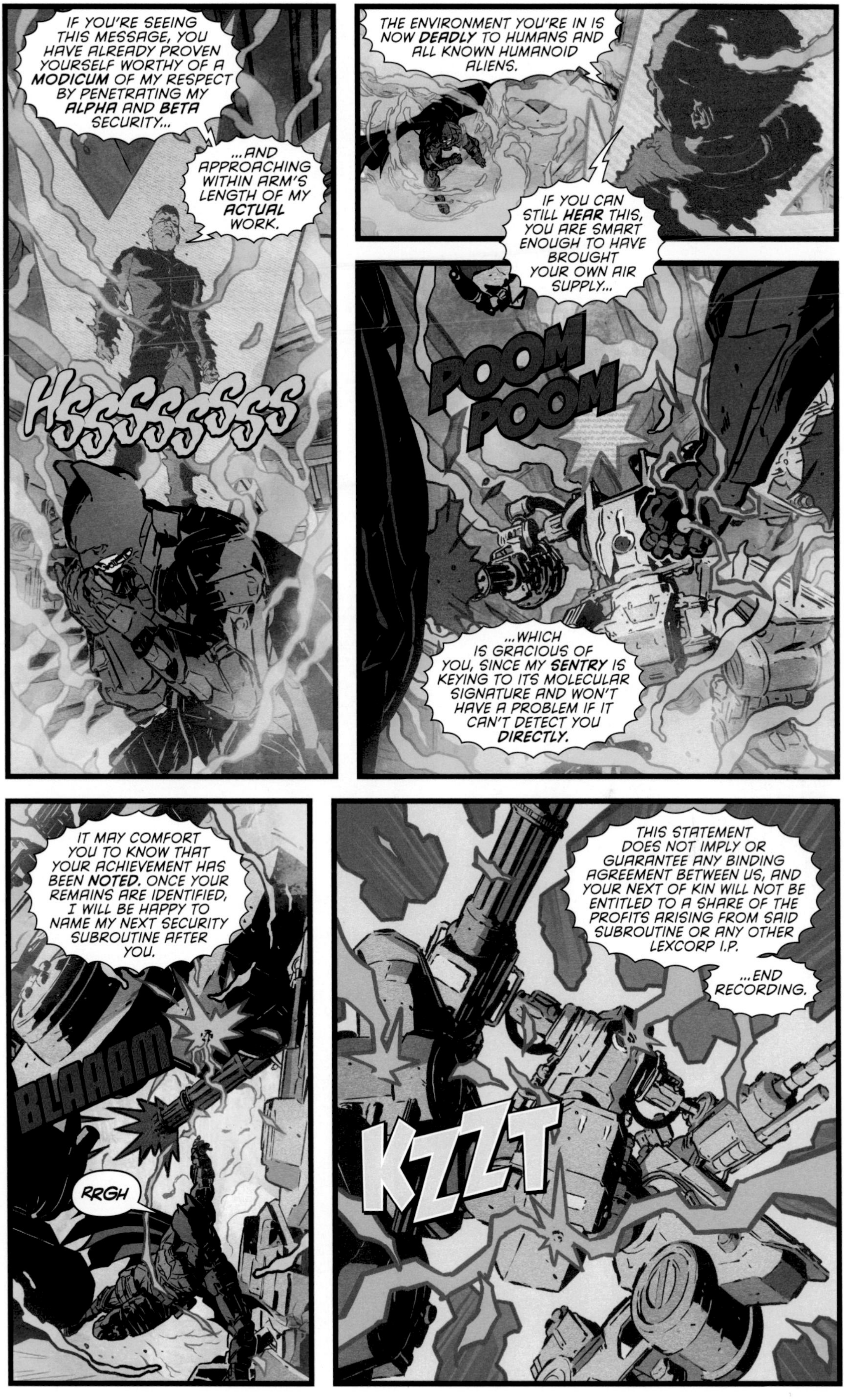
IF YOU'RE SEEING THIS MESSAGE, YOU HAVE ALREADY PROVEN YOURSELF WORTHY OF A MODICUM OF MY RESPECT BY PENETRATING MY ALPHA AND BETA SECURITY...
...AND APPROACHING WITHIN ARM'S LENGTH OF MY ACTUAL WORK.
HSSSSSSSS
THE ENVIRONMENT YOU'RE IN IS NOW DEADLY TO HUMANS AND ALL KNOWN HUMANOID ALIENS.
IF YOU CAN STILL HEAR THIS, YOU ARE SMART ENOUGH TO HAVE BROUGHT YOUR OWN AIR SUPPLY...
POOM POOM
...WHICH IS GRACIOUS OF YOU, SINCE MY SENTRY IS KEYING TO ITS MOLECULAR SIGNATURE AND WON'T HAVE A PROBLEM IF IT CAN'T DETECT YOU DIRECTLY.
IT MAY COMFORT YOU TO KNOW THAT YOUR ACHIEVEMENT HAS BEEN NOTED. ONCE YOUR REMAINS ARE IDENTIFIED, I WILL BE HAPPY TO NAME MY NEXT SECURITY SUBROUTINE AFTER YOU.
BLAAAM
RRGH
THIS STATEMENT DOES NOT IMPLY OR GUARANTEE ANY BINDING AGREEMENT BETWEEN US, AND YOUR NEXT OF KIN WILL NOT BE ENTITLED TO A SHARE OF THE PROFITS ARISING FROM SAID SUBROUTINE OR ANY OTHER LEXCORP I.P.
...END RECORDING.
KZZT

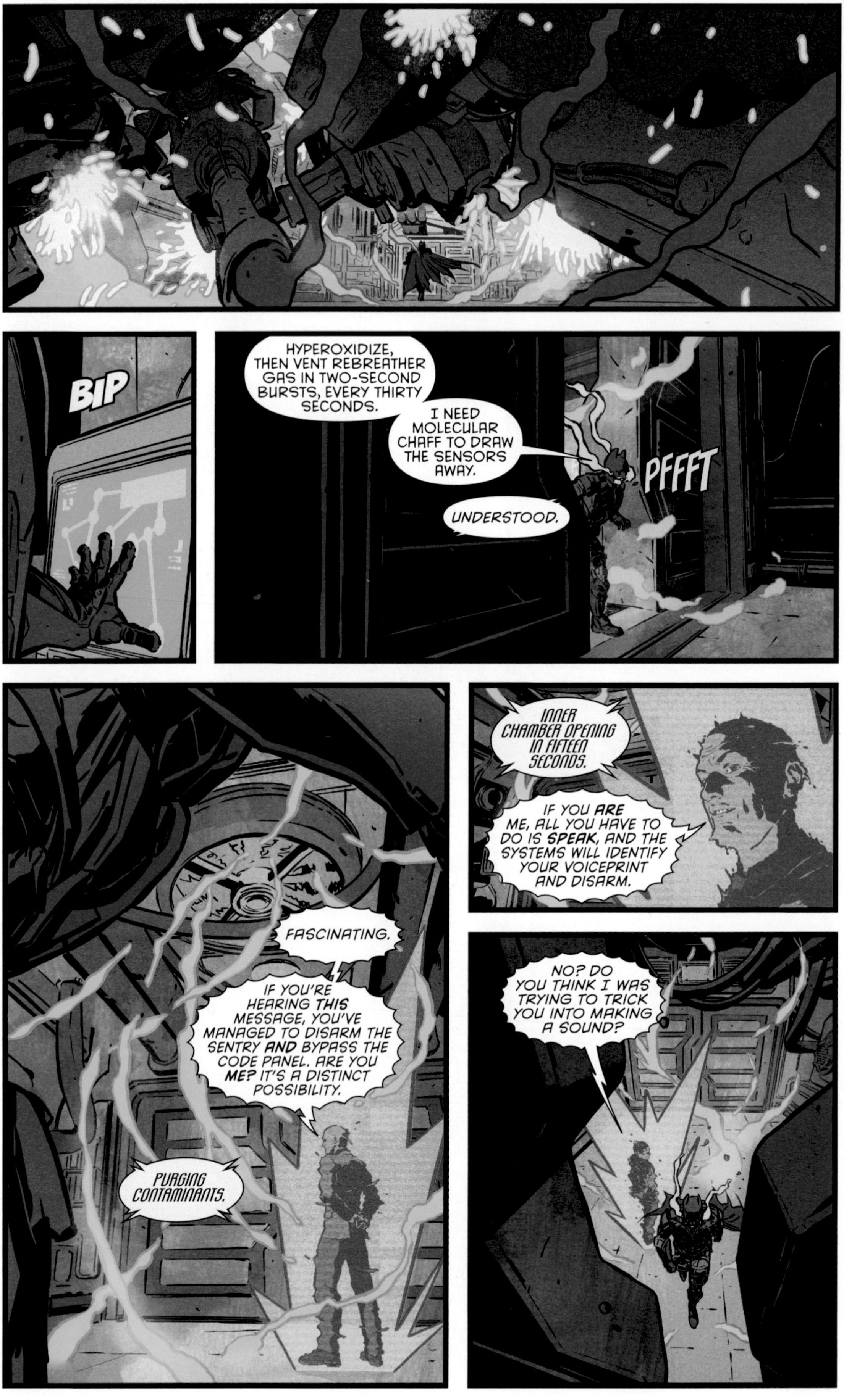
BIP
HYPEROXIDIZE, THEN VENT REBREATHER GAS IN TWO-SECOND BURSTS, EVERY THIRTY SECONDS.
I NEED MOLECULAR CHAFF TO DRAW THE SENSORS AWAY.
UNDERSTOOD.
PFFFT
FASCINATING.
IF YOU'RE HEARING THIS MESSAGE, YOU'VE MANAGED TO DISARM THE SENTRY AND BYPASS THE CODE PANEL. ARE YOU ME? IT'S A DISTINCT POSSIBILITY.
PURGING CONTAMINANTS.
INNER CHAMBER OPENING IN FIFTEEN SECONDS.
IF YOU ARE ME, ALL YOU HAVE TO DO IS SPEAK, AND THE SYSTEMS WILL IDENTIFY YOUR VOICEPRINT AND DISARM.
NO? DO YOU THINK I WAS TRYING TO TRICK YOU INTO MAKING A SOUND?

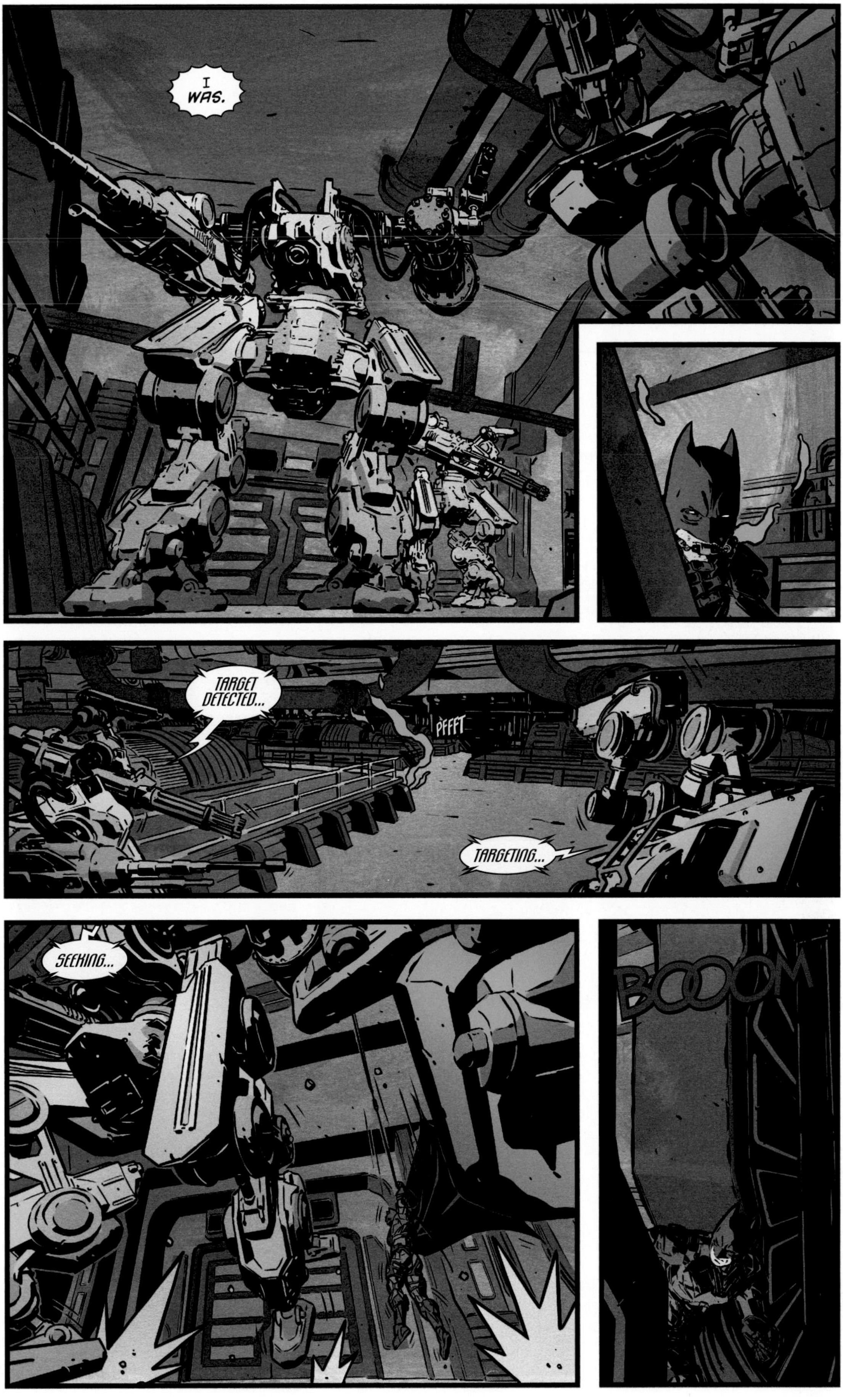
I WAS.
TARGET DETECTED...
PFFFT
TARGETING...
SEEKING...
BOOOM

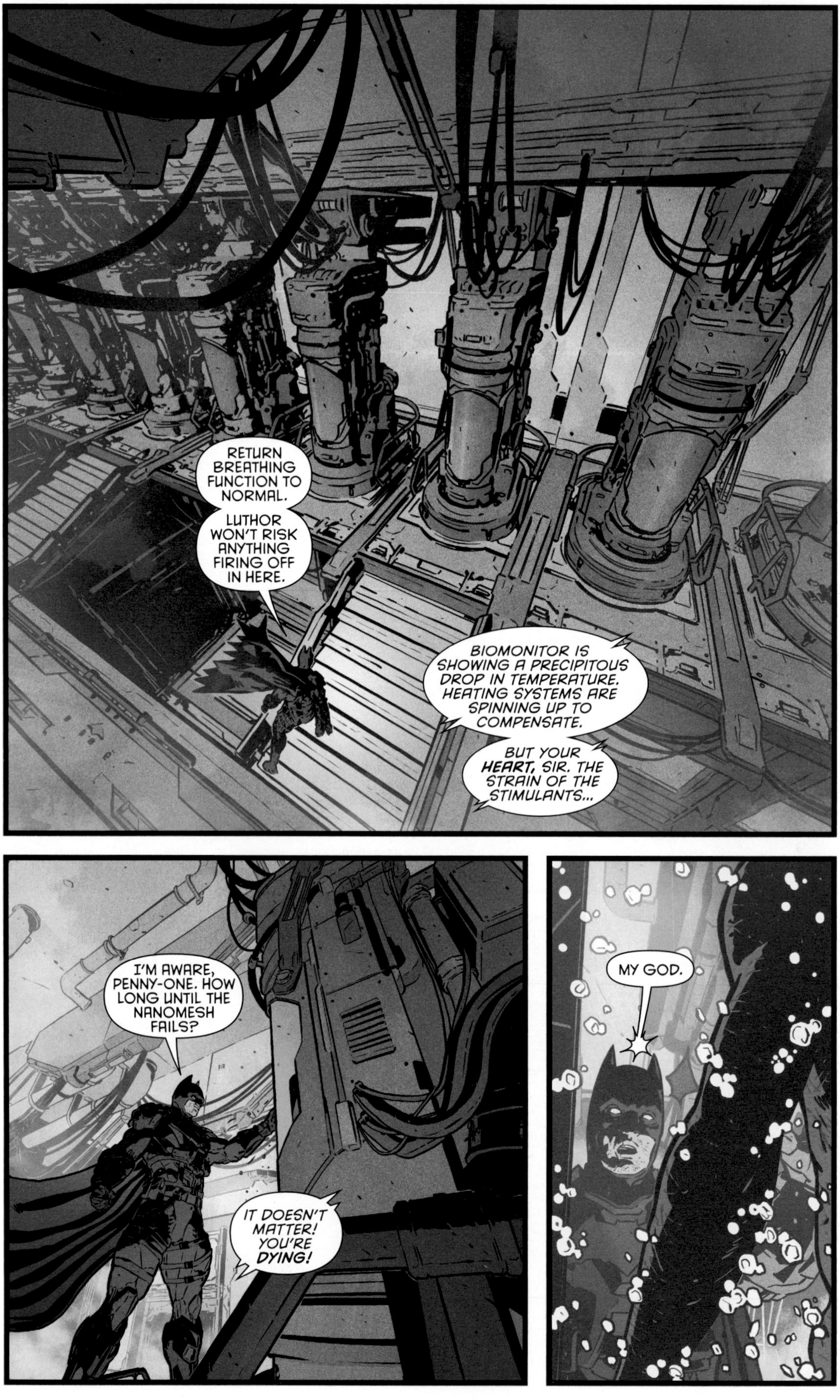
RETURN BREATHING FUNCTION TO NORMAL.
LUTHOR WON'T RISK ANYTHING FIRING OFF IN HERE.
BIOMONITOR IS SHOWING A PRECIPITOUS DROP IN TEMPERATURE. HEATING SYSTEMS ARE SPINNING UP TO COMPENSATE.
BUT YOUR HEART, SIR. THE STRAIN OF THE STIMULANTS...
I'M AWARE, PENNY-ONE. HOW LONG UNTIL THE NANOMESH FAILS?
IT DOESN'T MATTER! YOU'RE DYING!
MY GOD.

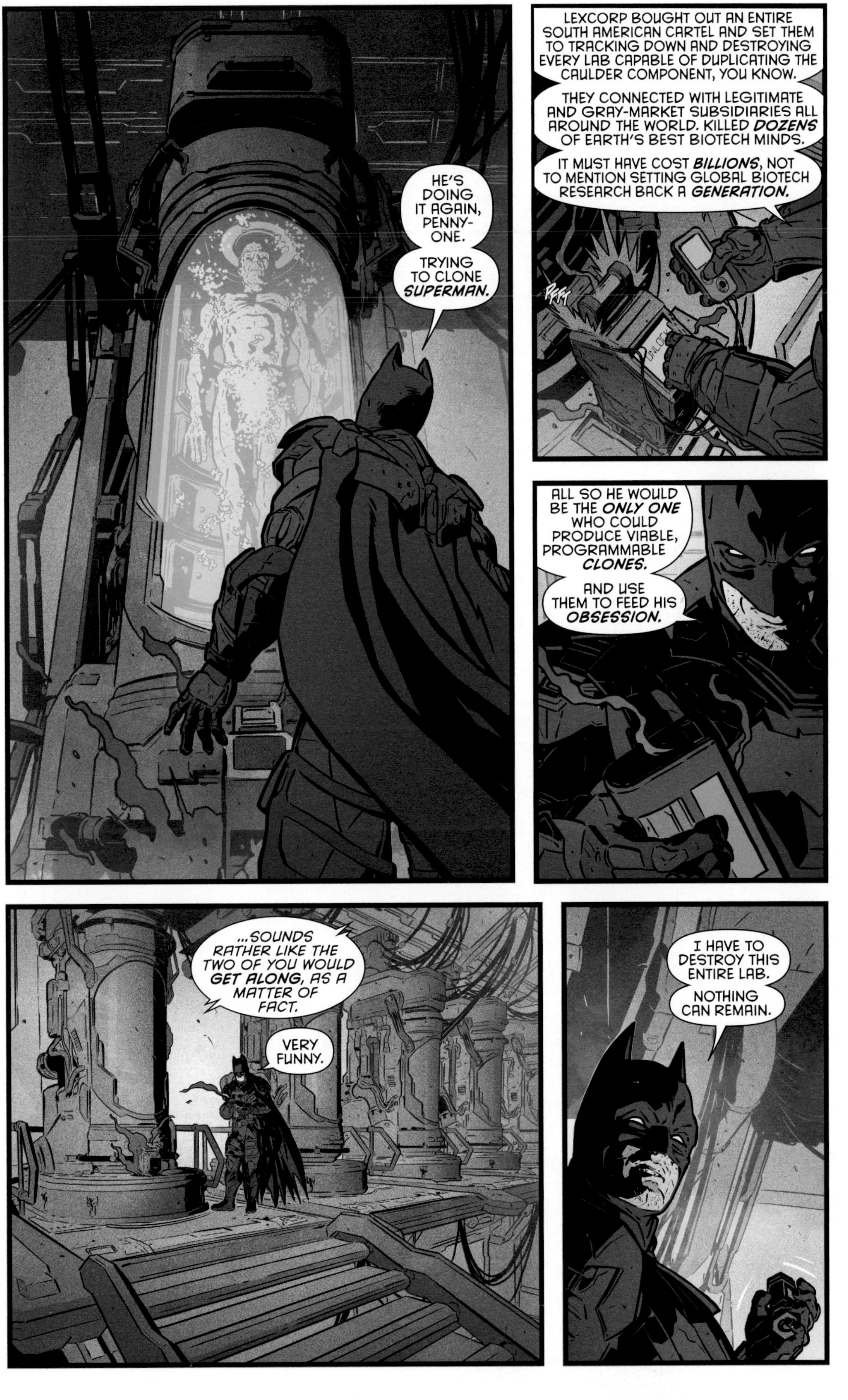
HE'S DOING IT AGAIN, PENNY-ONE.
TRYING TO CLONE *SUPERMAN.*
LEXCORP BOUGHT OUT AN ENTIRE SOUTH AMERICAN CARTEL AND SET THEM TO TRACKING DOWN AND DESTROYING EVERY LAB CAPABLE OF DUPLICATING THE CAULDER COMPONENT, YOU KNOW.
THEY CONNECTED WITH LEGITIMATE AND GRAY-MARKET SUBSIDIARIES ALL AROUND THE WORLD. KILLED *DOZENS* OF EARTH'S BEST BIOTECH MINDS.
IT MUST HAVE COST *BILLIONS*, NOT TO MENTION SETTING GLOBAL BIOTECH RESEARCH BACK A *GENERATION.*
PFFT
UNLOCK
ALL SO HE WOULD BE THE *ONLY ONE* WHO COULD PRODUCE VIABLE, PROGRAMMABLE *CLONES.*
AND USE THEM TO FEED HIS *OBSESSION.*
...SOUNDS RATHER LIKE THE TWO OF YOU WOULD *GET ALONG*, AS A MATTER OF FACT.
VERY FUNNY.
I HAVE TO DESTROY THIS ENTIRE LAB.
NOTHING CAN REMAIN.

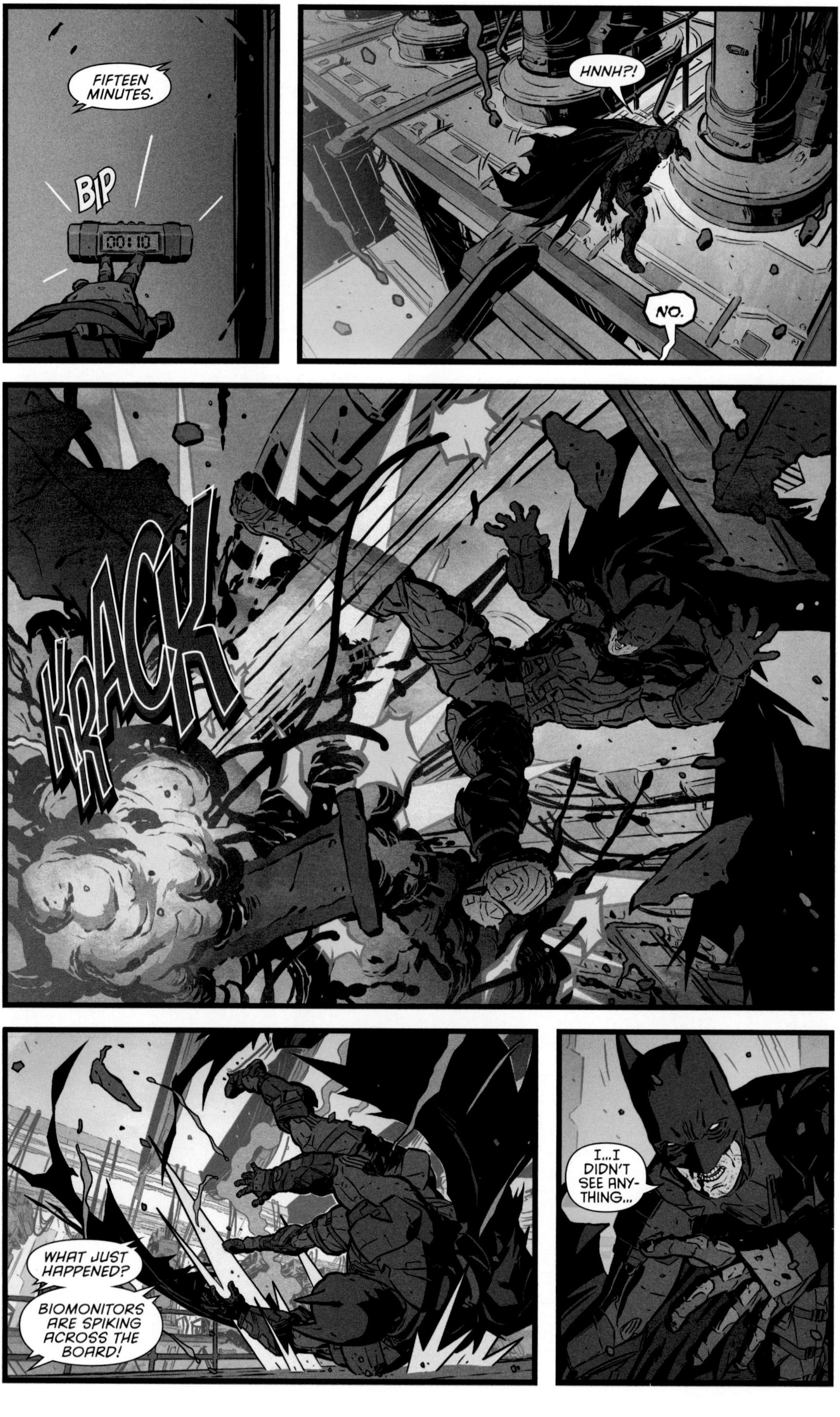
FIFTEEN MINUTES.
BIP
00:10
HNNH?!
NO.
KRACK
WHAT JUST HAPPENED?
BIOMONITORS ARE SPIKING ACROSS THE BOARD!
I...I DIDN'T SEE ANY-THING...

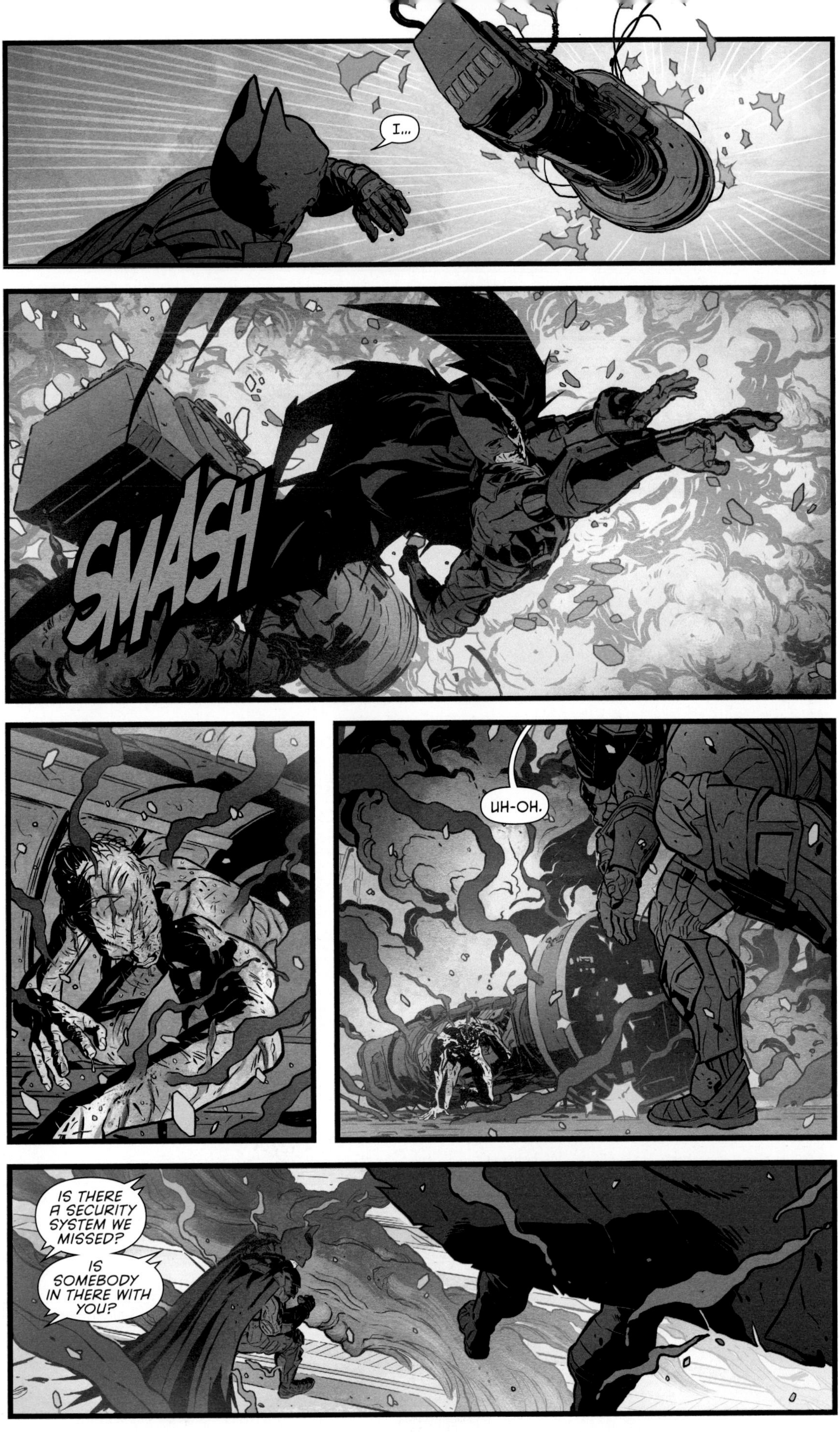
I...
SMASH
UH-OH.
IS THERE A SECURITY SYSTEM WE MISSED?
IS SOMEBODY IN THERE WITH YOU?

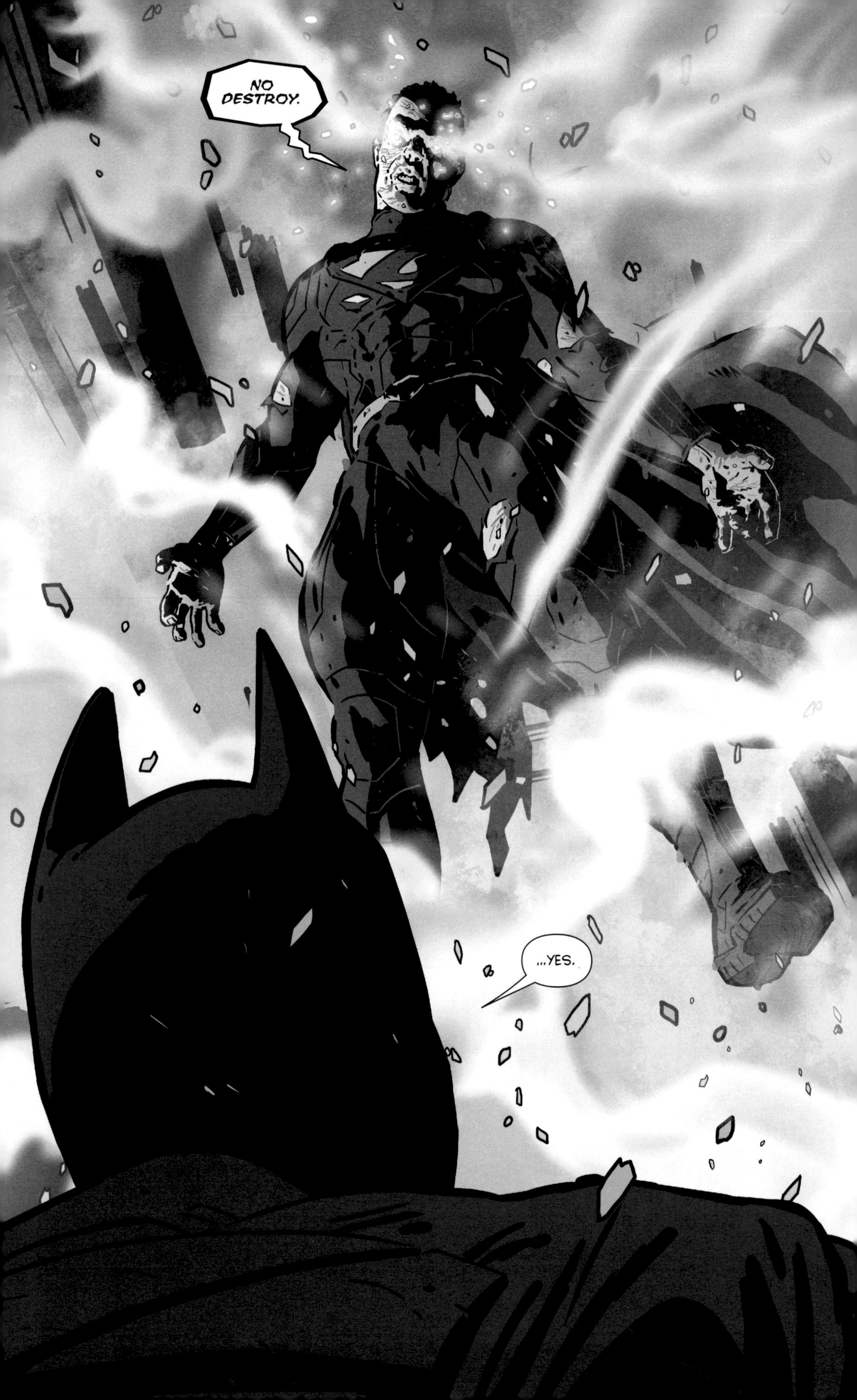
NO DESTROY.
...YES.

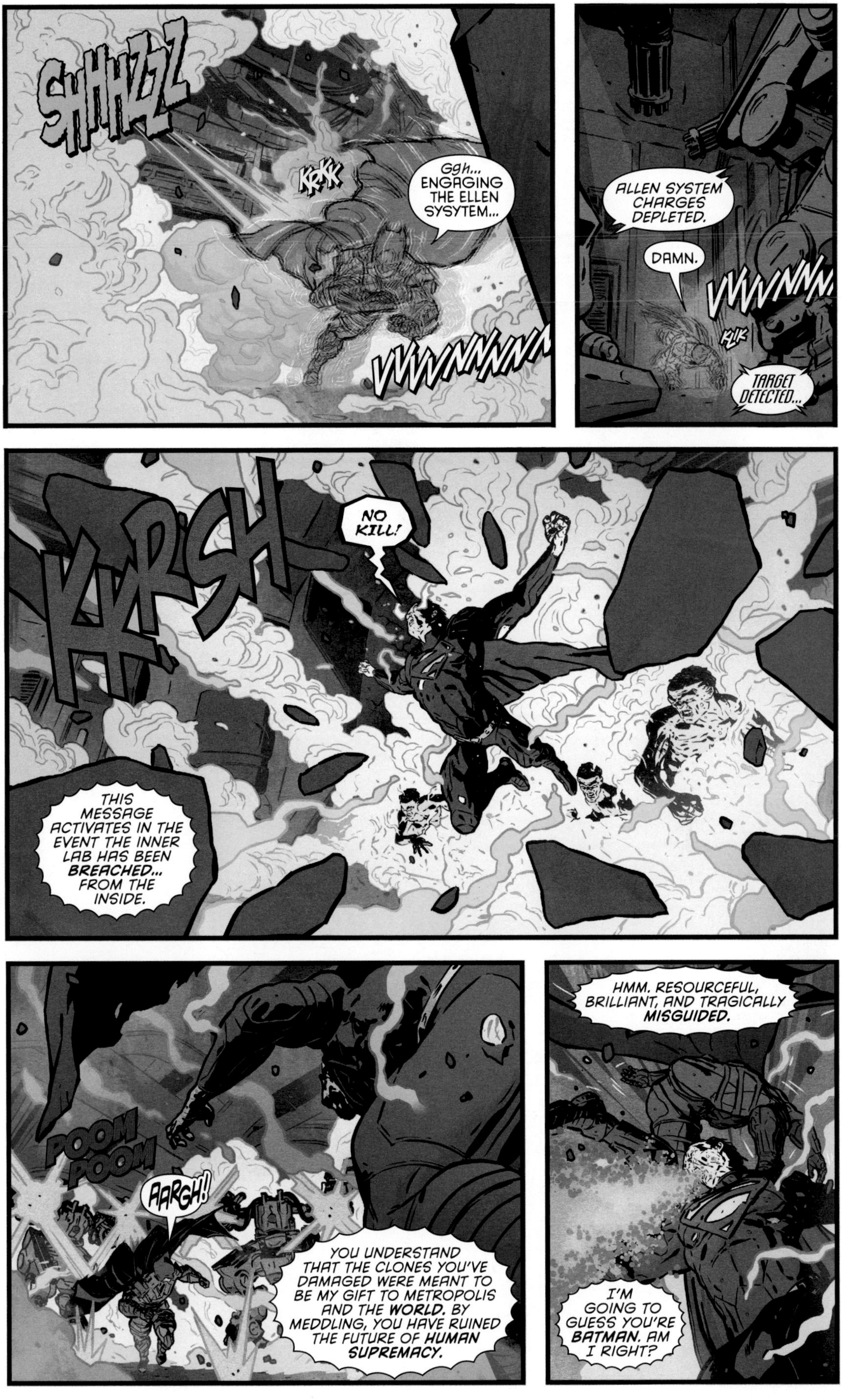
SHHZZZ
KRKK
Ggh... ENGAGING THE ELLEN SYSYTEM...
VVVVNNNNN
ALLEN SYSTEM CHARGES DEPLETED.
DAMN.
VVVVNNNN
KLIK
TARGET DETECTED...
KKRSH
NO KILL!
THIS MESSAGE ACTIVATES IN THE EVENT THE INNER LAB HAS BEEN BREACHED... FROM THE INSIDE.
POOM POOM
AARGH!
YOU UNDERSTAND THAT THE CLONES YOU'VE DAMAGED WERE MEANT TO BE MY GIFT TO METROPOLIS AND THE WORLD. BY MEDDLING, YOU HAVE RUINED THE FUTURE OF HUMAN SUPREMACY.
HMM. RESOURCEFUL, BRILLIANT, AND TRAGICALLY MISGUIDED.
I'M GOING TO GUESS YOU'RE BATMAN. AM I RIGHT?

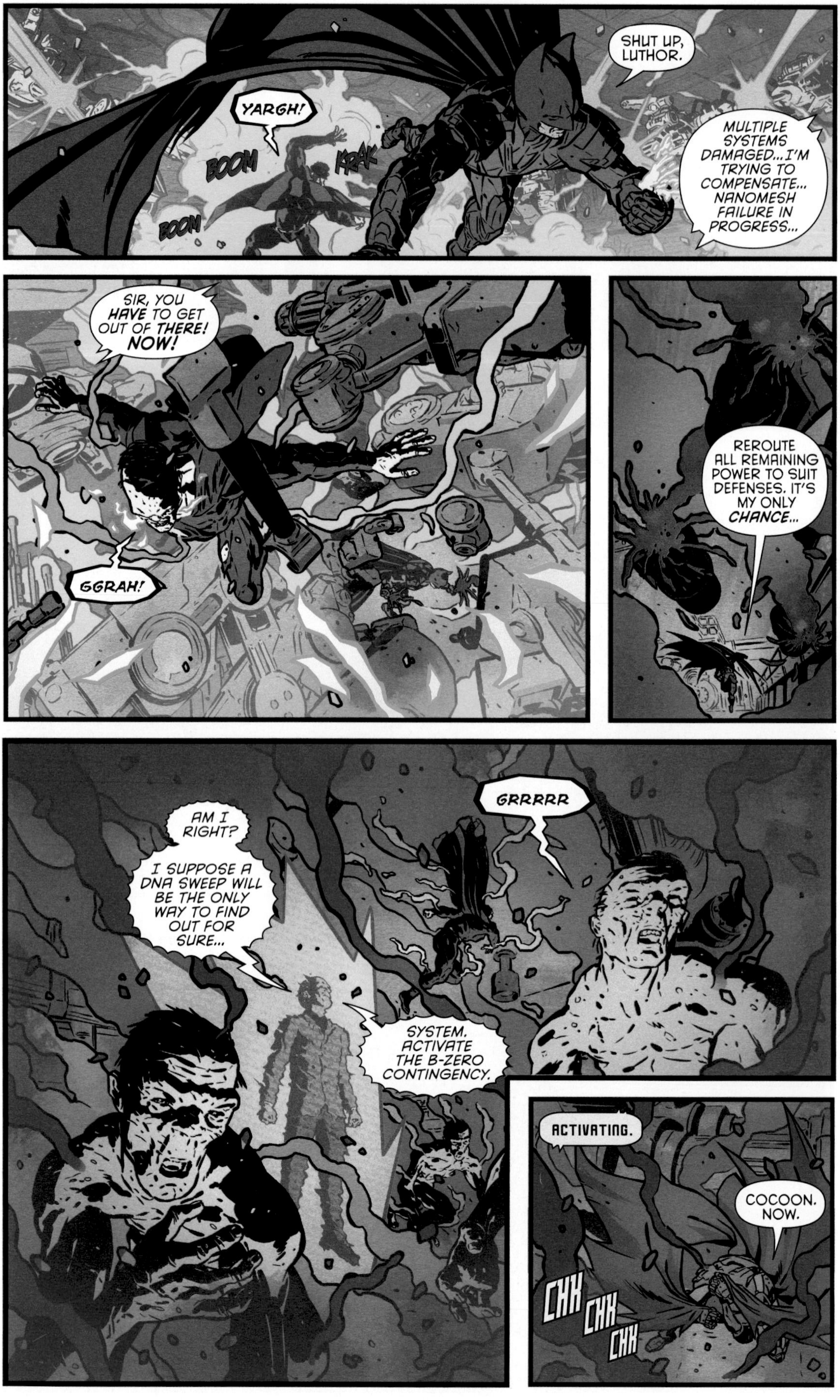

SHUT UP, LUTHOR.
YARGH!
BOOM
KRAK
BOOM
MULTIPLE SYSTEMS DAMAGED...I'M TRYING TO COMPENSATE... NANOMESH FAILURE IN PROGRESS...
SIR, YOU HAVE TO GET OUT OF THERE! NOW!
GGRAH!
REROUTE ALL REMAINING POWER TO SUIT DEFENSES. IT'S MY ONLY CHANCE...
AM I RIGHT?
I SUPPOSE A DNA SWEEP WILL BE THE ONLY WAY TO FIND OUT FOR SURE...
GRRRRR
SYSTEM. ACTIVATE THE B-ZERO CONTINGENCY.
ACTIVATING.
COCOON. NOW.
CHK
CHK
CHK

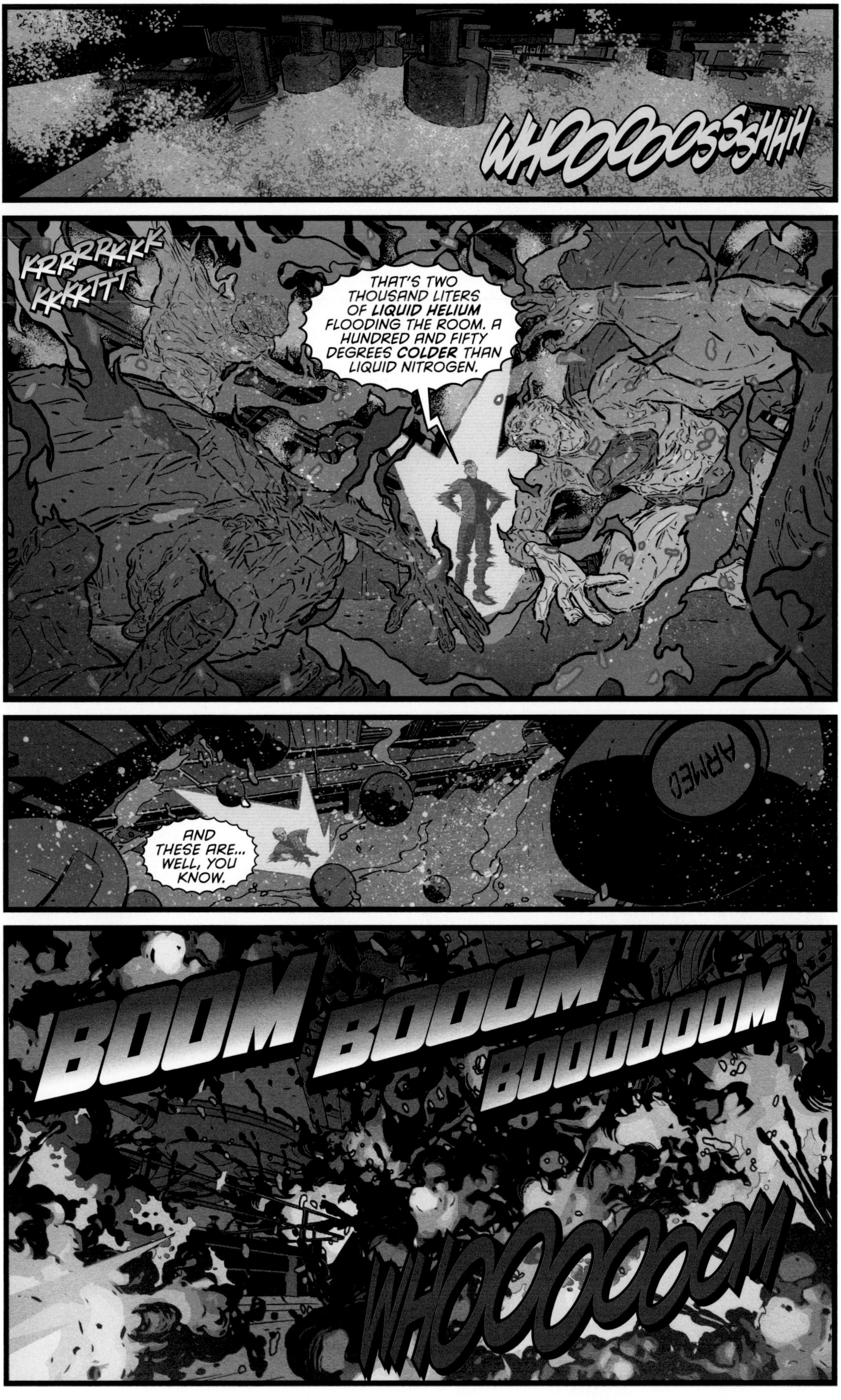
WHOOOOOSSHHH
KRRRRKKK
KKKKTTT
THAT'S TWO THOUSAND LITERS OF LIQUID HELIUM FLOODING THE ROOM. A HUNDRED AND FIFTY DEGREES COLDER THAN LIQUID NITROGEN.
ARMED
AND THESE ARE... WELL, YOU KNOW.
BOOM BOOOM BOOOOOOM
WHOOOOOOM

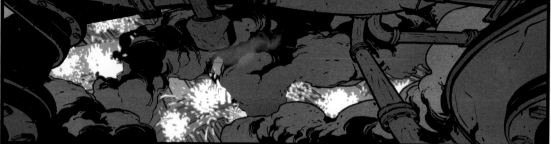

"MASTER BRUCE...ARE YOU THERE?"

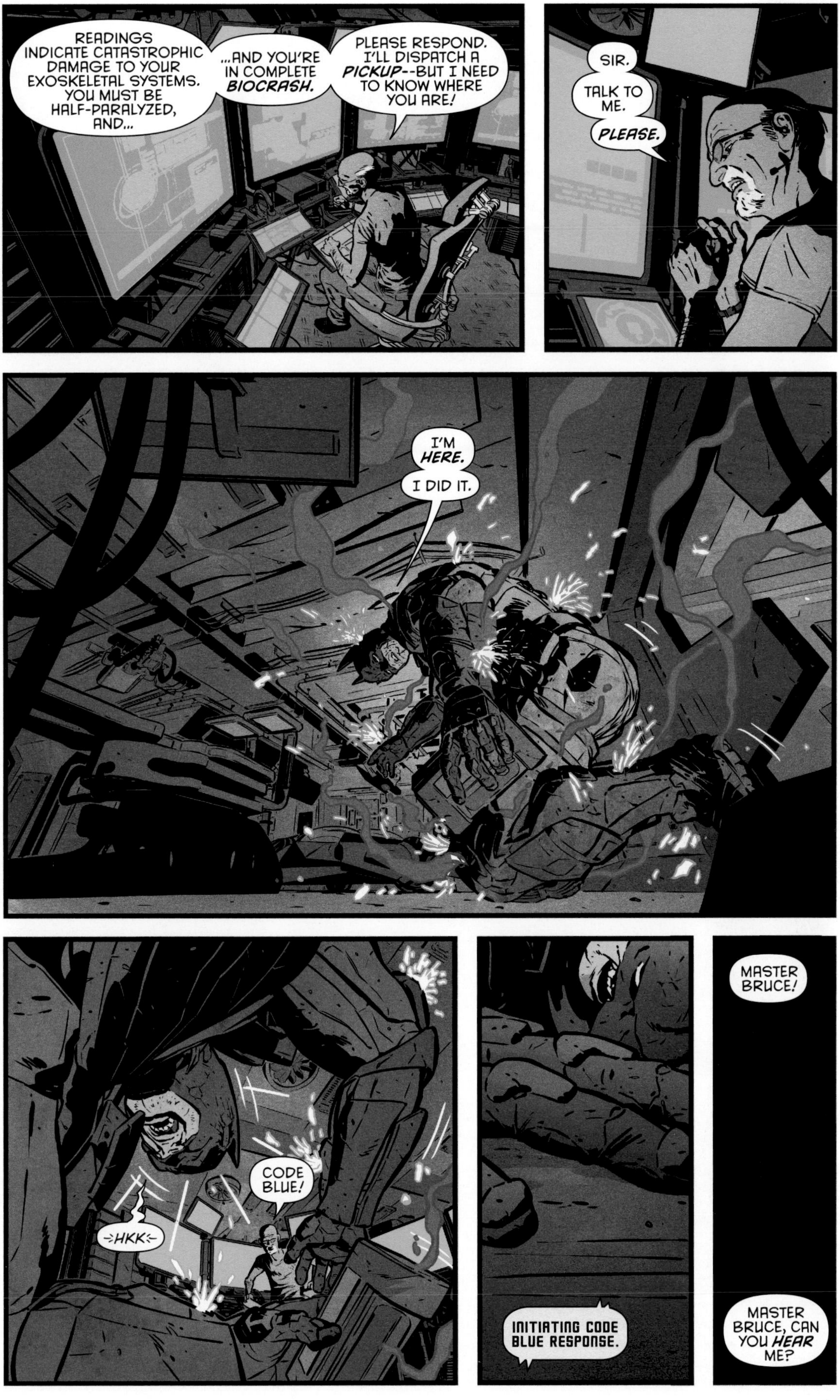
READINGS INDICATE CATASTROPHIC DAMAGE TO YOUR EXOSKELETAL SYSTEMS. YOU MUST BE HALF-PARALYZED, AND...
...AND YOU'RE IN COMPLETE BIOCRASH.
PLEASE RESPOND. I'LL DISPATCH A PICKUP--BUT I NEED TO KNOW WHERE YOU ARE!
SIR.
TALK TO ME.
PLEASE.
I'M HERE.
I DID IT.
CODE BLUE!
HKK
INITIATING CODE BLUE RESPONSE.
MASTER BRUCE!
MASTER BRUCE, CAN YOU HEAR ME?

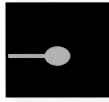

SAY IT AGAIN.

NINE MONTHS LATER.

YOU WERE RIGHT. ALL READINGS ARE *POSITIVE.*

THE CLONE IS *VIABLE.*

ACTIVATE THE MEMORY IMPLANTS. ALL RECORDINGS UP TO THE NIGHT IN MY FATHER'S STUDY.

ACCESSING

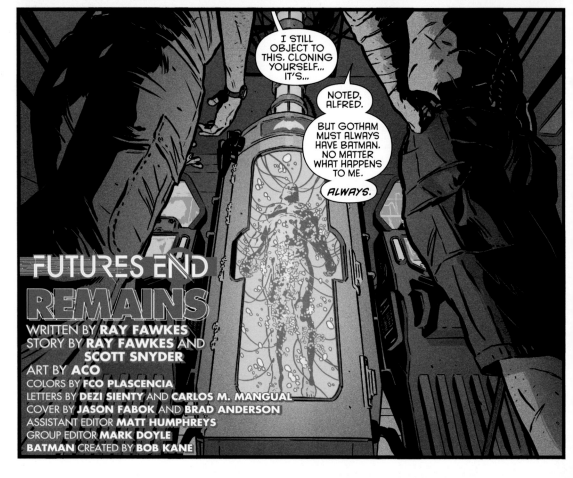

I STILL OBJECT TO THIS. CLONING YOURSELF... IT'S...

NOTED, ALFRED.

BUT GOTHAM MUST ALWAYS HAVE BATMAN. NO MATTER WHAT HAPPENS TO ME.

ALWAYS.

FUTURES END
REMAINS
WRITTEN BY **RAY FAWKES**
STORY BY **RAY FAWKES** AND **SCOTT SNYDER**
ART BY **ACO**
COLORS BY **FCO PLASCENCIA**
LETTERS BY **DEZI SIENTY** AND **CARLOS M. MANGUAL**
COVER BY **JASON FABOK** AND **BRAD ANDERSON**
ASSISTANT EDITOR **MATT HUMPHREYS**
GROUP EDITOR **MARK DOYLE**
BATMAN CREATED BY **BOB KANE**

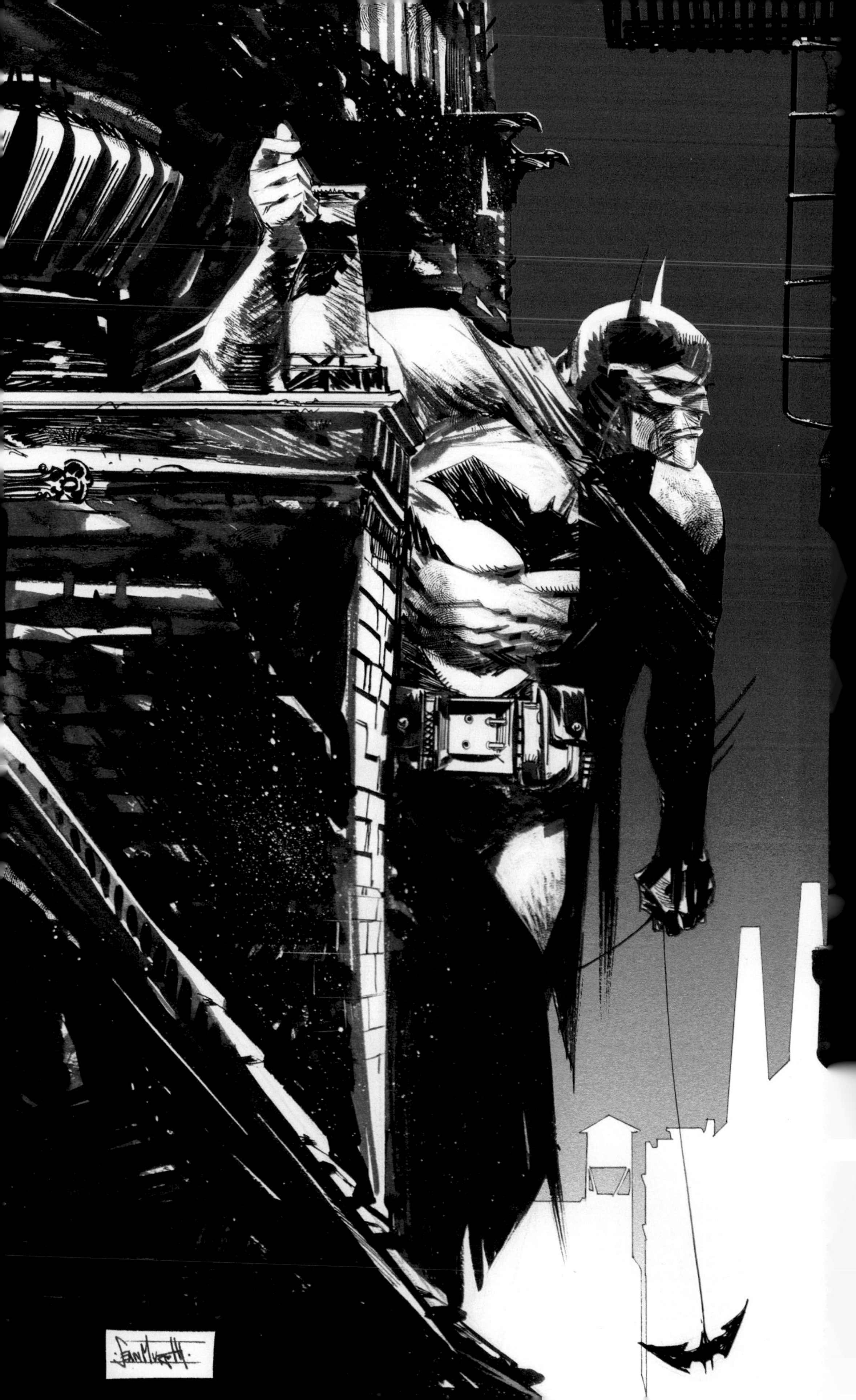

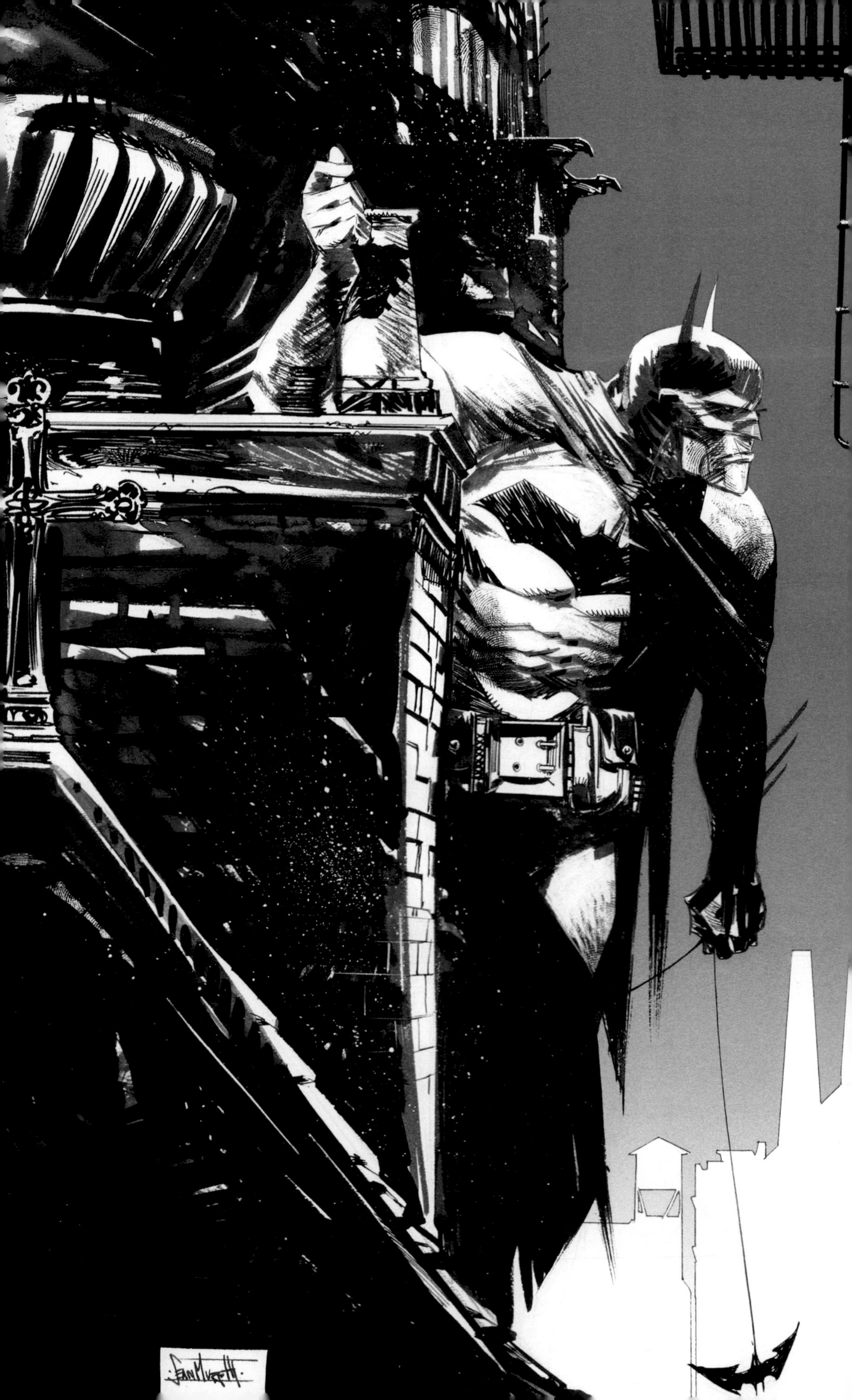

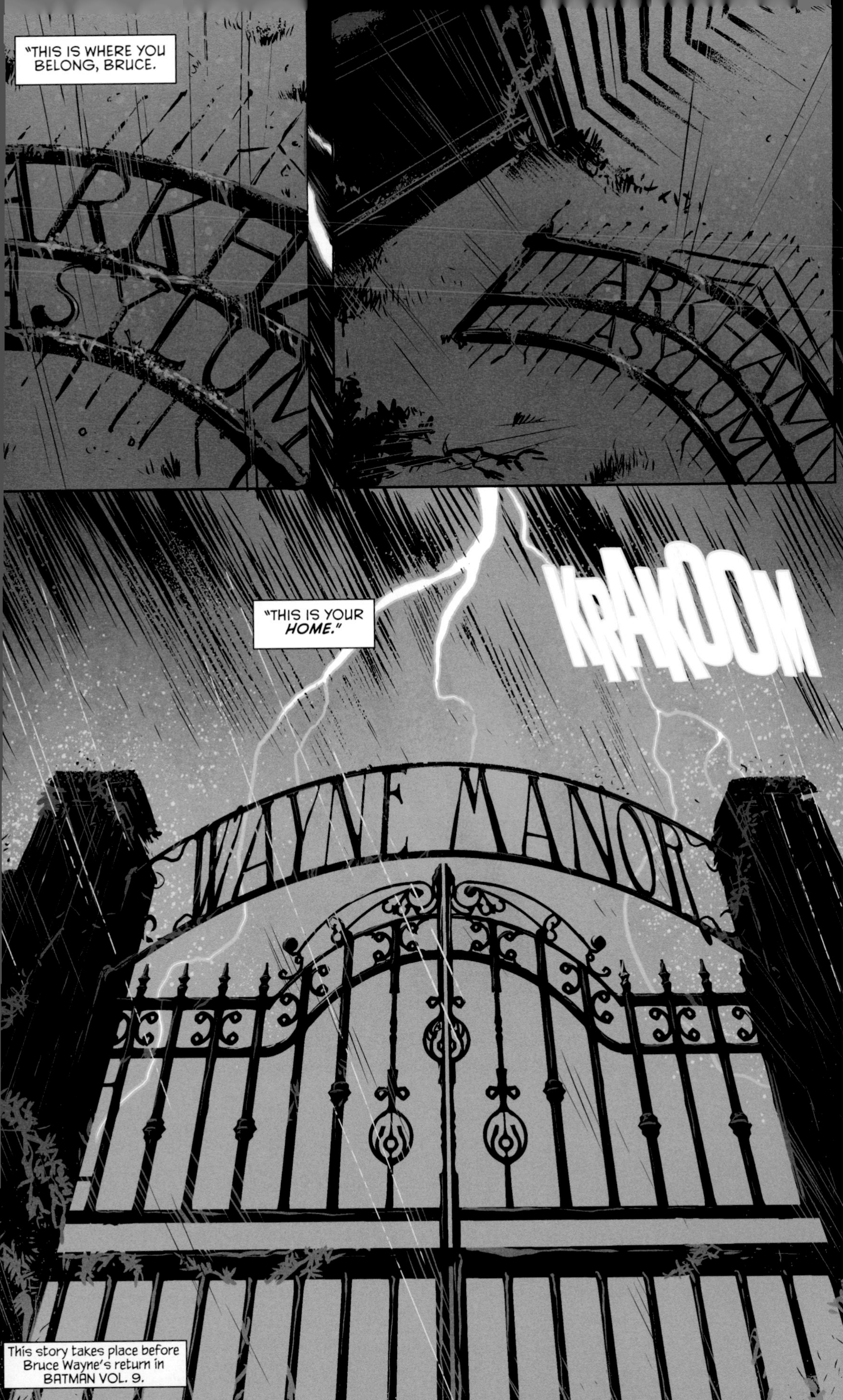
"THIS IS WHERE YOU BELONG, BRUCE.
ARKHAM ASYLUM
ARKHAM ASYLUM
KRAKOOM
"THIS IS YOUR HOME."
WAYNE MANOR
This story takes place before Bruce Wayne's return in BATMAN VOL. 9.

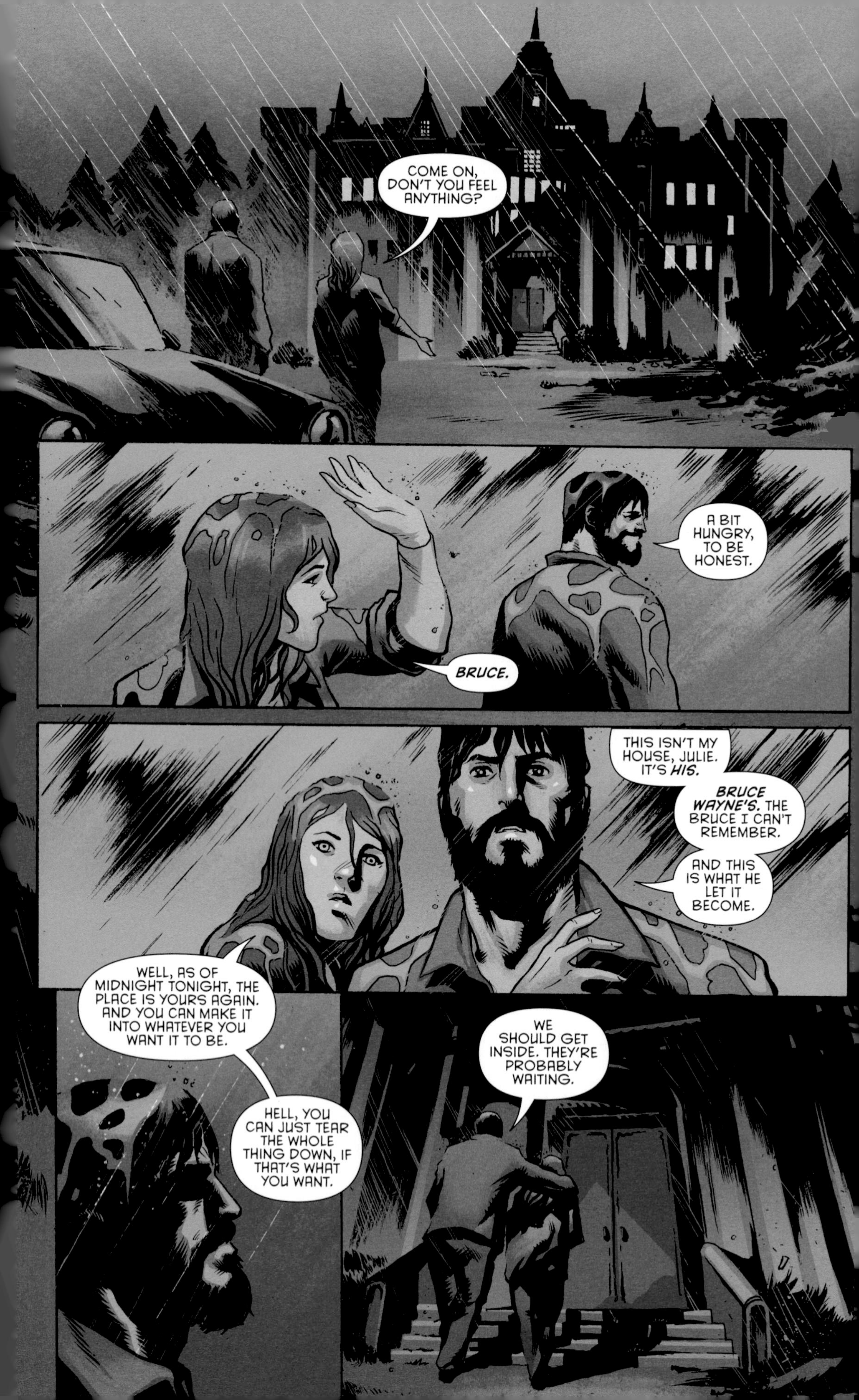
COME ON, DON'T YOU FEEL ANYTHING?
A BIT HUNGRY, TO BE HONEST.
BRUCE.
THIS ISN'T MY HOUSE, JULIE. IT'S HIS.
BRUCE WAYNE'S. THE BRUCE I CAN'T REMEMBER.
AND THIS IS WHAT HE LET IT BECOME.
WELL, AS OF MIDNIGHT TONIGHT, THE PLACE IS YOURS AGAIN. AND YOU CAN MAKE IT INTO WHATEVER YOU WANT IT TO BE.
HELL, YOU CAN JUST TEAR THE WHOLE THING DOWN, IF THAT'S WHAT YOU WANT.
WE SHOULD GET INSIDE. THEY'RE PROBABLY WAITING.

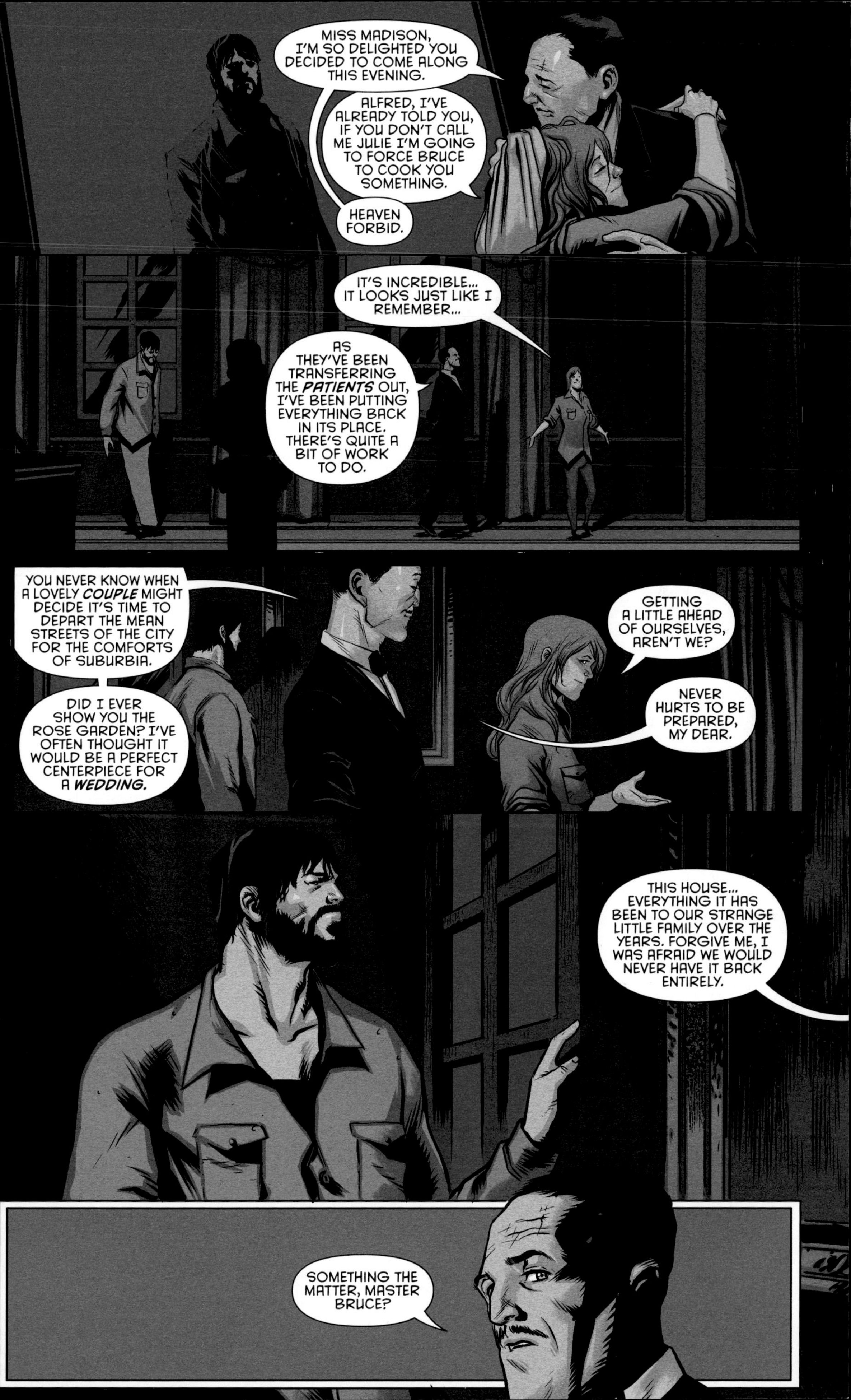
MISS MADISON, I'M SO DELIGHTED YOU DECIDED TO COME ALONG THIS EVENING.
ALFRED, I'VE ALREADY TOLD YOU, IF YOU DON'T CALL ME JULIE I'M GOING TO FORCE BRUCE TO COOK YOU SOMETHING.
HEAVEN FORBID.
IT'S INCREDIBLE... IT LOOKS JUST LIKE I REMEMBER...
AS THEY'VE BEEN TRANSFERRING THE *PATIENTS* OUT, I'VE BEEN PUTTING EVERYTHING BACK IN ITS PLACE. THERE'S QUITE A BIT OF WORK TO DO.
YOU NEVER KNOW WHEN A LOVELY *COUPLE* MIGHT DECIDE IT'S TIME TO DEPART THE MEAN STREETS OF THE CITY FOR THE COMFORTS OF SUBURBIA.
DID I EVER SHOW YOU THE ROSE GARDEN? I'VE OFTEN THOUGHT IT WOULD BE A PERFECT CENTERPIECE FOR A *WEDDING.*
GETTING A LITTLE AHEAD OF OURSELVES, AREN'T WE?
NEVER HURTS TO BE PREPARED, MY DEAR.
THIS HOUSE... EVERYTHING IT HAS BEEN TO OUR STRANGE LITTLE FAMILY OVER THE YEARS. FORGIVE ME, I WAS AFRAID WE WOULD NEVER HAVE IT BACK ENTIRELY.
SOMETHING THE MATTER, MASTER BRUCE?

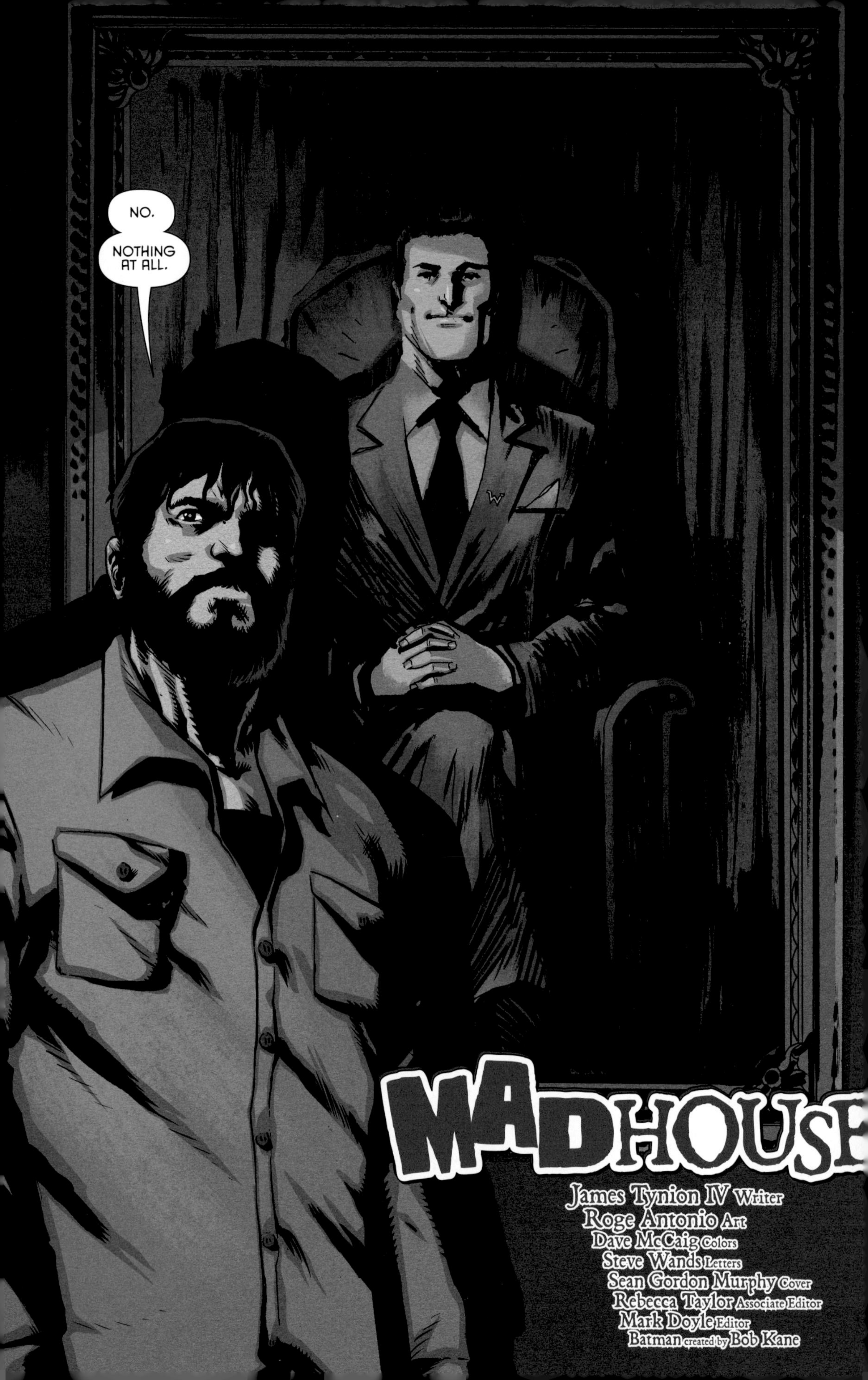
NO.
NOTHING AT ALL.
MADHOUSE
James Tynion IV Writer
Roge Antonio Art
Dave McCaig Colors
Steve Wands Letters
Sean Gordon Murphy Cover
Rebecca Taylor Associate Editor
Mark Doyle Editor
Batman created by Bob Kane

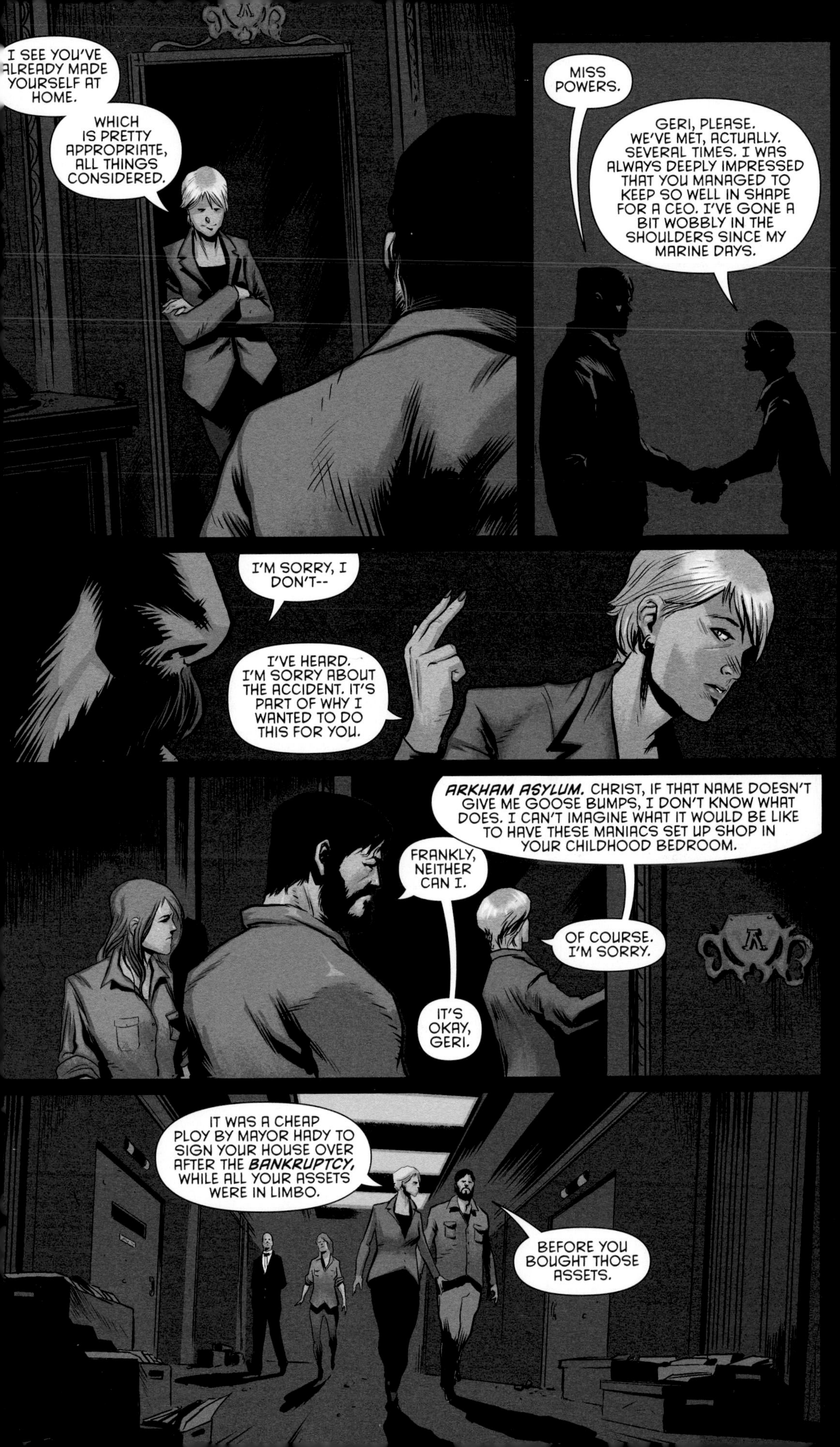

I SEE YOU'VE ALREADY MADE YOURSELF AT HOME.
WHICH IS PRETTY APPROPRIATE, ALL THINGS CONSIDERED.
MISS POWERS.
GERI, PLEASE. WE'VE MET, ACTUALLY. SEVERAL TIMES. I WAS ALWAYS DEEPLY IMPRESSED THAT YOU MANAGED TO KEEP SO WELL IN SHAPE FOR A CEO. I'VE GONE A BIT WOBBLY IN THE SHOULDERS SINCE MY MARINE DAYS.
I'M SORRY, I DON'T--
I'VE HEARD. I'M SORRY ABOUT THE ACCIDENT. IT'S PART OF WHY I WANTED TO DO THIS FOR YOU.
ARKHAM ASYLUM. CHRIST, IF THAT NAME DOESN'T GIVE ME GOOSE BUMPS, I DON'T KNOW WHAT DOES. I CAN'T IMAGINE WHAT IT WOULD BE LIKE TO HAVE THESE MANIACS SET UP SHOP IN YOUR CHILDHOOD BEDROOM.
FRANKLY, NEITHER CAN I.
OF COURSE. I'M SORRY.
IT'S OKAY, GERI.
IT WAS A CHEAP PLOY BY MAYOR HADY TO SIGN YOUR HOUSE OVER AFTER THE BANKRUPTCY, WHILE ALL YOUR ASSETS WERE IN LIMBO.
BEFORE YOU BOUGHT THOSE ASSETS.

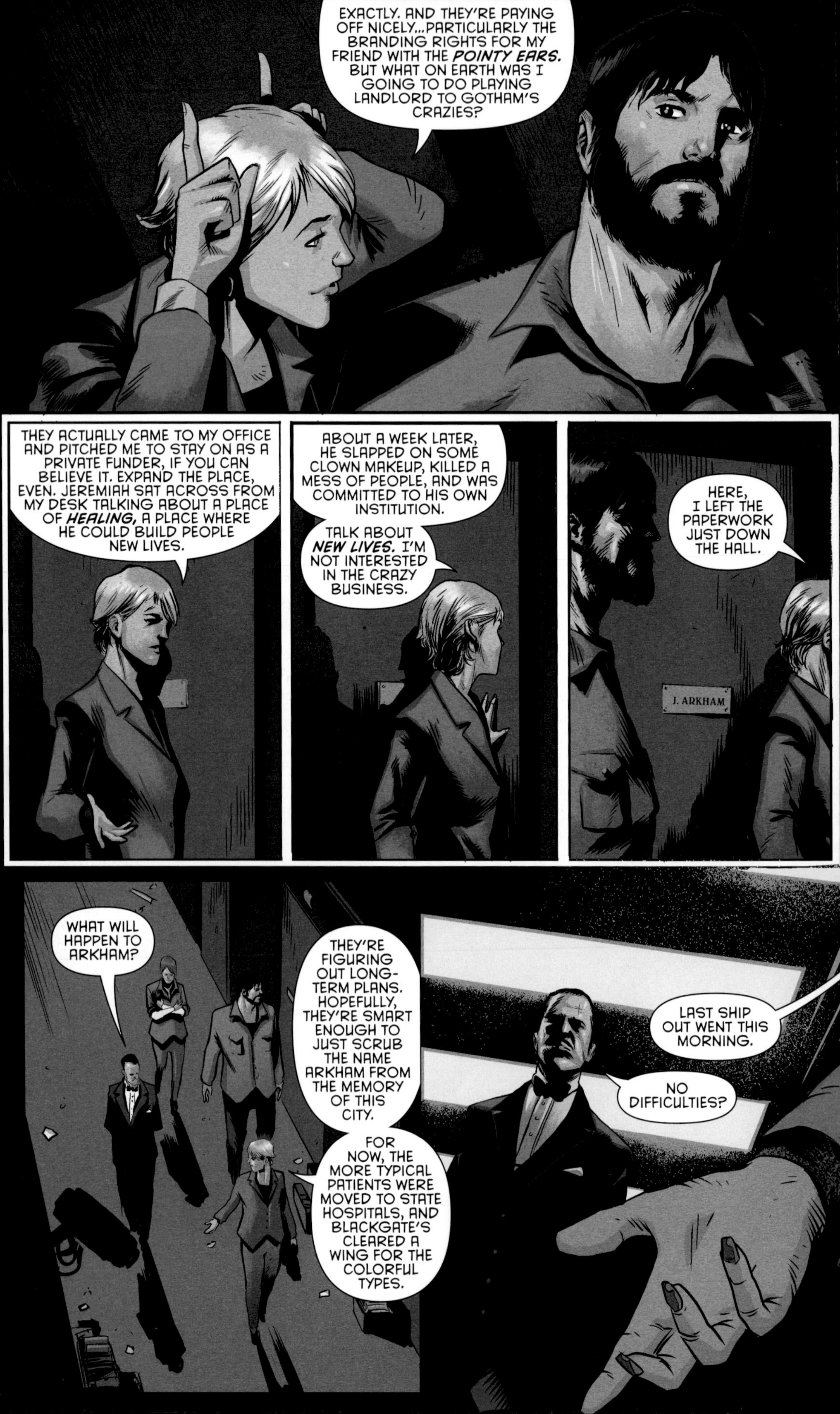
EXACTLY. AND THEY'RE PAYING OFF NICELY...PARTICULARLY THE BRANDING RIGHTS FOR MY FRIEND WITH THE *POINTY EARS.* BUT WHAT ON EARTH WAS I GOING TO DO PLAYING LANDLORD TO GOTHAM'S CRAZIES?
THEY ACTUALLY CAME TO MY OFFICE AND PITCHED ME TO STAY ON AS A PRIVATE FUNDER, IF YOU CAN BELIEVE IT. EXPAND THE PLACE, EVEN. JEREMIAH SAT ACROSS FROM MY DESK TALKING ABOUT A PLACE OF *HEALING,* A PLACE WHERE HE COULD BUILD PEOPLE NEW LIVES.
ABOUT A WEEK LATER, HE SLAPPED ON SOME CLOWN MAKEUP, KILLED A MESS OF PEOPLE, AND WAS COMMITTED TO HIS OWN INSTITUTION.
TALK ABOUT *NEW LIVES.* I'M NOT INTERESTED IN THE CRAZY BUSINESS.
HERE, I LEFT THE PAPERWORK JUST DOWN THE HALL.
J. ARKHAM
WHAT WILL HAPPEN TO ARKHAM?
THEY'RE FIGURING OUT LONG-TERM PLANS. HOPEFULLY, THEY'RE SMART ENOUGH TO JUST SCRUB THE NAME ARKHAM FROM THE MEMORY OF THIS CITY.
FOR NOW, THE MORE TYPICAL PATIENTS WERE MOVED TO STATE HOSPITALS, AND BLACKGATE'S CLEARED A WING FOR THE COLORFUL TYPES.
LAST SHIP OUT WENT THIS MORNING.
NO DIFFICULTIES?

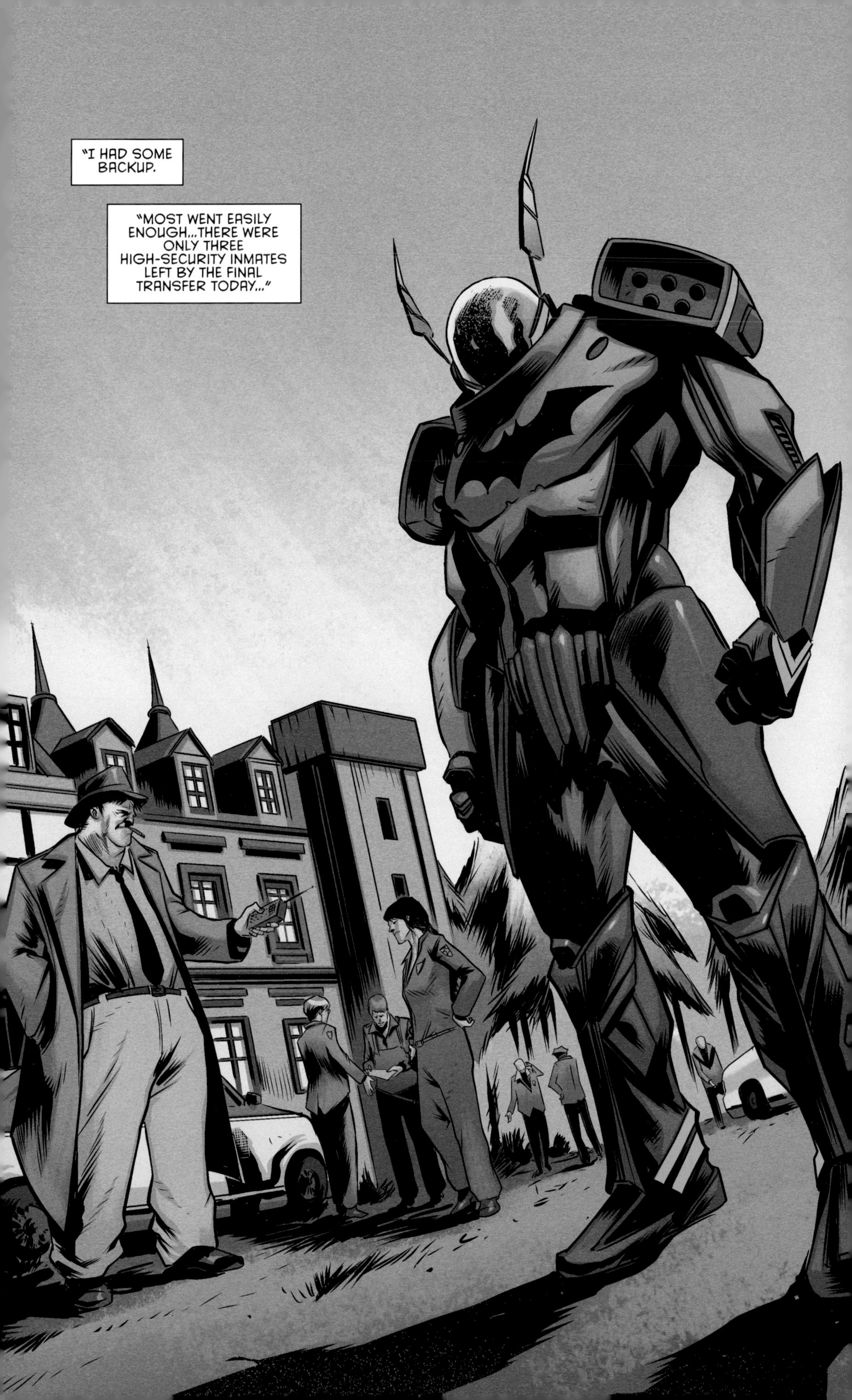
"I HAD SOME BACKUP.
"MOST WENT EASILY ENOUGH...THERE WERE ONLY THREE HIGH-SECURITY INMATES LEFT BY THE FINAL TRANSFER TODAY..."

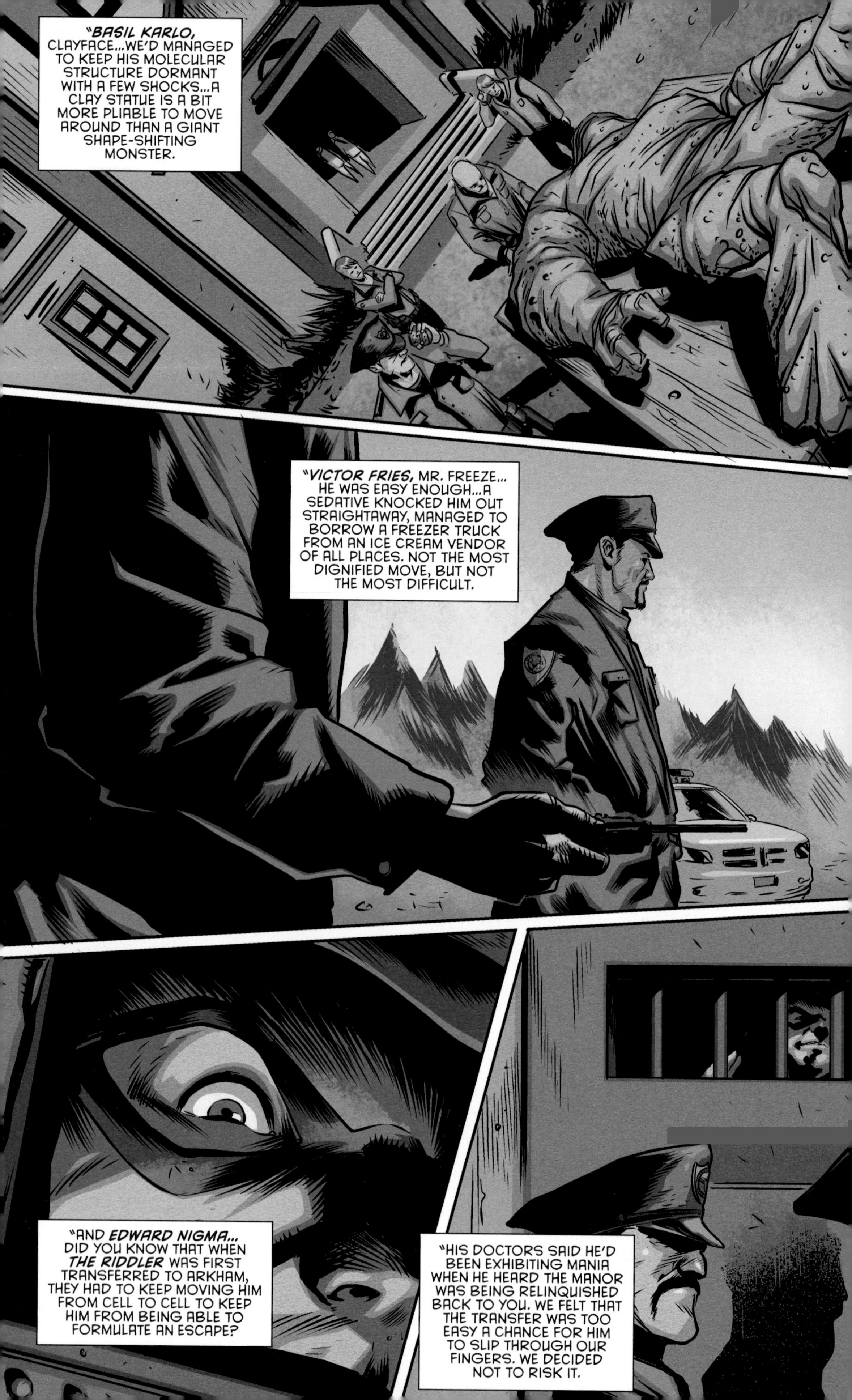
"BASIL KARLO, CLAYFACE...WE'D MANAGED TO KEEP HIS MOLECULAR STRUCTURE DORMANT WITH A FEW SHOCKS...A CLAY STATUE IS A BIT MORE PLIABLE TO MOVE AROUND THAN A GIANT SHAPE-SHIFTING MONSTER.
"VICTOR FRIES, MR. FREEZE... HE WAS EASY ENOUGH...A SEDATIVE KNOCKED HIM OUT STRAIGHTAWAY, MANAGED TO BORROW A FREEZER TRUCK FROM AN ICE CREAM VENDOR OF ALL PLACES. NOT THE MOST DIGNIFIED MOVE, BUT NOT THE MOST DIFFICULT.
"AND EDWARD NIGMA... DID YOU KNOW THAT WHEN THE RIDDLER WAS FIRST TRANSFERRED TO ARKHAM, THEY HAD TO KEEP MOVING HIM FROM CELL TO CELL TO KEEP HIM FROM BEING ABLE TO FORMULATE AN ESCAPE?
"HIS DOCTORS SAID HE'D BEEN EXHIBITING MANIA WHEN HE HEARD THE MANOR WAS BEING RELINQUISHED BACK TO YOU. WE FELT THAT THE TRANSFER WAS TOO EASY A CHANCE FOR HIM TO SLIP THROUGH OUR FINGERS. WE DECIDED NOT TO RISK IT.

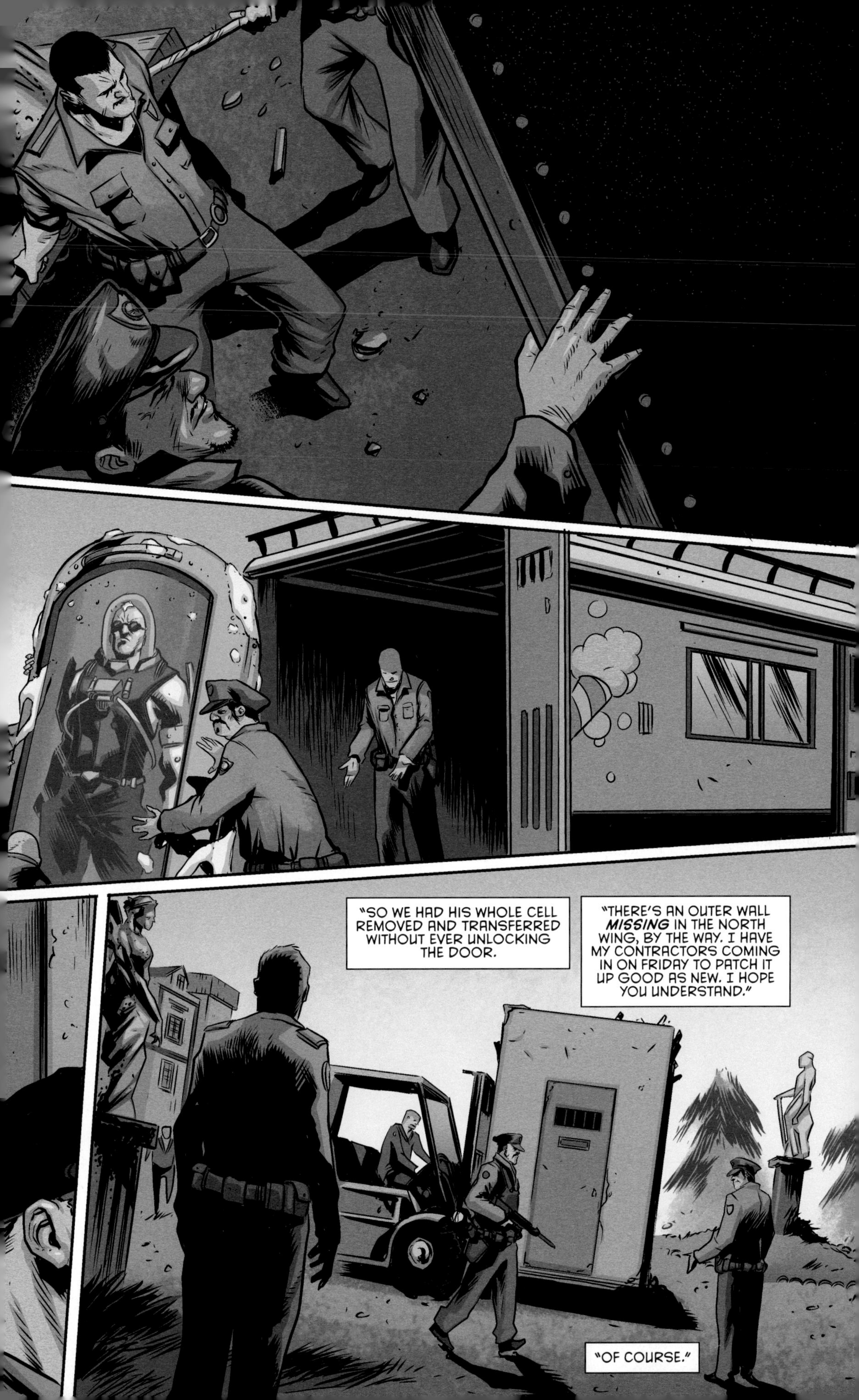
"SO WE HAD HIS WHOLE CELL REMOVED AND TRANSFERRED WITHOUT EVER UNLOCKING THE DOOR.
"THERE'S AN OUTER WALL *MISSING* IN THE NORTH WING, BY THE WAY. I HAVE MY CONTRACTORS COMING IN ON FRIDAY TO PATCH IT UP GOOD AS NEW. I HOPE YOU UNDERSTAND."
"OF COURSE."

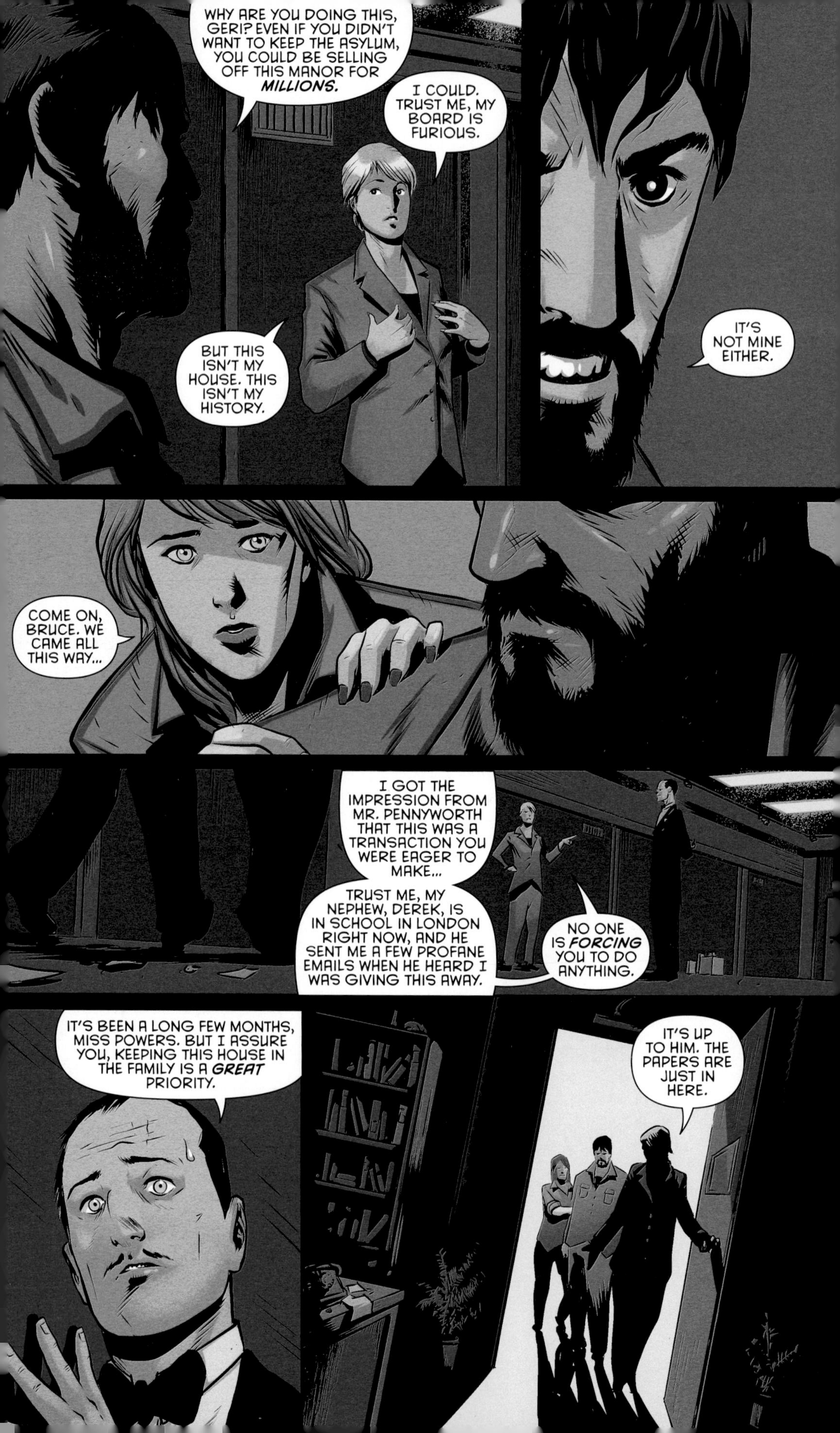
WHY ARE YOU DOING THIS, GERI? EVEN IF YOU DIDN'T WANT TO KEEP THE ASYLUM, YOU COULD BE SELLING OFF THIS MANOR FOR MILLIONS.
I COULD. TRUST ME, MY BOARD IS FURIOUS.
BUT THIS ISN'T MY HOUSE. THIS ISN'T MY HISTORY.
IT'S NOT MINE EITHER.
COME ON, BRUCE. WE CAME ALL THIS WAY...
I GOT THE IMPRESSION FROM MR. PENNYWORTH THAT THIS WAS A TRANSACTION YOU WERE EAGER TO MAKE...
TRUST ME, MY NEPHEW, DEREK, IS IN SCHOOL IN LONDON RIGHT NOW, AND HE SENT ME A FEW PROFANE EMAILS WHEN HE HEARD I WAS GIVING THIS AWAY.
NO ONE IS FORCING YOU TO DO ANYTHING.
IT'S BEEN A LONG FEW MONTHS, MISS POWERS. BUT I ASSURE YOU, KEEPING THIS HOUSE IN THE FAMILY IS A GREAT PRIORITY.
IT'S UP TO HIM. THE PAPERS ARE JUST IN HERE.

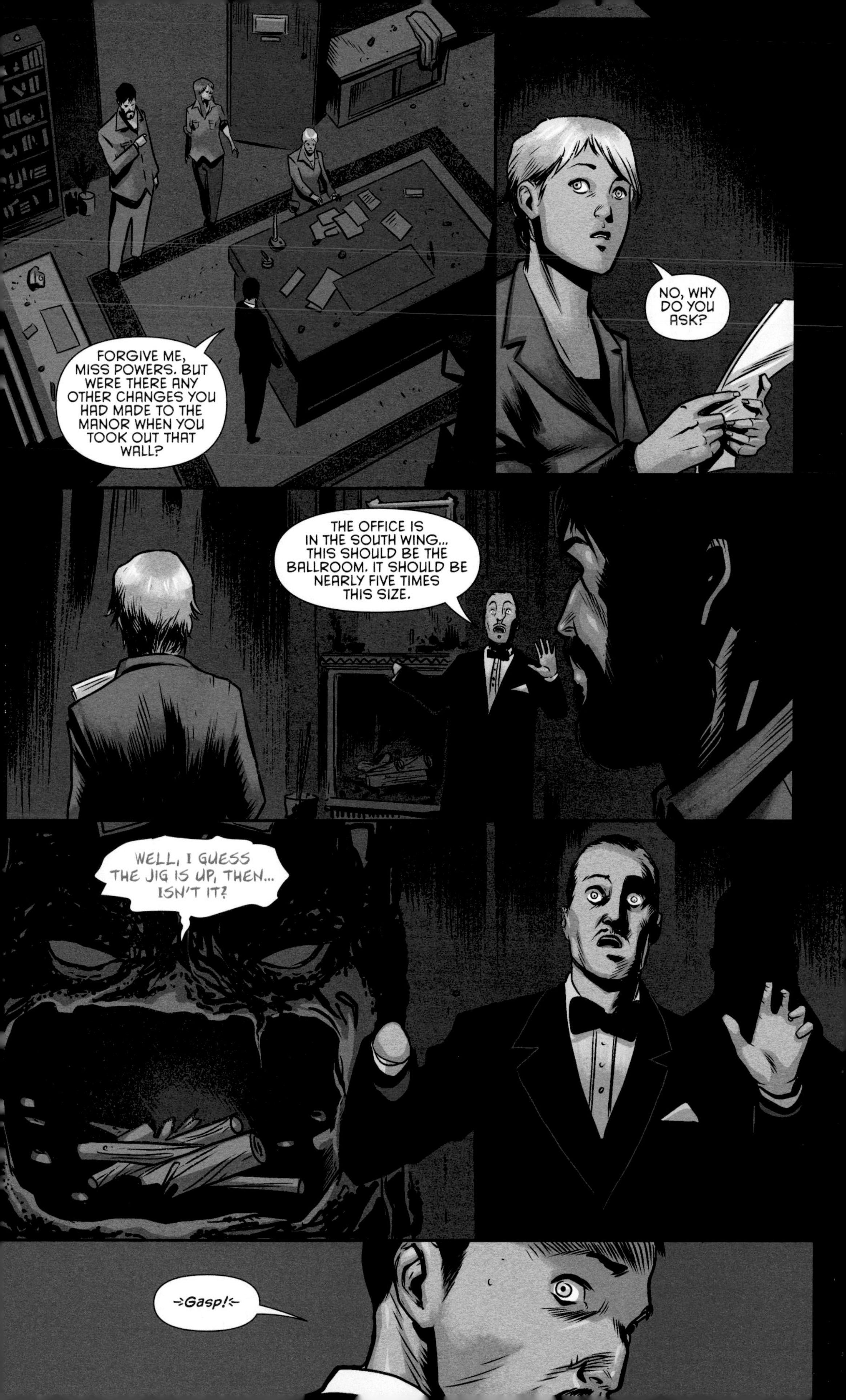
FORGIVE ME, MISS POWERS. BUT WERE THERE ANY OTHER CHANGES YOU HAD MADE TO THE MANOR WHEN YOU TOOK OUT THAT WALL?
NO, WHY DO YOU ASK?
THE OFFICE IS IN THE SOUTH WING... THIS SHOULD BE THE BALLROOM. IT SHOULD BE NEARLY FIVE TIMES THIS SIZE.
WELL, I GUESS THE JIG IS UP, THEN... ISN'T IT?
-Gasp!-

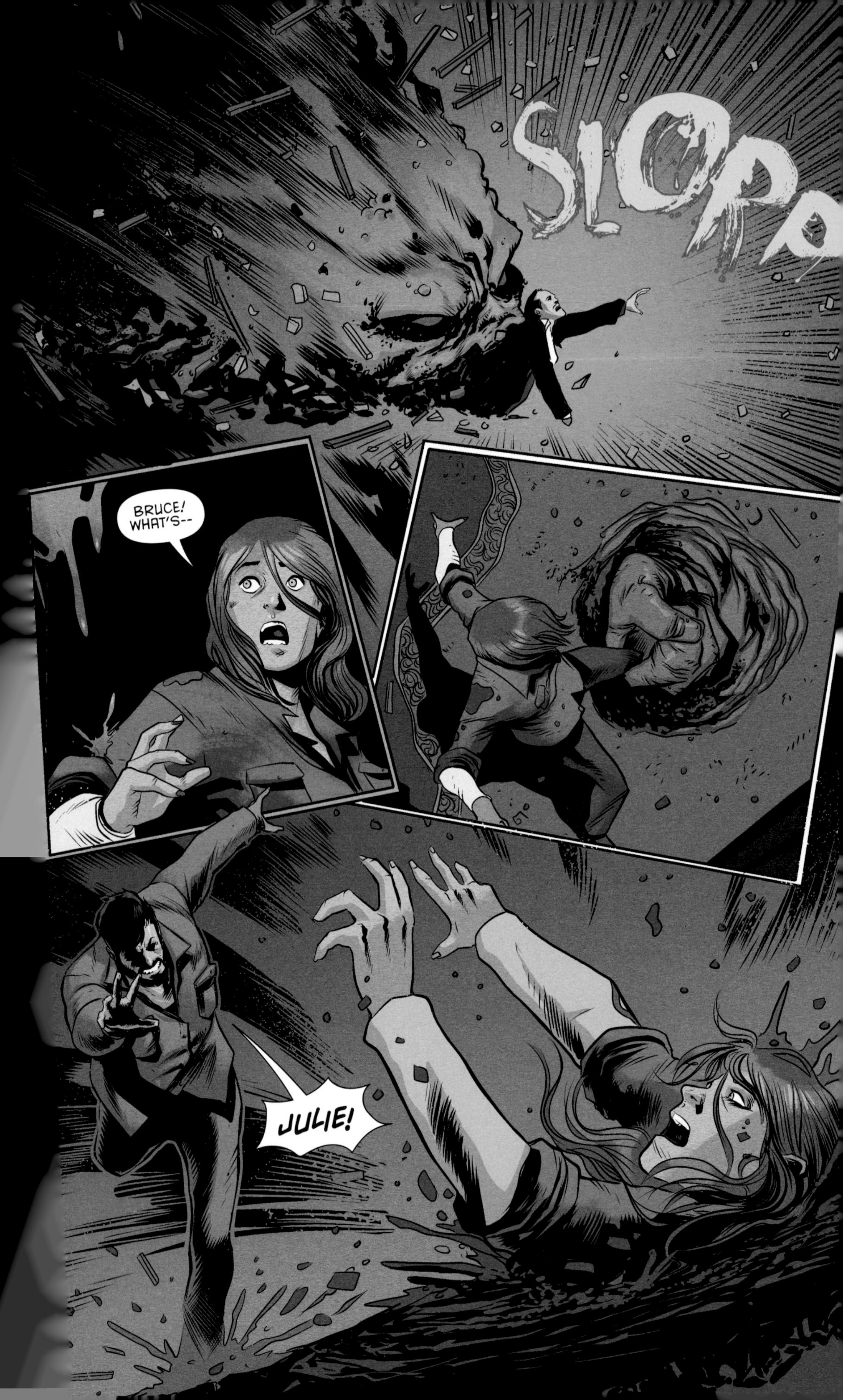
SLORP
BRUCE! WHAT'S--
JULIE!

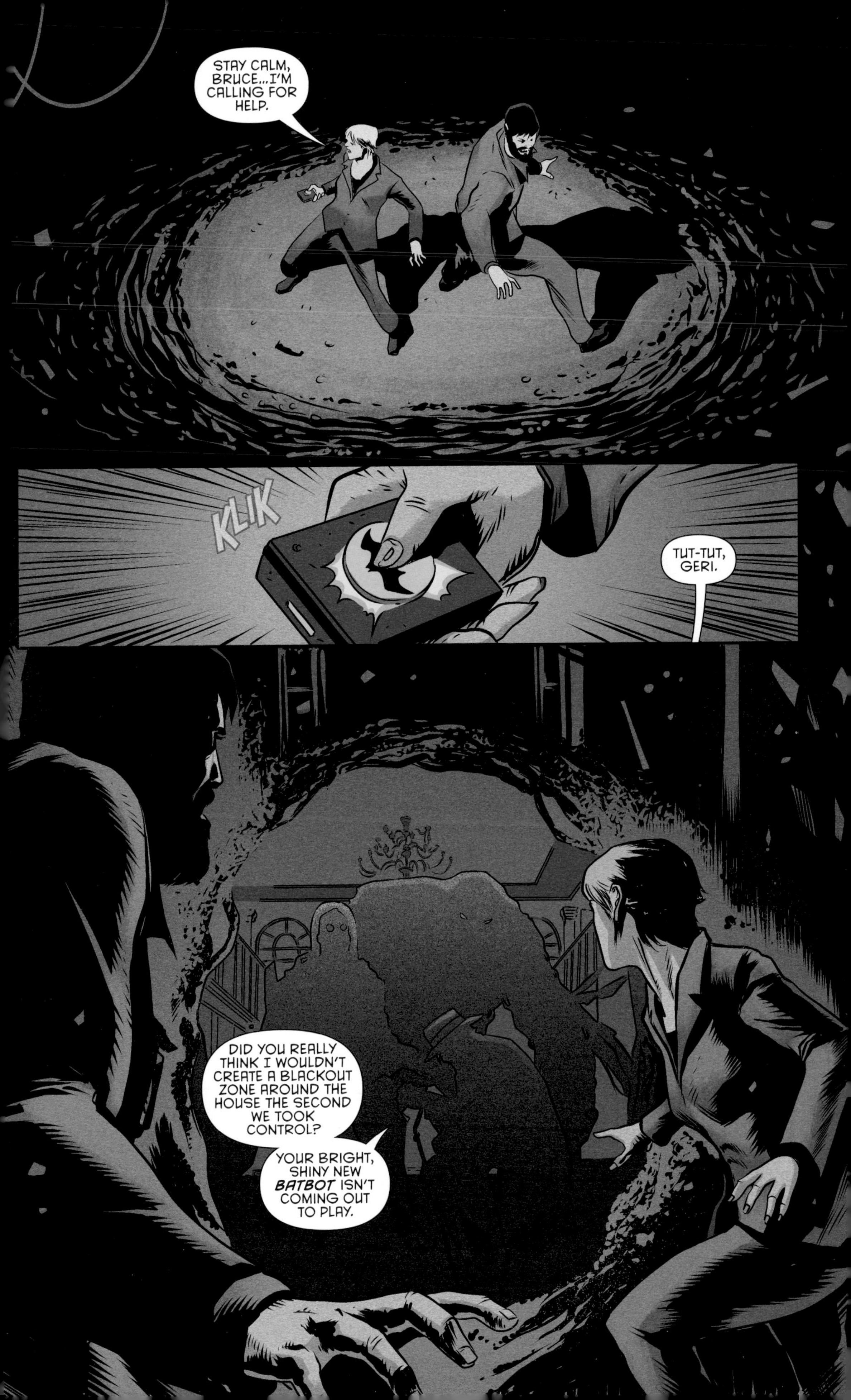
STAY CALM, BRUCE...I'M CALLING FOR HELP.
KLIK
TUT-TUT, GERI.
DID YOU REALLY THINK I WOULDN'T CREATE A BLACKOUT ZONE AROUND THE HOUSE THE SECOND WE TOOK CONTROL?
YOUR BRIGHT, SHINY NEW *BATBOT* ISN'T COMING OUT TO PLAY.

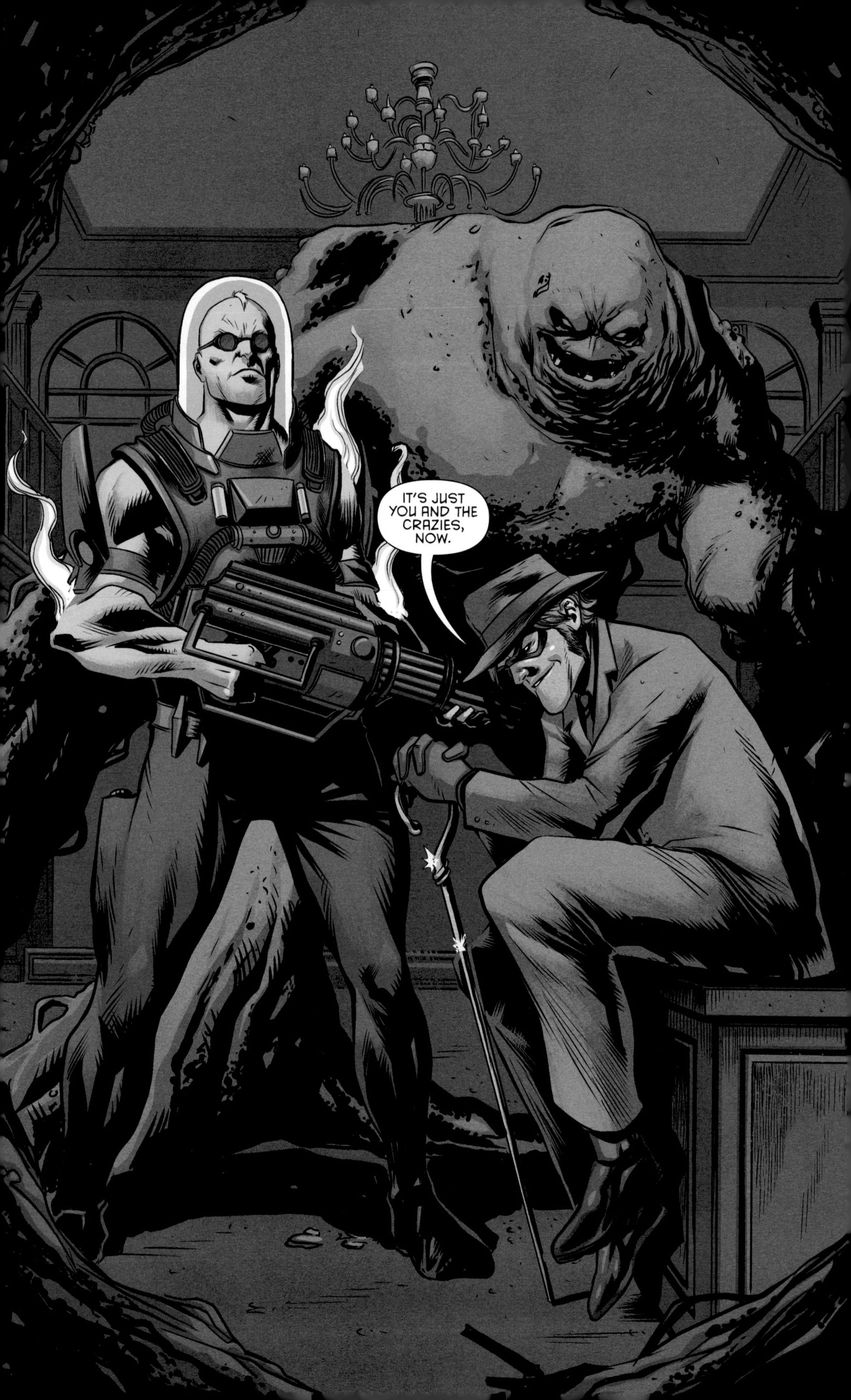
IT'S JUST YOU AND THE CRAZIES, NOW.

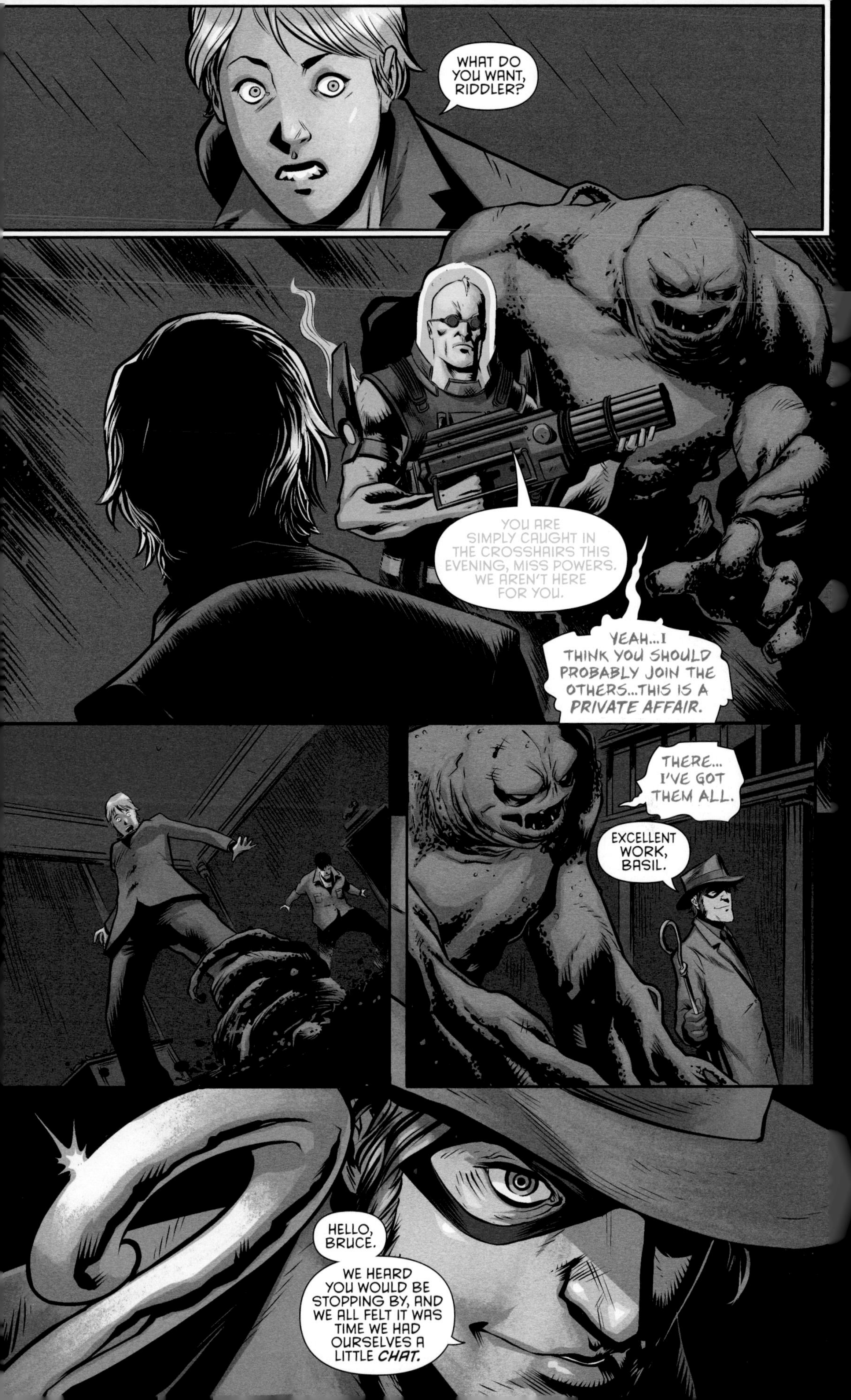
WHAT DO YOU WANT, RIDDLER?
YOU ARE SIMPLY CAUGHT IN THE CROSSHAIRS THIS EVENING, MISS POWERS. WE AREN'T HERE FOR YOU.
YEAH...I THINK YOU SHOULD PROBABLY JOIN THE OTHERS...THIS IS A PRIVATE AFFAIR.
THERE... I'VE GOT THEM ALL.
EXCELLENT WORK, BASIL.
HELLO, BRUCE.
WE HEARD YOU WOULD BE STOPPING BY, AND WE ALL FELT IT WAS TIME WE HAD OURSELVES A LITTLE CHAT.

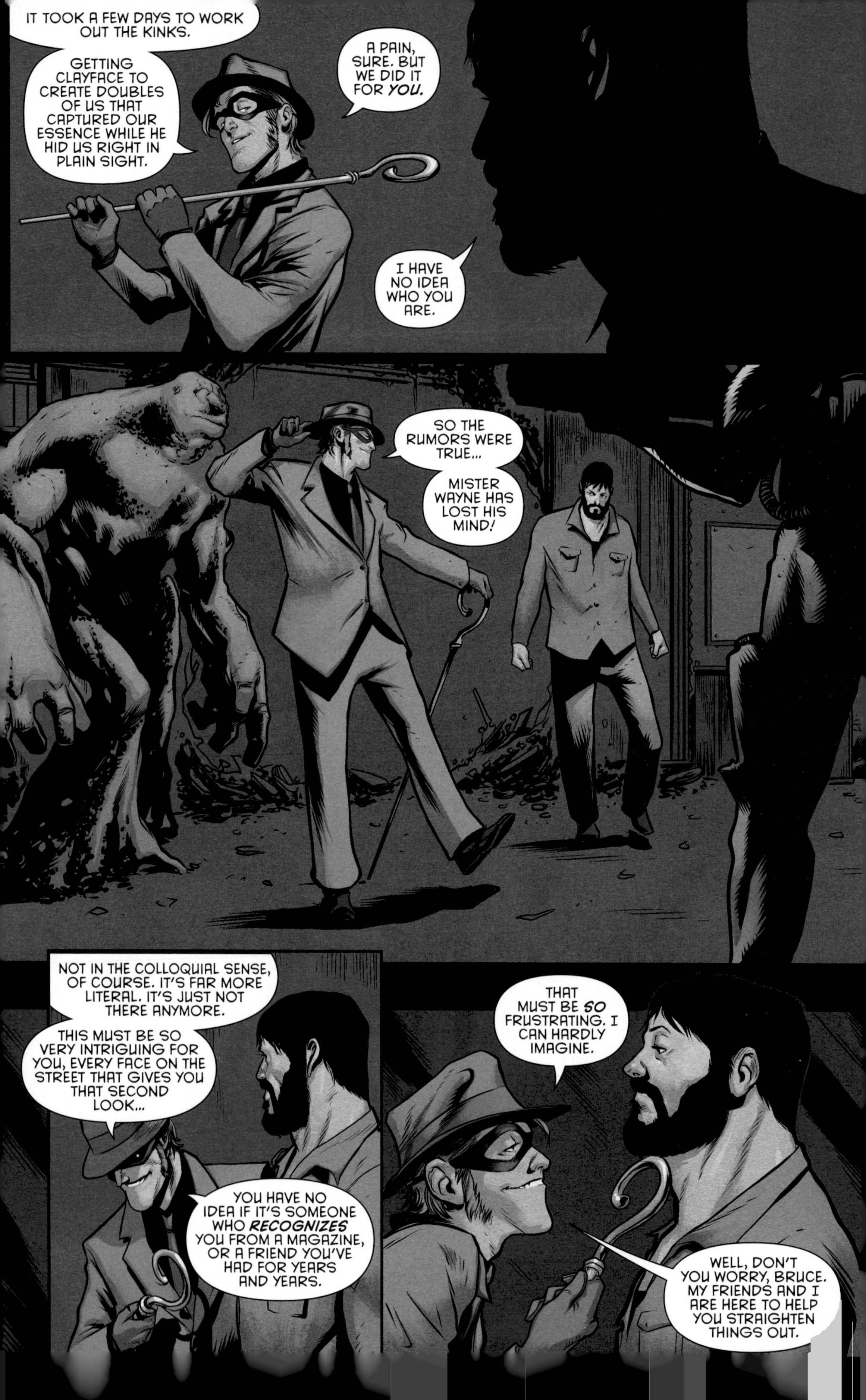
IT TOOK A FEW DAYS TO WORK OUT THE KINKS.
GETTING CLAYFACE TO CREATE DOUBLES OF US THAT CAPTURED OUR ESSENCE WHILE HE HID US RIGHT IN PLAIN SIGHT.
A PAIN, SURE. BUT WE DID IT FOR YOU.
I HAVE NO IDEA WHO YOU ARE.
SO THE RUMORS WERE TRUE...
MISTER WAYNE HAS LOST HIS MIND!
NOT IN THE COLLOQUIAL SENSE, OF COURSE. IT'S FAR MORE LITERAL. IT'S JUST NOT THERE ANYMORE.
THIS MUST BE SO VERY INTRIGUING FOR YOU, EVERY FACE ON THE STREET THAT GIVES YOU THAT SECOND LOOK...
YOU HAVE NO IDEA IF IT'S SOMEONE WHO RECOGNIZES YOU FROM A MAGAZINE, OR A FRIEND YOU'VE HAD FOR YEARS AND YEARS.
THAT MUST BE SO FRUSTRATING. I CAN HARDLY IMAGINE.
WELL, DON'T YOU WORRY, BRUCE. MY FRIENDS AND I ARE HERE TO HELP YOU STRAIGHTEN THINGS OUT.

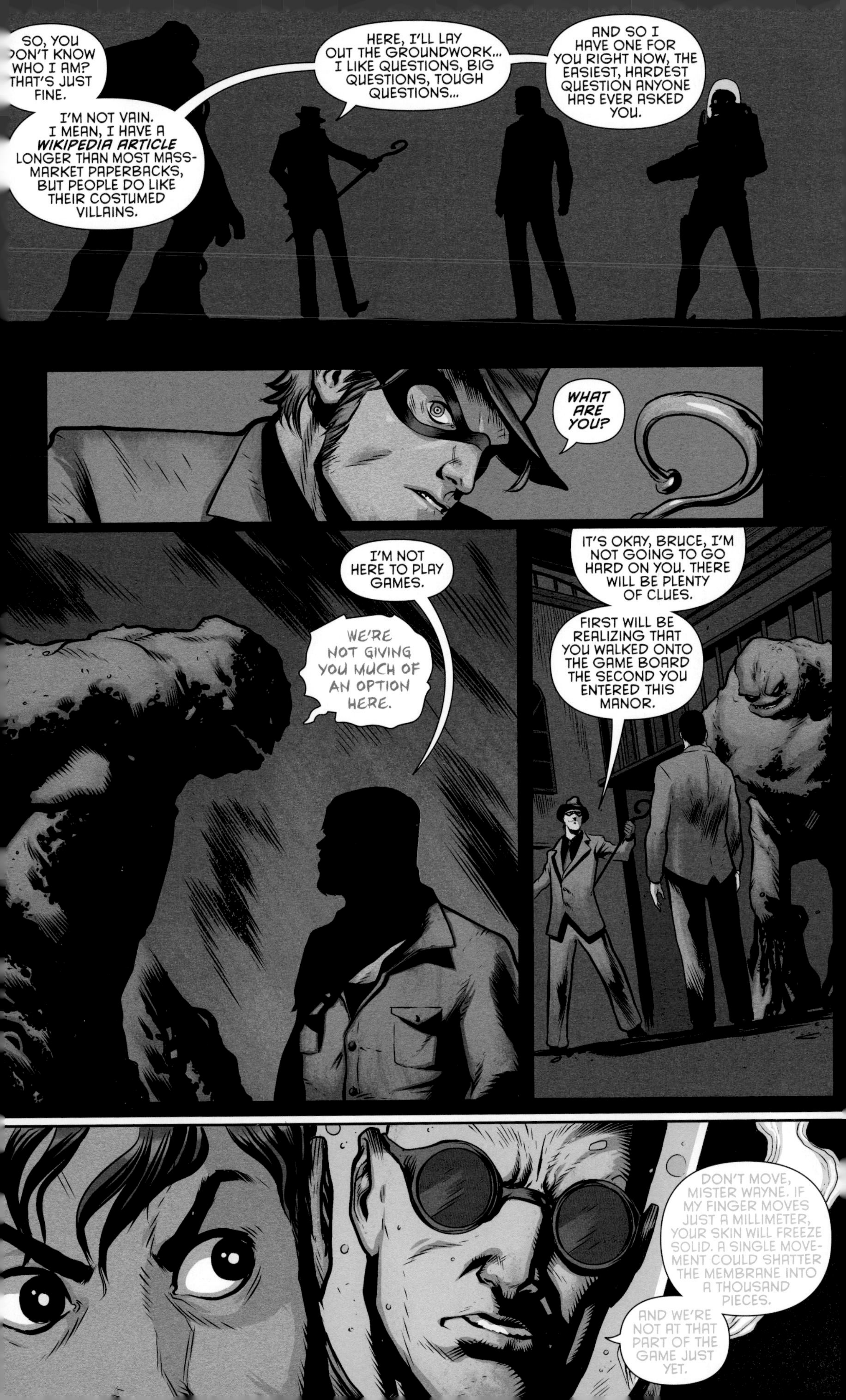
SO, YOU DON'T KNOW WHO I AM? THAT'S JUST FINE.
I'M NOT VAIN. I MEAN, I HAVE A WIKIPEDIA ARTICLE LONGER THAN MOST MASS-MARKET PAPERBACKS, BUT PEOPLE DO LIKE THEIR COSTUMED VILLAINS.
HERE, I'LL LAY OUT THE GROUNDWORK... I LIKE QUESTIONS, BIG QUESTIONS, TOUGH QUESTIONS...
AND SO I HAVE ONE FOR YOU RIGHT NOW, THE EASIEST, HARDEST QUESTION ANYONE HAS EVER ASKED YOU.
WHAT ARE YOU?
I'M NOT HERE TO PLAY GAMES.
WE'RE NOT GIVING YOU MUCH OF AN OPTION HERE.
IT'S OKAY, BRUCE, I'M NOT GOING TO GO HARD ON YOU. THERE WILL BE PLENTY OF CLUES.
FIRST WILL BE REALIZING THAT YOU WALKED ONTO THE GAME BOARD THE SECOND YOU ENTERED THIS MANOR.
DON'T MOVE, MISTER WAYNE. IF MY FINGER MOVES JUST A MILLIMETER, YOUR SKIN WILL FREEZE SOLID. A SINGLE MOVEMENT COULD SHATTER THE MEMBRANE INTO A THOUSAND PIECES.
AND WE'RE NOT AT THAT PART OF THE GAME JUST YET.

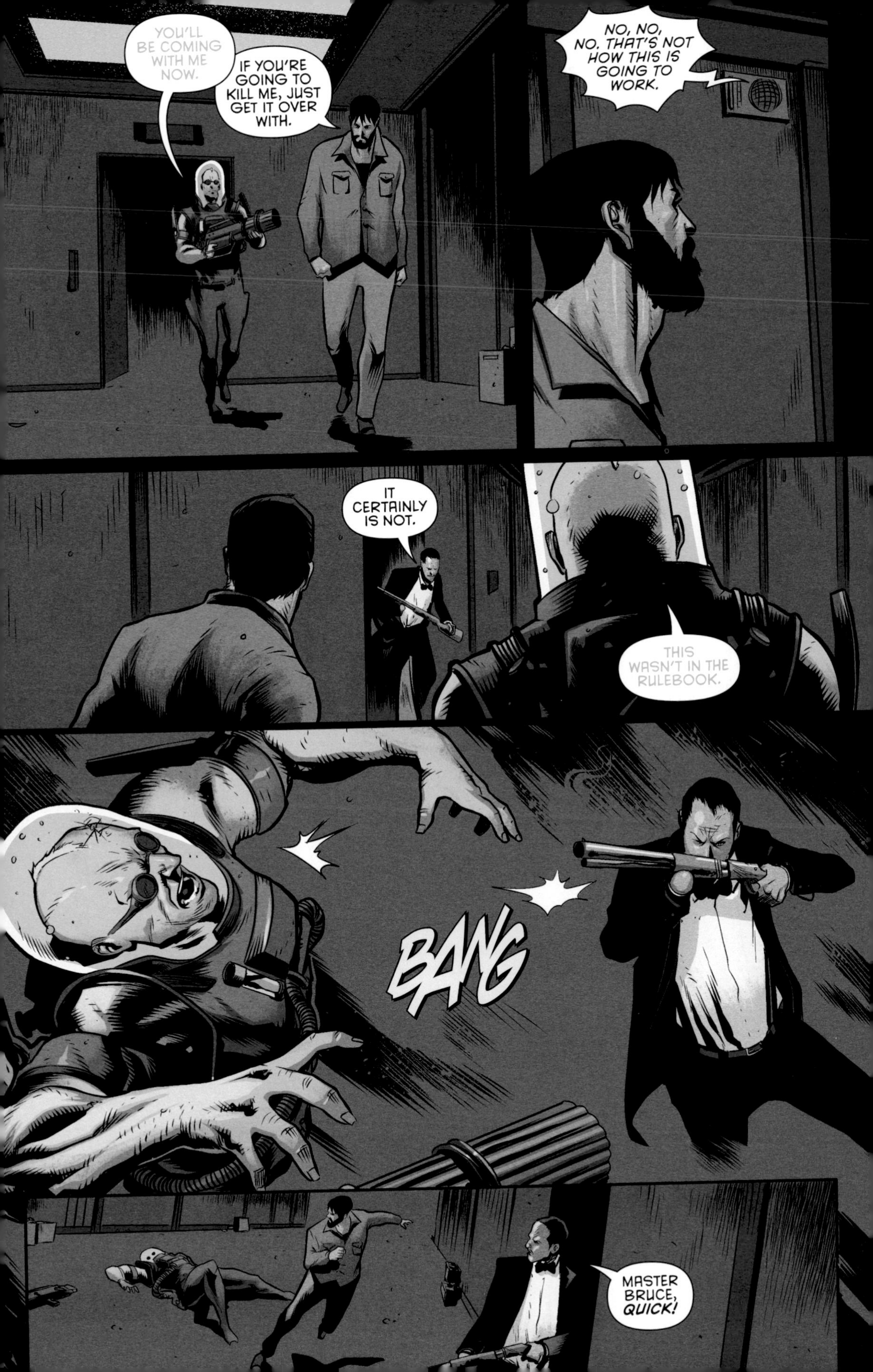
YOU'LL BE COMING WITH ME NOW.
IF YOU'RE GOING TO KILL ME, JUST GET IT OVER WITH.
NO, NO, NO. THAT'S NOT HOW THIS IS GOING TO WORK.
IT CERTAINLY IS NOT.
THIS WASN'T IN THE RULEBOOK.
BANG
MASTER BRUCE, QUICK!

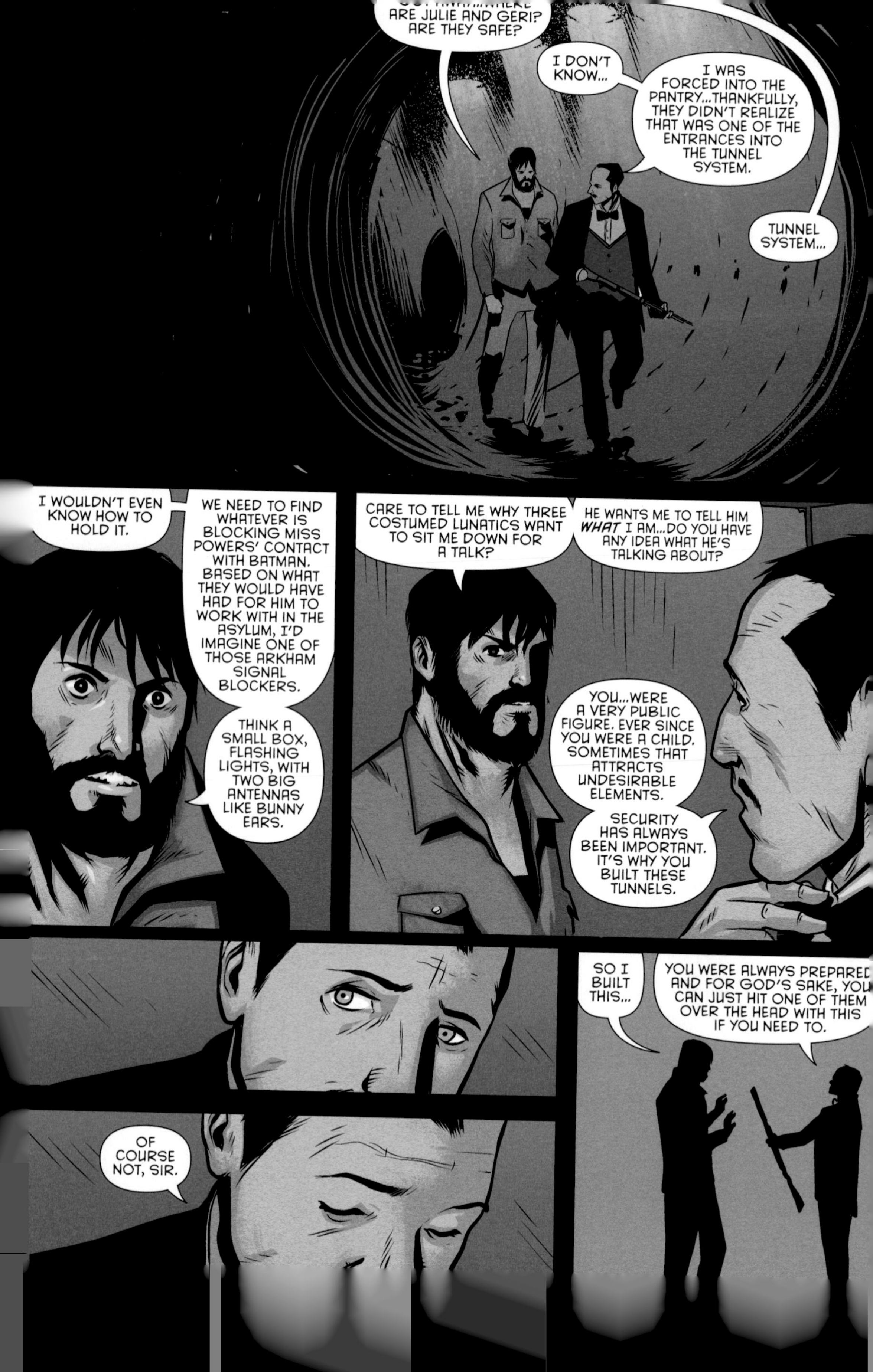

ARE JULIE AND GERI? ARE THEY SAFE?
I DON'T KNOW...
I WAS FORCED INTO THE PANTRY...THANKFULLY, THEY DIDN'T REALIZE THAT WAS ONE OF THE ENTRANCES INTO THE TUNNEL SYSTEM.
TUNNEL SYSTEM...
I WOULDN'T EVEN KNOW HOW TO HOLD IT.
WE NEED TO FIND WHATEVER IS BLOCKING MISS POWERS' CONTACT WITH BATMAN. BASED ON WHAT THEY WOULD HAVE HAD FOR HIM TO WORK WITH IN THE ASYLUM, I'D IMAGINE ONE OF THOSE ARKHAM SIGNAL BLOCKERS.
THINK A SMALL BOX, FLASHING LIGHTS, WITH TWO BIG ANTENNAS LIKE BUNNY EARS.
CARE TO TELL ME WHY THREE COSTUMED LUNATICS WANT TO SIT ME DOWN FOR A TALK?
HE WANTS ME TO TELL HIM *WHAT* I AM...DO YOU HAVE ANY IDEA WHAT HE'S TALKING ABOUT?
YOU...WERE A VERY PUBLIC FIGURE. EVER SINCE YOU WERE A CHILD. SOMETIMES THAT ATTRACTS UNDESIRABLE ELEMENTS.
SECURITY HAS ALWAYS BEEN IMPORTANT. IT'S WHY YOU BUILT THESE TUNNELS.
SO I BUILT THIS...
YOU WERE ALWAYS PREPARED AND FOR GOD'S SAKE, YOU CAN JUST HIT ONE OF THEM OVER THE HEAD WITH THIS IF YOU NEED TO.
OF COURSE NOT, SIR.

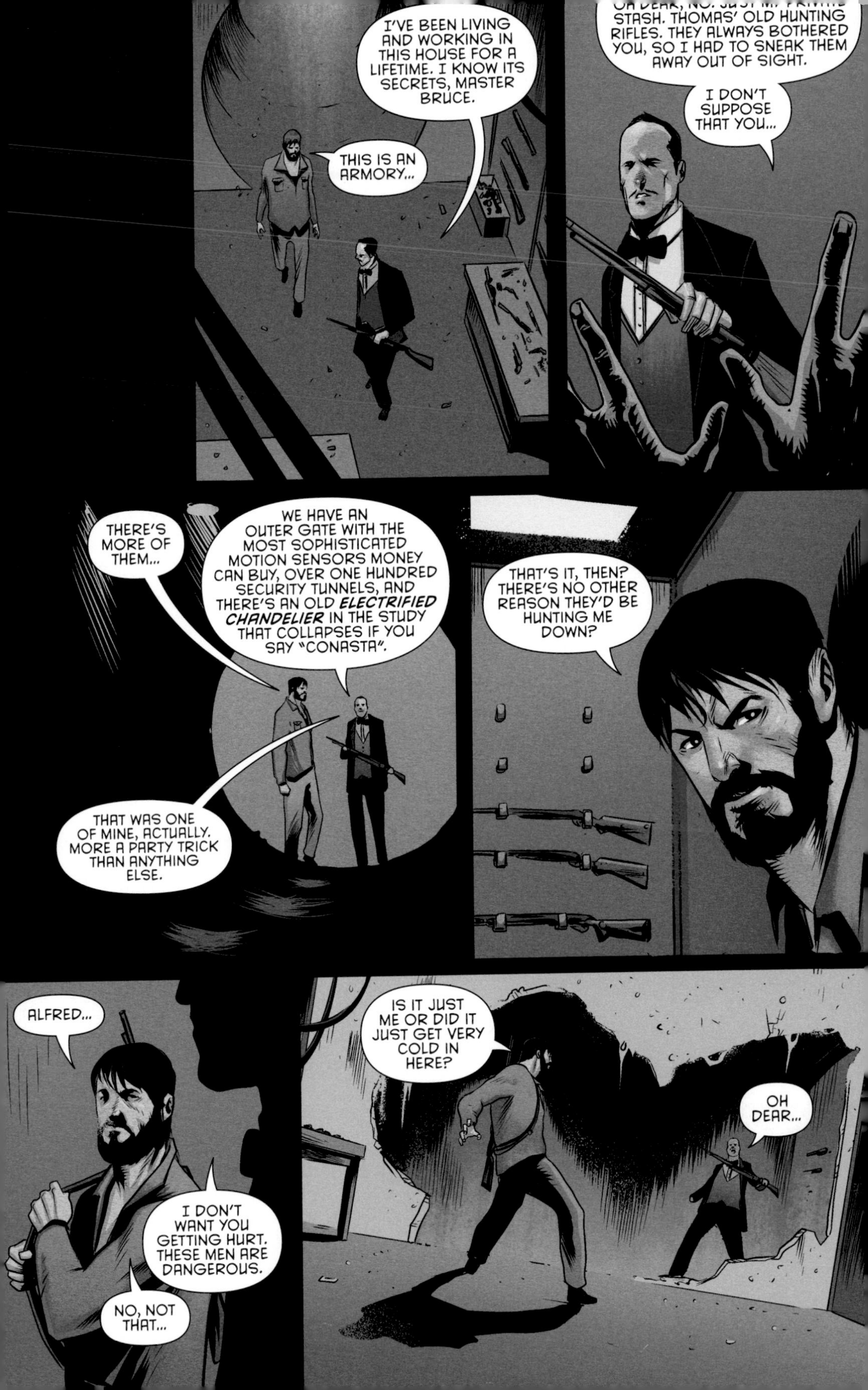
I'VE BEEN LIVING AND WORKING IN THIS HOUSE FOR A LIFETIME. I KNOW ITS SECRETS, MASTER BRUCE.
THIS IS AN ARMORY...
STASH. THOMAS' OLD HUNTING RIFLES. THEY ALWAYS BOTHERED YOU, SO I HAD TO SNEAK THEM AWAY OUT OF SIGHT.
I DON'T SUPPOSE THAT YOU...
THERE'S MORE OF THEM...
WE HAVE AN OUTER GATE WITH THE MOST SOPHISTICATED MOTION SENSORS MONEY CAN BUY, OVER ONE HUNDRED SECURITY TUNNELS, AND THERE'S AN OLD *ELECTRIFIED CHANDELIER* IN THE STUDY THAT COLLAPSES IF YOU SAY "CONASTA".
THAT WAS ONE OF MINE, ACTUALLY. MORE A PARTY TRICK THAN ANYTHING ELSE.
THAT'S IT, THEN? THERE'S NO OTHER REASON THEY'D BE HUNTING ME DOWN?
ALFRED...
I DON'T WANT YOU GETTING HURT. THESE MEN ARE DANGEROUS.
NO, NOT THAT...
IS IT JUST ME OR DID IT JUST GET VERY COLD IN HERE?
OH DEAR...

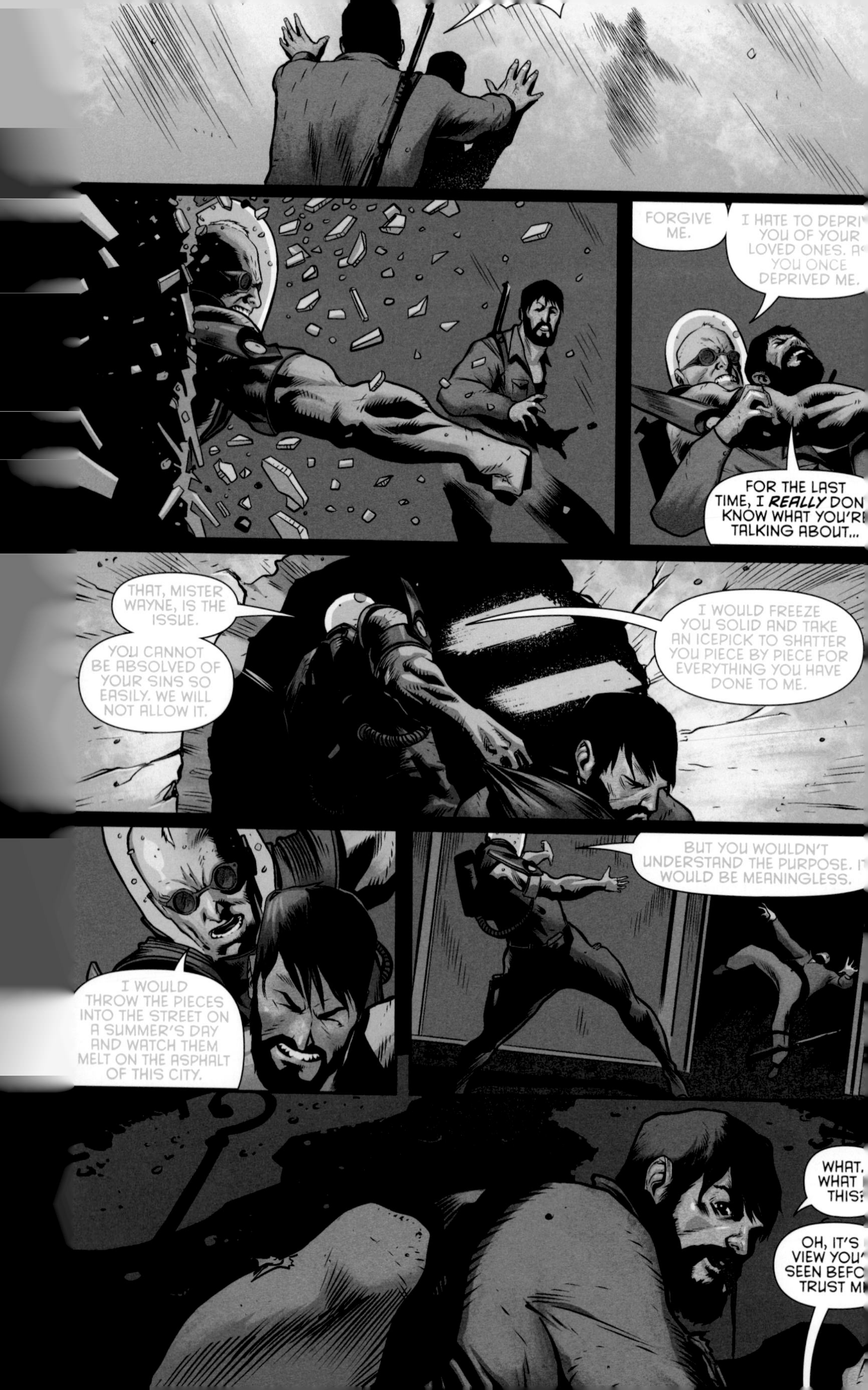
FORGIVE ME.
I HATE TO DEPRI YOU OF YOUR LOVED ONES. A YOU ONCE DEPRIVED ME.
FOR THE LAST TIME, I *REALLY* DON KNOW WHAT YOU'R TALKING ABOUT...
THAT, MISTER WAYNE, IS THE ISSUE.
YOU CANNOT BE ABSOLVED OF YOUR SINS SO EASILY. WE WILL NOT ALLOW IT.
I WOULD FREEZE YOU SOLID AND TAKE AN ICEPICK TO SHATTER YOU PIECE BY PIECE FOR EVERYTHING YOU HAVE DONE TO ME.
I WOULD THROW THE PIECES INTO THE STREET ON A SUMMER'S DAY AND WATCH THEM MELT ON THE ASPHALT OF THIS CITY.
BUT YOU WOULDN'T UNDERSTAND THE PURPOSE. I WOULD BE MEANINGLESS.
WHAT, WHAT THIS?
OH, IT'S VIEW YOU SEEN BEFO TRUST M

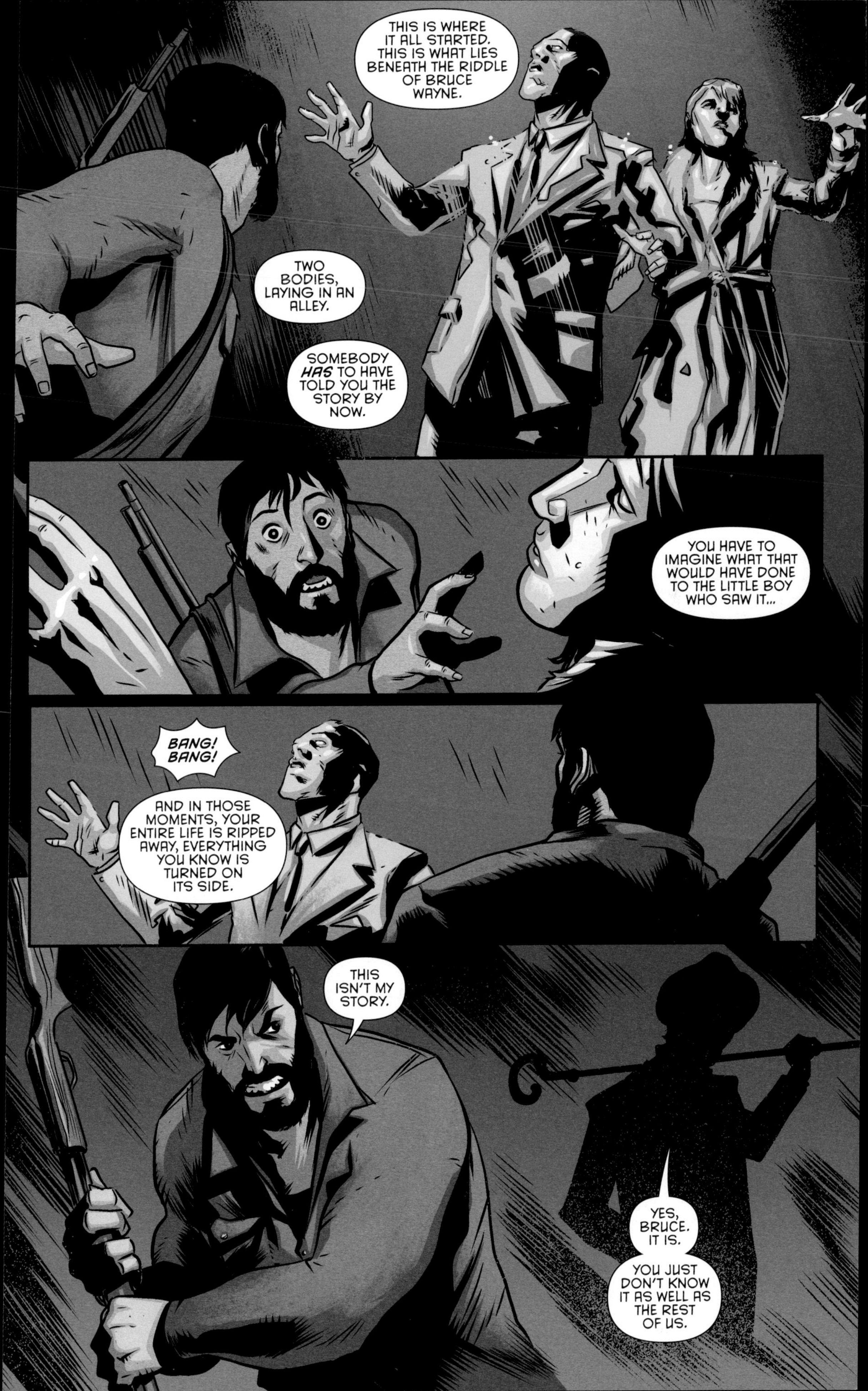
THIS IS WHERE IT ALL STARTED. THIS IS WHAT LIES BENEATH THE RIDDLE OF BRUCE WAYNE.
TWO BODIES, LAYING IN AN ALLEY.
SOMEBODY *HAS* TO HAVE TOLD YOU THE STORY BY NOW.
YOU HAVE TO IMAGINE WHAT THAT WOULD HAVE DONE TO THE LITTLE BOY WHO SAW IT...
BANG! BANG!
AND IN THOSE MOMENTS, YOUR ENTIRE LIFE IS RIPPED AWAY, EVERYTHING YOU KNOW IS TURNED ON ITS SIDE.
THIS ISN'T MY STORY.
YES, BRUCE. IT IS.
YOU JUST DON'T KNOW IT AS WELL AS THE REST OF US.

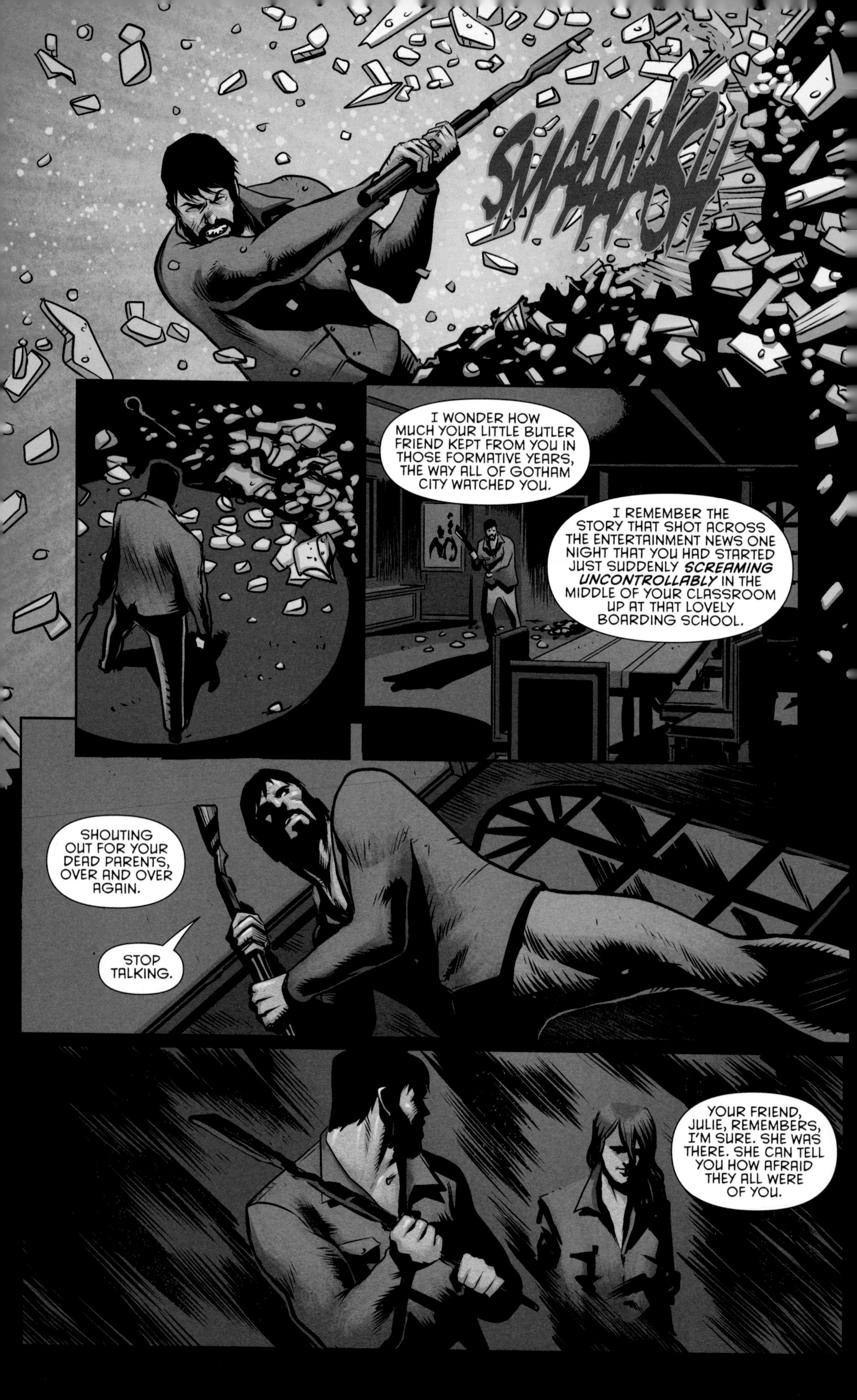
SMAAASH
I WONDER HOW MUCH YOUR LITTLE BUTLER FRIEND KEPT FROM YOU IN THOSE FORMATIVE YEARS, THE WAY ALL OF GOTHAM CITY WATCHED YOU.
I REMEMBER THE STORY THAT SHOT ACROSS THE ENTERTAINMENT NEWS ONE NIGHT THAT YOU HAD STARTED JUST SUDDENLY *SCREAMING UNCONTROLLABLY* IN THE MIDDLE OF YOUR CLASSROOM UP AT THAT LOVELY BOARDING SCHOOL.
SHOUTING OUT FOR YOUR DEAD PARENTS, OVER AND OVER AGAIN.
STOP TALKING.
YOUR FRIEND, JULIE, REMEMBERS, I'M SURE. SHE WAS THERE. SHE CAN TELL YOU HOW AFRAID THEY ALL WERE OF YOU.

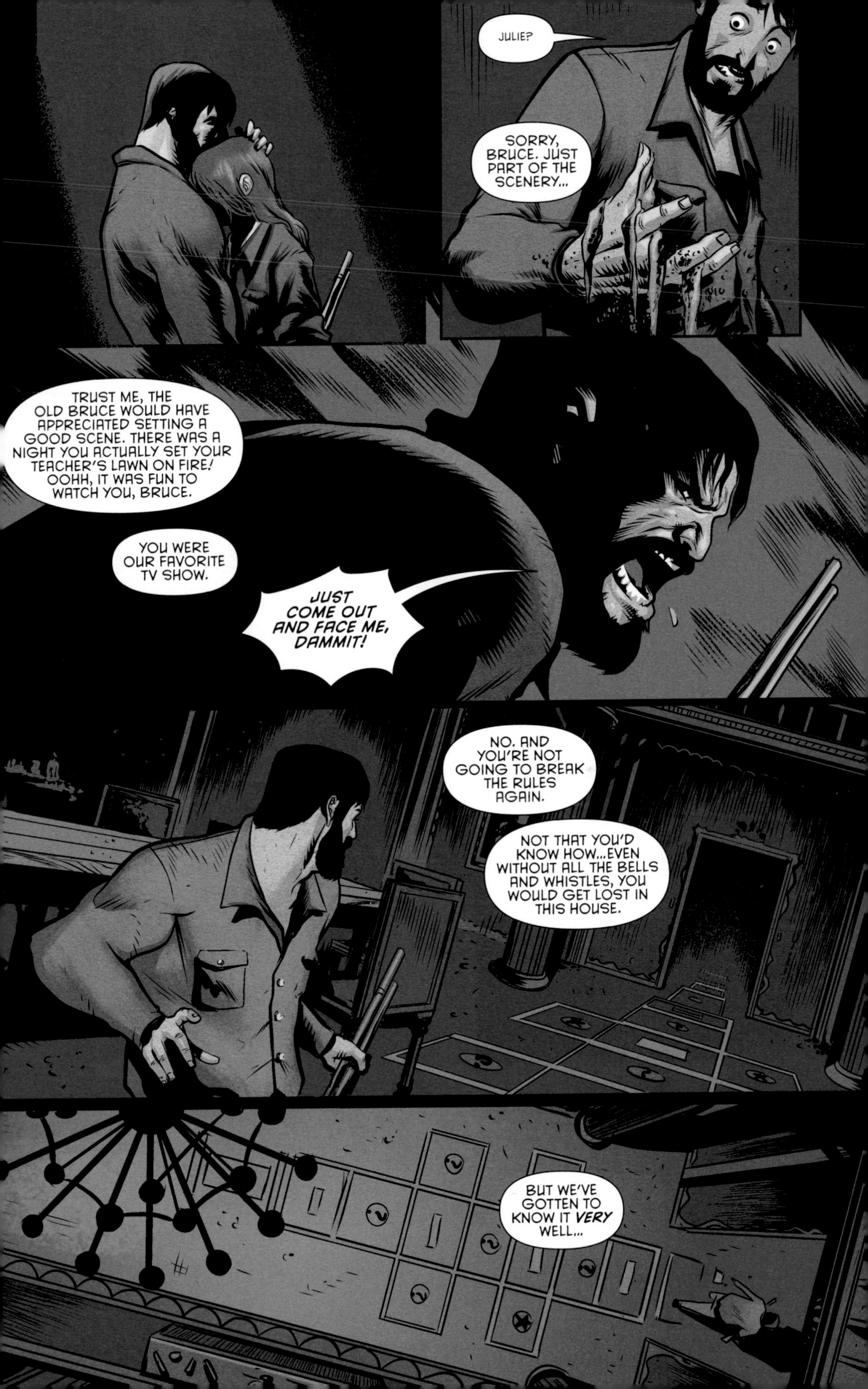
JULIE?
SORRY, BRUCE. JUST PART OF THE SCENERY...
TRUST ME, THE OLD BRUCE WOULD HAVE APPRECIATED SETTING A GOOD SCENE. THERE WAS A NIGHT YOU ACTUALLY SET YOUR TEACHER'S LAWN ON FIRE! OOHH, IT WAS FUN TO WATCH YOU, BRUCE.
YOU WERE OUR FAVORITE TV SHOW.
JUST COME OUT AND FACE ME, DAMMIT!
NO. AND YOU'RE NOT GOING TO BREAK THE RULES AGAIN.
NOT THAT YOU'D KNOW HOW...EVEN WITHOUT ALL THE BELLS AND WHISTLES, YOU WOULD GET LOST IN THIS HOUSE.
BUT WE'VE GOTTEN TO KNOW IT VERY WELL...

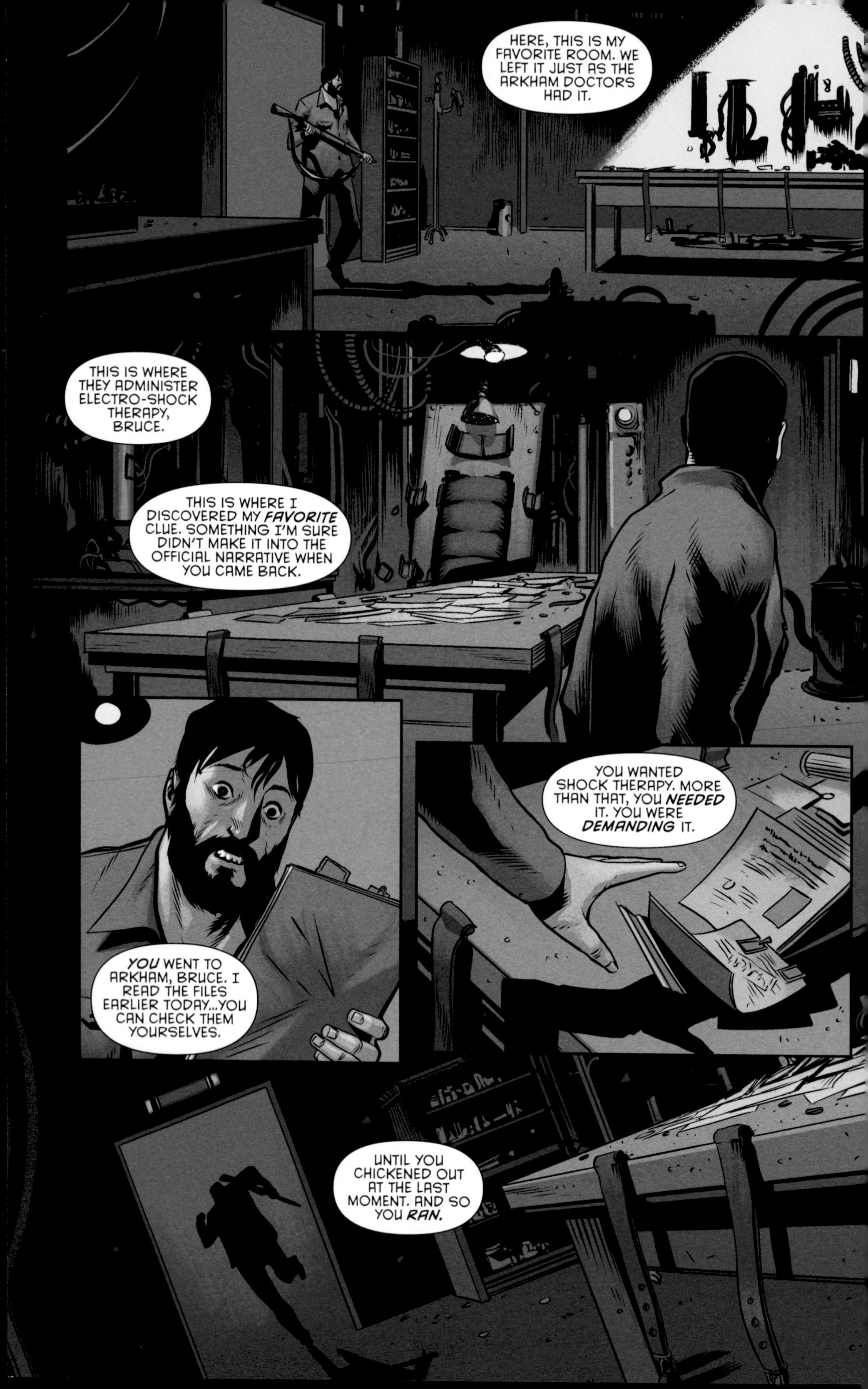
HERE, THIS IS MY FAVORITE ROOM. WE LEFT IT JUST AS THE ARKHAM DOCTORS HAD IT.
THIS IS WHERE THEY ADMINISTER ELECTRO-SHOCK THERAPY, BRUCE.
THIS IS WHERE I DISCOVERED MY *FAVORITE* CLUE. SOMETHING I'M SURE DIDN'T MAKE IT INTO THE OFFICIAL NARRATIVE WHEN YOU CAME BACK.
YOU WENT TO ARKHAM, BRUCE. I READ THE FILES EARLIER TODAY...YOU CAN CHECK THEM YOURSELVES.
YOU WANTED SHOCK THERAPY. MORE THAN THAT, YOU *NEEDED* IT. YOU WERE *DEMANDING* IT.
UNTIL YOU CHICKENED OUT AT THE LAST MOMENT. AND SO YOU *RAN.*

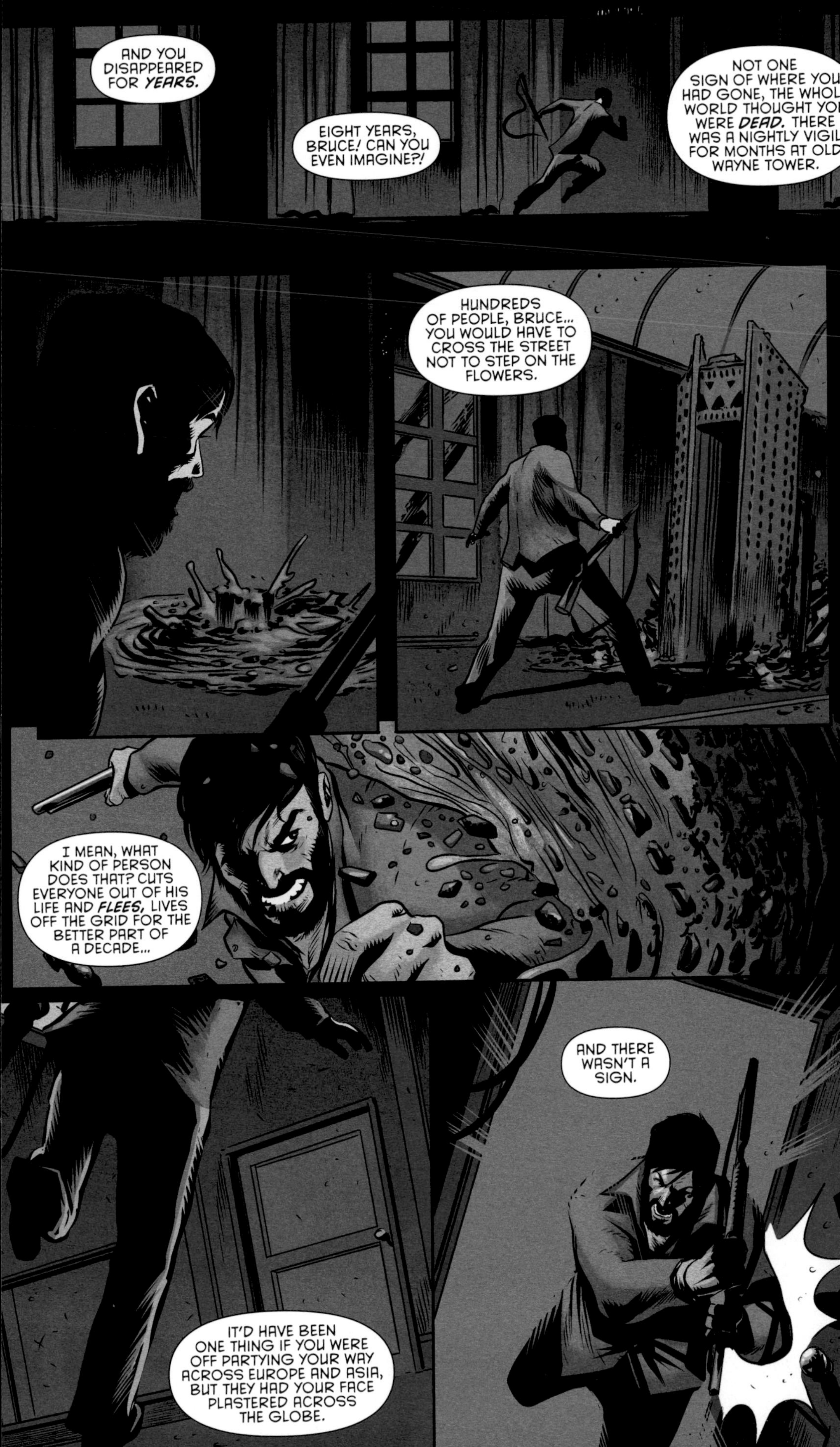
AND YOU DISAPPEARED FOR *YEARS.*
EIGHT YEARS, BRUCE! CAN YOU EVEN IMAGINE?!
NOT ONE SIGN OF WHERE YOU HAD GONE, THE WHOL WORLD THOUGHT YOU WERE *DEAD.* THERE WAS A NIGHTLY VIGIL FOR MONTHS AT OLD WAYNE TOWER.
HUNDREDS OF PEOPLE, BRUCE... YOU WOULD HAVE TO CROSS THE STREET NOT TO STEP ON THE FLOWERS.
I MEAN, WHAT KIND OF PERSON DOES THAT? CUTS EVERYONE OUT OF HIS LIFE AND *FLEES,* LIVES OFF THE GRID FOR THE BETTER PART OF A DECADE...
IT'D HAVE BEEN ONE THING IF YOU WERE OFF PARTYING YOUR WAY ACROSS EUROPE AND ASIA, BUT THEY HAD YOUR FACE PLASTERED ACROSS THE GLOBE.
AND THERE WASN'T A SIGN.

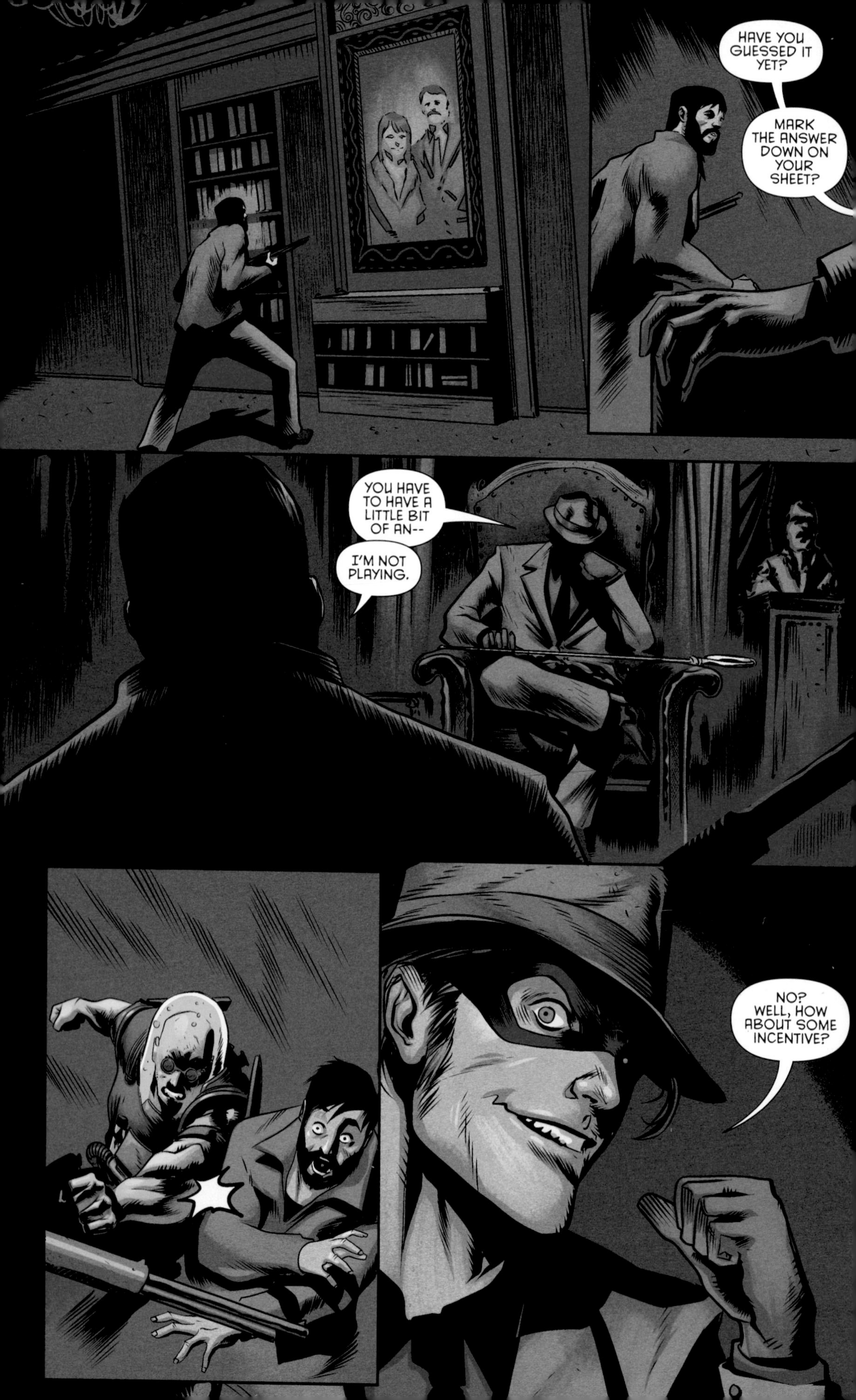
HAVE YOU GUESSED IT YET?
MARK THE ANSWER DOWN ON YOUR SHEET?
YOU HAVE TO HAVE A LITTLE BIT OF AN--
I'M NOT PLAYING.
NO? WELL, HOW ABOUT SOME INCENTIVE?

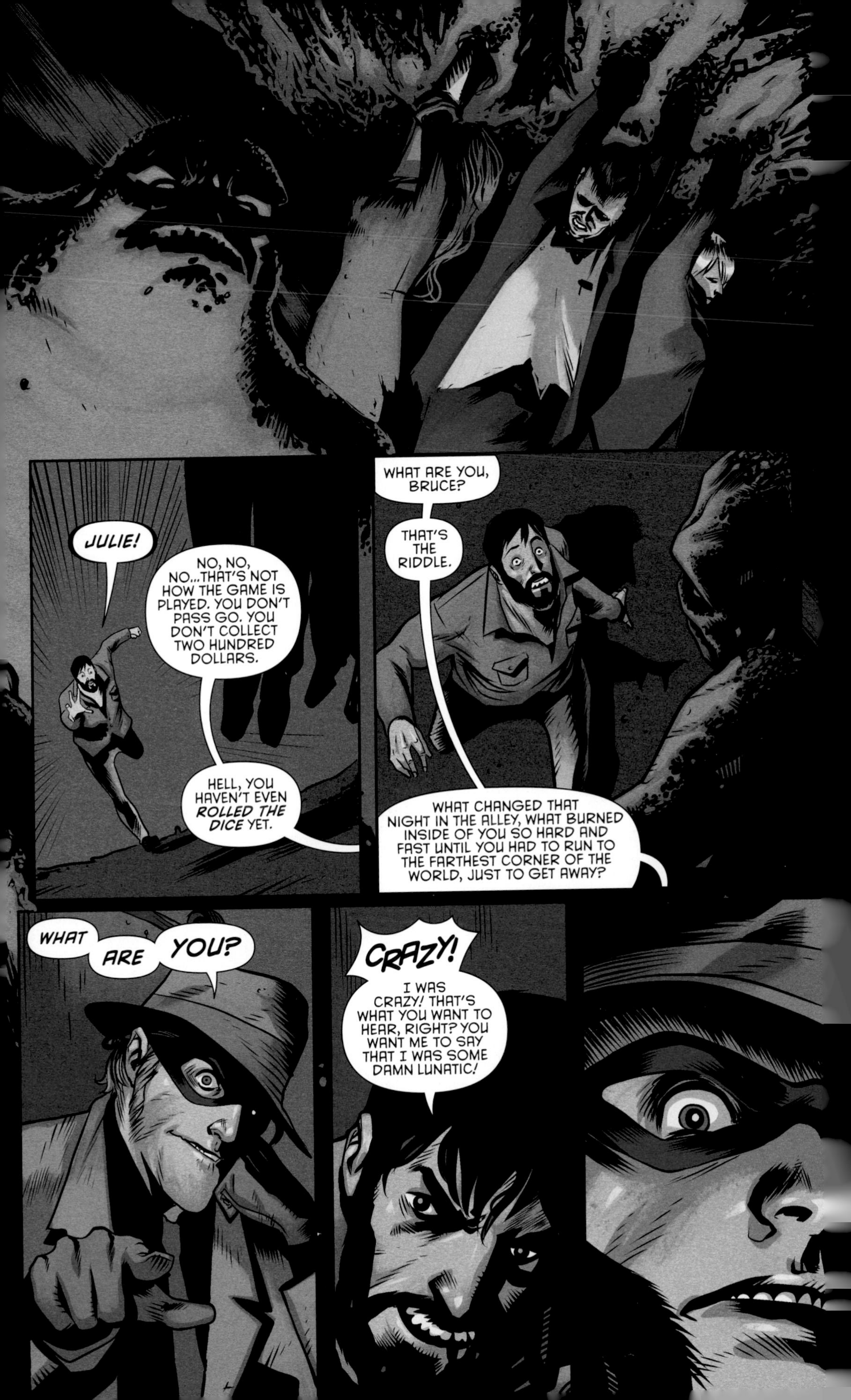
JULIE!
NO, NO, NO...THAT'S NOT HOW THE GAME IS PLAYED. YOU DON'T PASS GO. YOU DON'T COLLECT TWO HUNDRED DOLLARS.
HELL, YOU HAVEN'T EVEN ROLLED THE DICE YET.
WHAT ARE YOU, BRUCE?
THAT'S THE RIDDLE.
WHAT CHANGED THAT NIGHT IN THE ALLEY, WHAT BURNED INSIDE OF YOU SO HARD AND FAST UNTIL YOU HAD TO RUN TO THE FARTHEST CORNER OF THE WORLD, JUST TO GET AWAY?
WHAT
ARE
YOU?
CRAZY!
I WAS CRAZY! THAT'S WHAT YOU WANT TO HEAR, RIGHT? YOU WANT ME TO SAY THAT I WAS SOME DAMN LUNATIC!

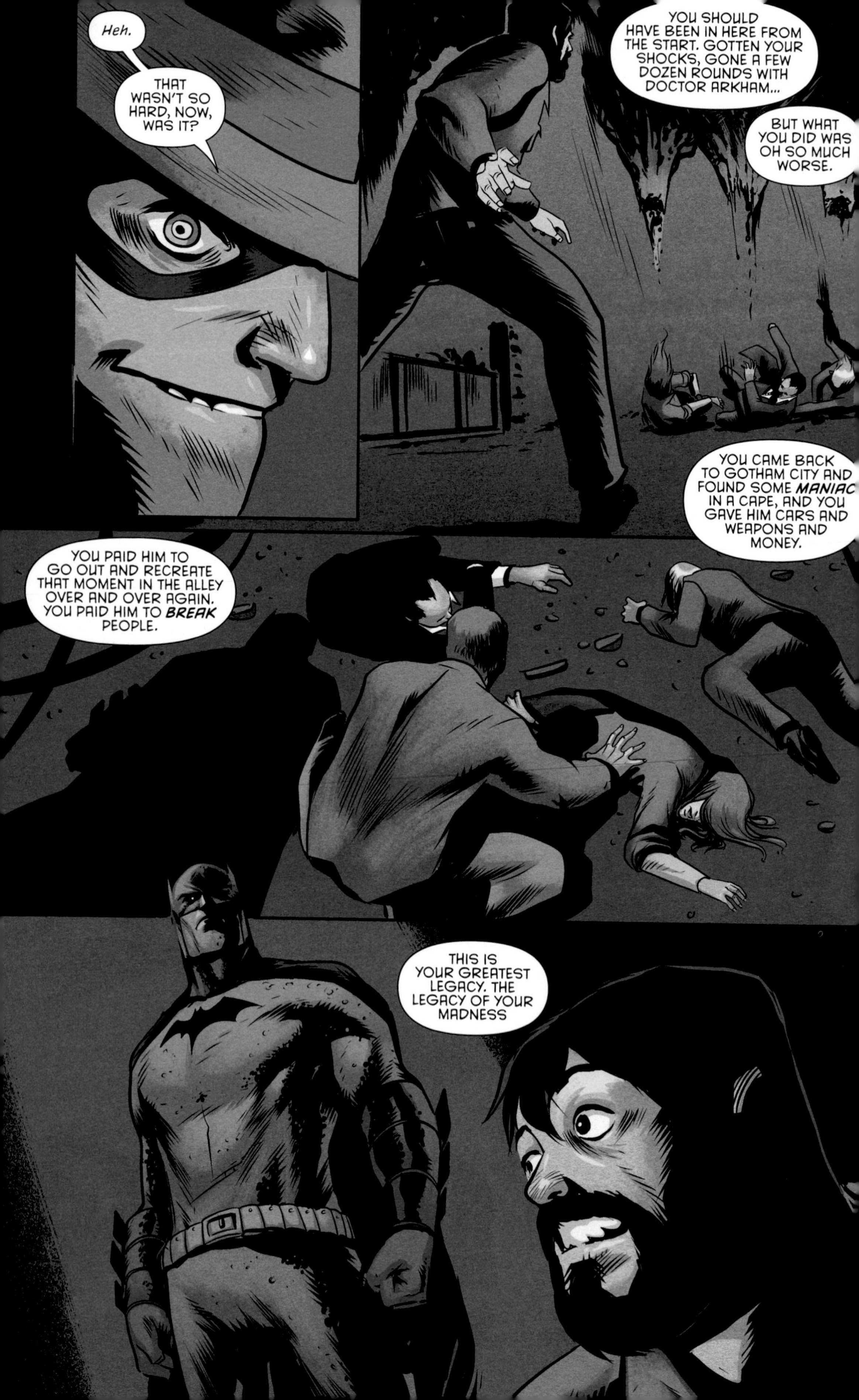
Heh.
THAT WASN'T SO HARD, NOW, WAS IT?
YOU SHOULD HAVE BEEN IN HERE FROM THE START. GOTTEN YOUR SHOCKS, GONE A FEW DOZEN ROUNDS WITH DOCTOR ARKHAM...
BUT WHAT YOU DID WAS OH SO MUCH WORSE.
YOU CAME BACK TO GOTHAM CITY AND FOUND SOME MANIAC IN A CAPE, AND YOU GAVE HIM CARS AND WEAPONS AND MONEY.
YOU PAID HIM TO GO OUT AND RECREATE THAT MOMENT IN THE ALLEY OVER AND OVER AGAIN. YOU PAID HIM TO BREAK PEOPLE.
THIS IS YOUR GREATEST LEGACY. THE LEGACY OF YOUR MADNESS

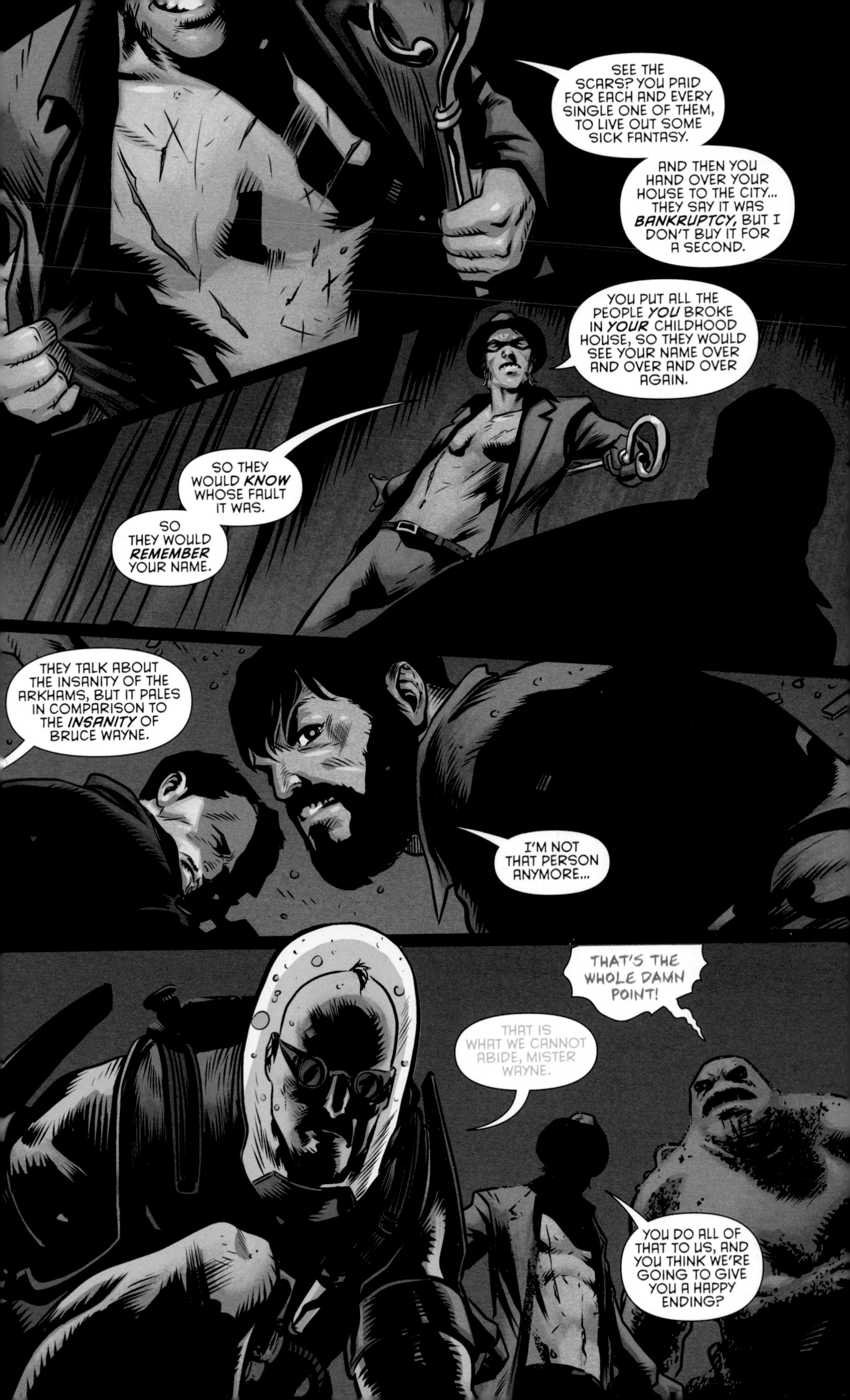
SEE THE SCARS? YOU PAID FOR EACH AND EVERY SINGLE ONE OF THEM, TO LIVE OUT SOME SICK FANTASY.
AND THEN YOU HAND OVER YOUR HOUSE TO THE CITY... THEY SAY IT WAS BANKRUPTCY, BUT I DON'T BUY IT FOR A SECOND.
YOU PUT ALL THE PEOPLE YOU BROKE IN YOUR CHILDHOOD HOUSE, SO THEY WOULD SEE YOUR NAME OVER AND OVER AND OVER AGAIN.
SO THEY WOULD KNOW WHOSE FAULT IT WAS.
SO THEY WOULD REMEMBER YOUR NAME.
THEY TALK ABOUT THE INSANITY OF THE ARKHAMS, BUT IT PALES IN COMPARISON TO THE INSANITY OF BRUCE WAYNE.
I'M NOT THAT PERSON ANYMORE...
THAT'S THE WHOLE DAMN POINT!
THAT IS WHAT WE CANNOT ABIDE, MISTER WAYNE.
YOU DO ALL OF THAT TO US, AND YOU THINK WE'RE GOING TO GIVE YOU A HAPPY ENDING?

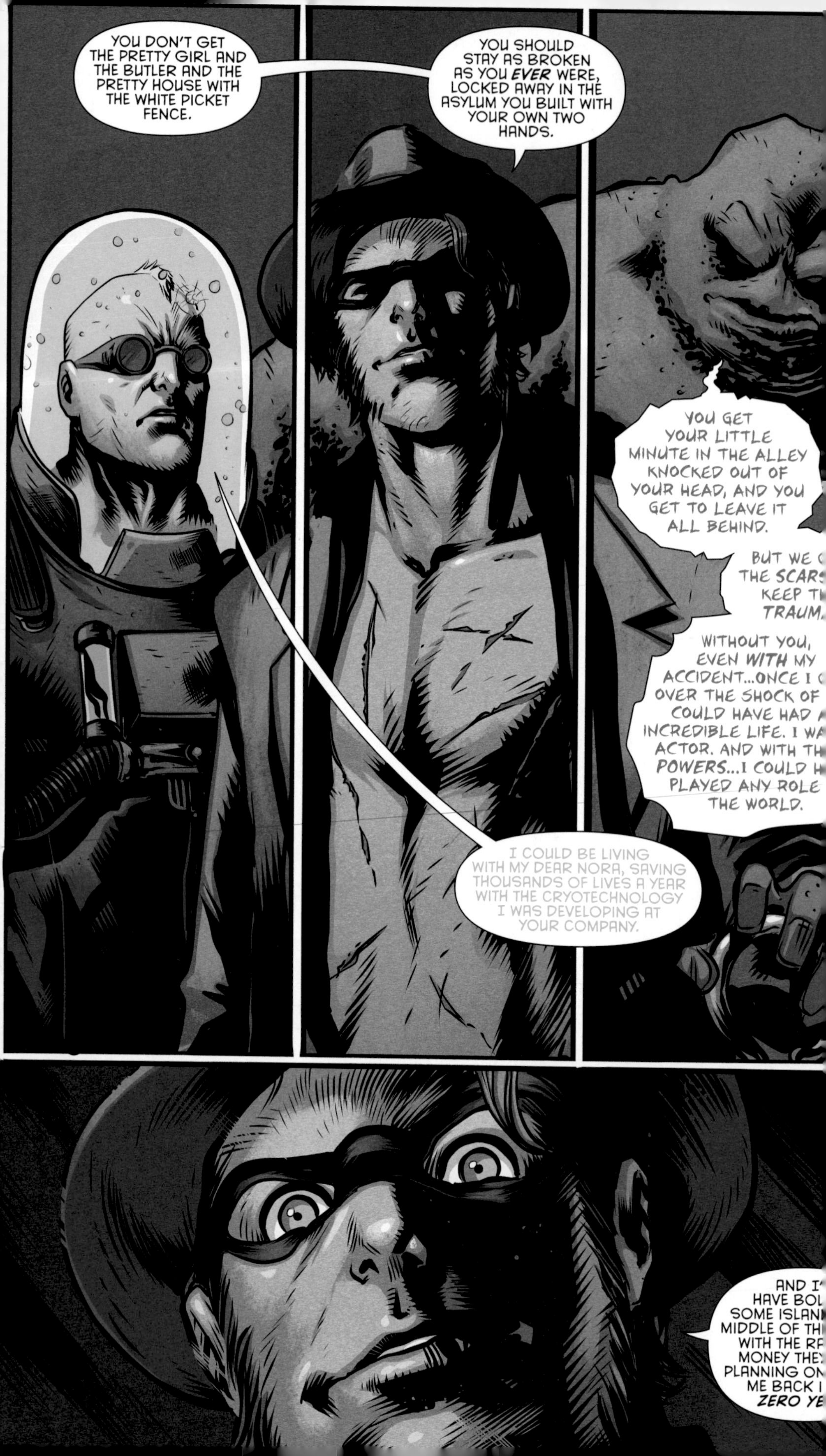
YOU DON'T GET THE PRETTY GIRL AND THE BUTLER AND THE PRETTY HOUSE WITH THE WHITE PICKET FENCE.
YOU SHOULD STAY AS BROKEN AS YOU *EVER* WERE, LOCKED AWAY IN THE ASYLUM YOU BUILT WITH YOUR OWN TWO HANDS.
YOU GET YOUR LITTLE MINUTE IN THE ALLEY KNOCKED OUT OF YOUR HEAD, AND YOU GET TO LEAVE IT ALL BEHIND.
BUT WE THE *SCAR* KEEP T *TRAUM*
WITHOUT YOU, EVEN *WITH* MY ACCIDENT...ONCE I OVER THE SHOCK OF COULD HAVE HAD INCREDIBLE LIFE. I WA ACTOR. AND WITH TH *POWERS*...I COULD PLAYED ANY ROLE THE WORLD.
I COULD BE LIVING WITH MY DEAR NORA, SAVING THOUSANDS OF LIVES A YEAR WITH THE CRYOTECHNOLOGY I WAS DEVELOPING AT YOUR COMPANY.
AND I HAVE BO SOME ISLAN MIDDLE OF TH WITH THE R MONEY THE PLANNING ON ME BACK *ZERO YE*

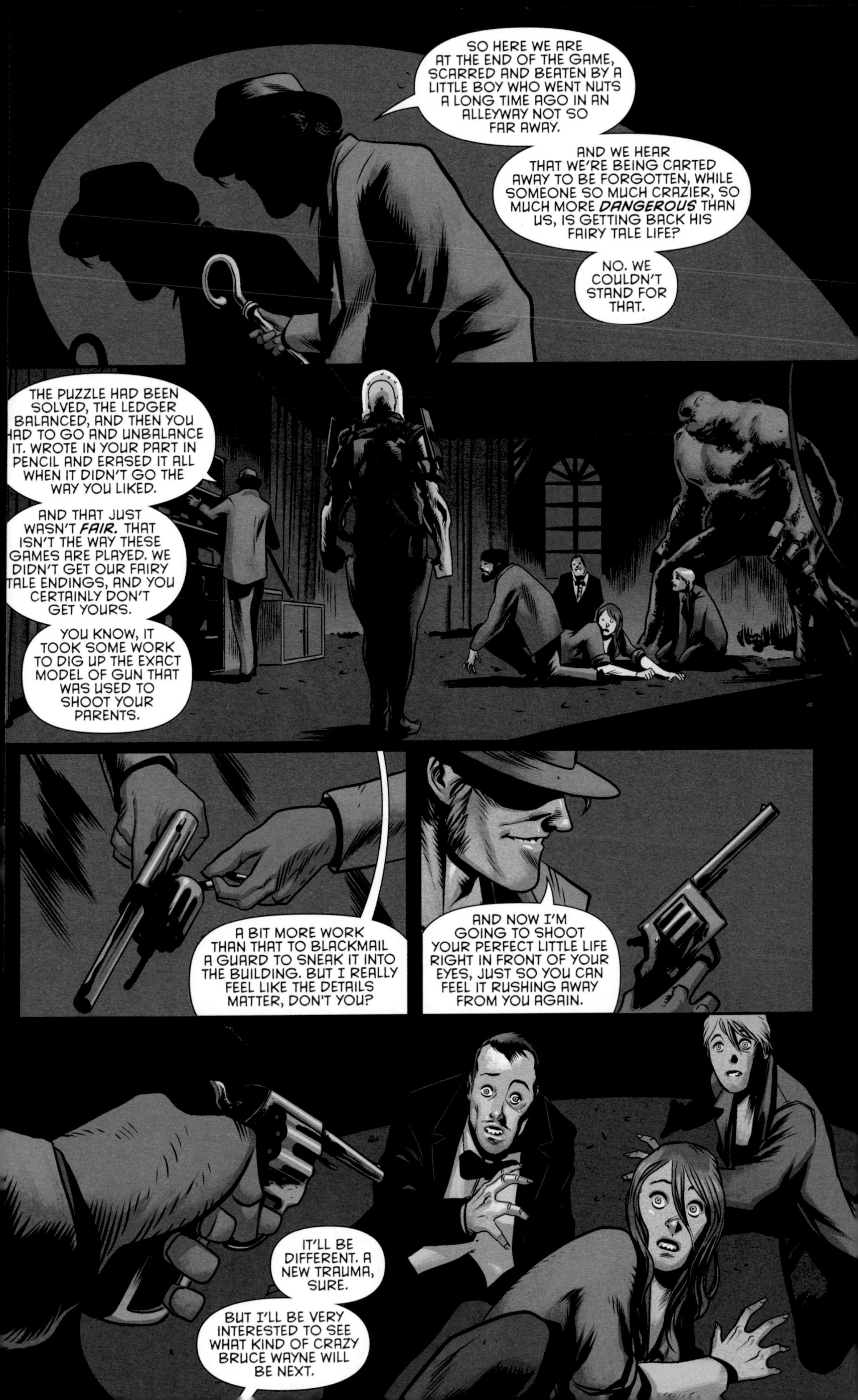
SO HERE WE ARE AT THE END OF THE GAME, SCARRED AND BEATEN BY A LITTLE BOY WHO WENT NUTS A LONG TIME AGO IN AN ALLEYWAY NOT SO FAR AWAY.
AND WE HEAR THAT WE'RE BEING CARTED AWAY TO BE FORGOTTEN, WHILE SOMEONE SO MUCH CRAZIER, SO MUCH MORE DANGEROUS THAN US, IS GETTING BACK HIS FAIRY TALE LIFE?
NO. WE COULDN'T STAND FOR THAT.
THE PUZZLE HAD BEEN SOLVED, THE LEDGER BALANCED, AND THEN YOU HAD TO GO AND UNBALANCE IT. WROTE IN YOUR PART IN PENCIL AND ERASED IT ALL WHEN IT DIDN'T GO THE WAY YOU LIKED.
AND THAT JUST WASN'T FAIR. THAT ISN'T THE WAY THESE GAMES ARE PLAYED. WE DIDN'T GET OUR FAIRY TALE ENDINGS, AND YOU CERTAINLY DON'T GET YOURS.
YOU KNOW, IT TOOK SOME WORK TO DIG UP THE EXACT MODEL OF GUN THAT WAS USED TO SHOOT YOUR PARENTS.
A BIT MORE WORK THAN THAT TO BLACKMAIL A GUARD TO SNEAK IT INTO THE BUILDING. BUT I REALLY FEEL LIKE THE DETAILS MATTER, DON'T YOU?
AND NOW I'M GOING TO SHOOT YOUR PERFECT LITTLE LIFE RIGHT IN FRONT OF YOUR EYES, JUST SO YOU CAN FEEL IT RUSHING AWAY FROM YOU AGAIN.
IT'LL BE DIFFERENT. A NEW TRAUMA, SURE.
BUT I'LL BE VERY INTERESTED TO SEE WHAT KIND OF CRAZY BRUCE WAYNE WILL BE NEXT.

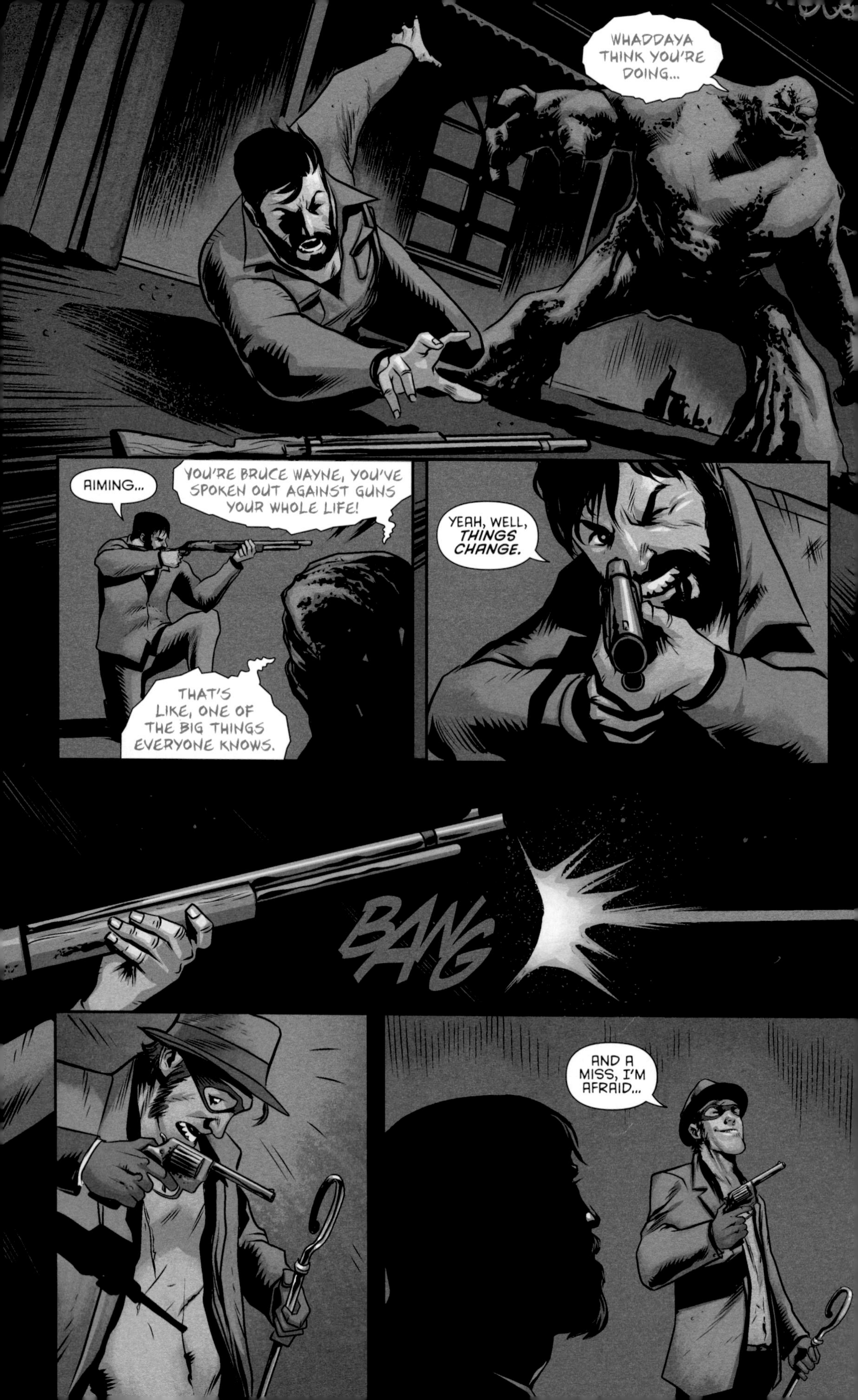
WHADDAYA THINK YOU'RE DOING...
AIMING...
YOU'RE BRUCE WAYNE, YOU'VE SPOKEN OUT AGAINST GUNS YOUR WHOLE LIFE!
THAT'S LIKE, ONE OF THE BIG THINGS EVERYONE KNOWS.
YEAH, WELL, *THINGS CHANGE.*
BANG
AND A MISS, I'M AFRAID...

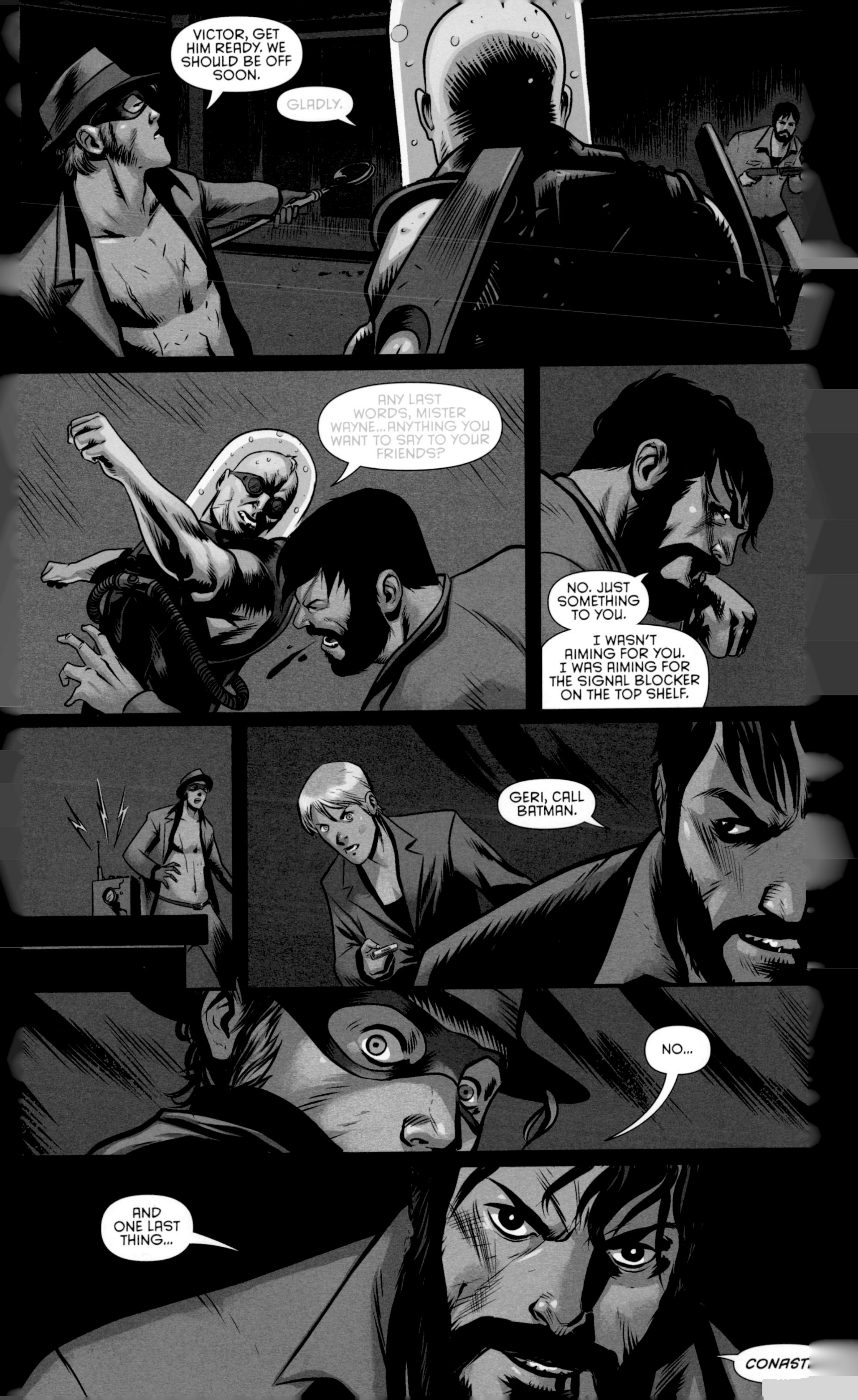
VICTOR, GET HIM READY. WE SHOULD BE OFF SOON.
GLADLY.
ANY LAST WORDS, MISTER WAYNE...ANYTHING YOU WANT TO SAY TO YOUR FRIENDS?
NO. JUST SOMETHING TO YOU.
I WASN'T AIMING FOR YOU. I WAS AIMING FOR THE SIGNAL BLOCKER ON THE TOP SHELF.
GERI, CALL BATMAN.
NO...
AND ONE LAST THING...

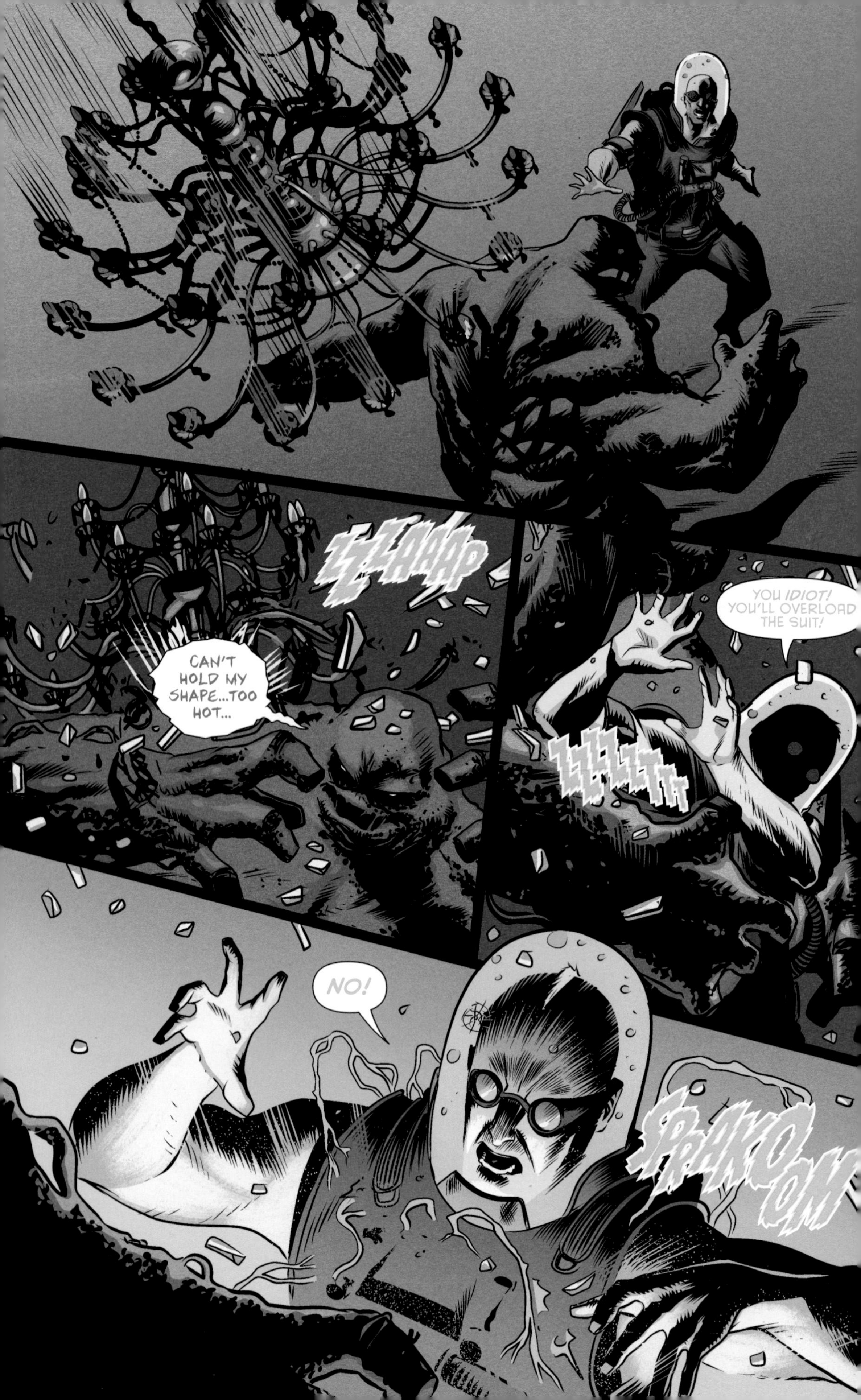
ZZZAAAP
CAN'T HOLD MY SHAPE...TOO HOT...
YOU IDIOT! YOU'LL OVERLOAD THE SUIT!
ZZZZZZTTT
NO!
SPRAKOOM

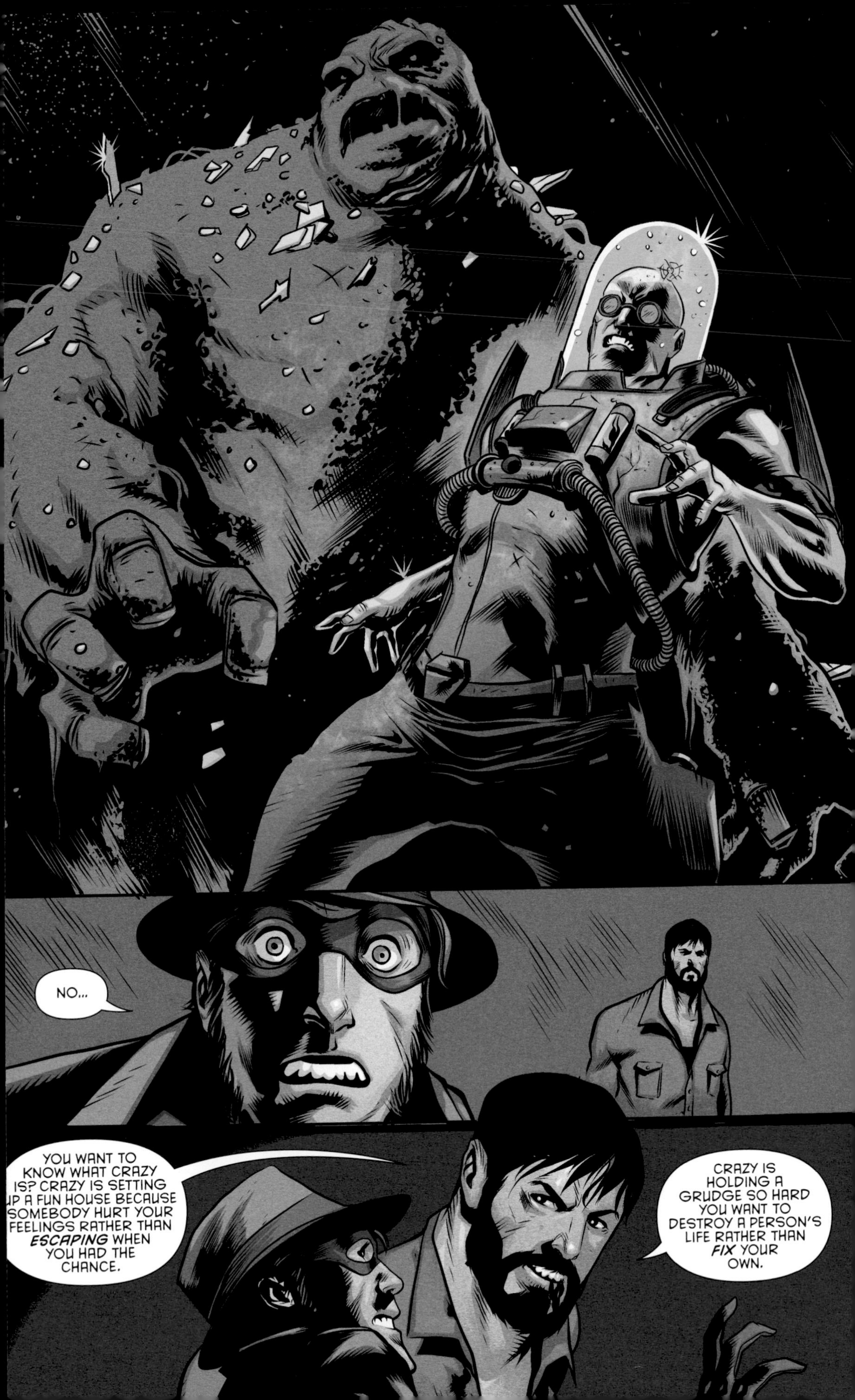
NO...
YOU WANT TO KNOW WHAT CRAZY IS? CRAZY IS SETTING UP A FUN HOUSE BECAUSE SOMEBODY HURT YOUR FEELINGS RATHER THAN *ESCAPING* WHEN YOU HAD THE CHANCE.
CRAZY IS HOLDING A GRUDGE SO HARD YOU WANT TO DESTROY A PERSON'S LIFE RATHER THAN *FIX* YOUR OWN.

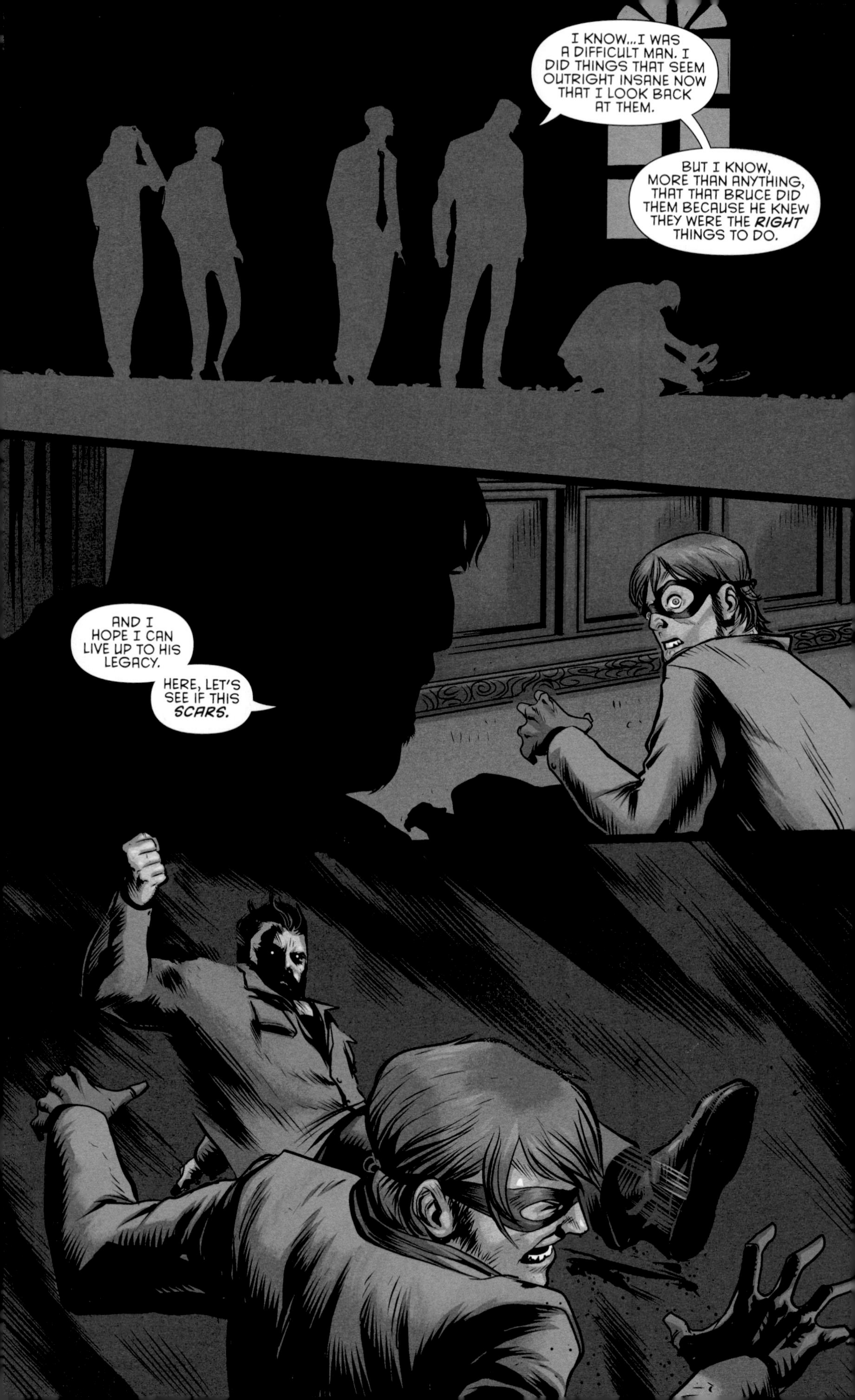
I KNOW...I WAS A DIFFICULT MAN. I DID THINGS THAT SEEM OUTRIGHT INSANE NOW THAT I LOOK BACK AT THEM.
BUT I KNOW, MORE THAN ANYTHING, THAT THAT BRUCE DID THEM BECAUSE HE KNEW THEY WERE THE *RIGHT* THINGS TO DO.
AND I HOPE I CAN LIVE UP TO HIS LEGACY.
HERE, LET'S SEE IF THIS *SCARS.*

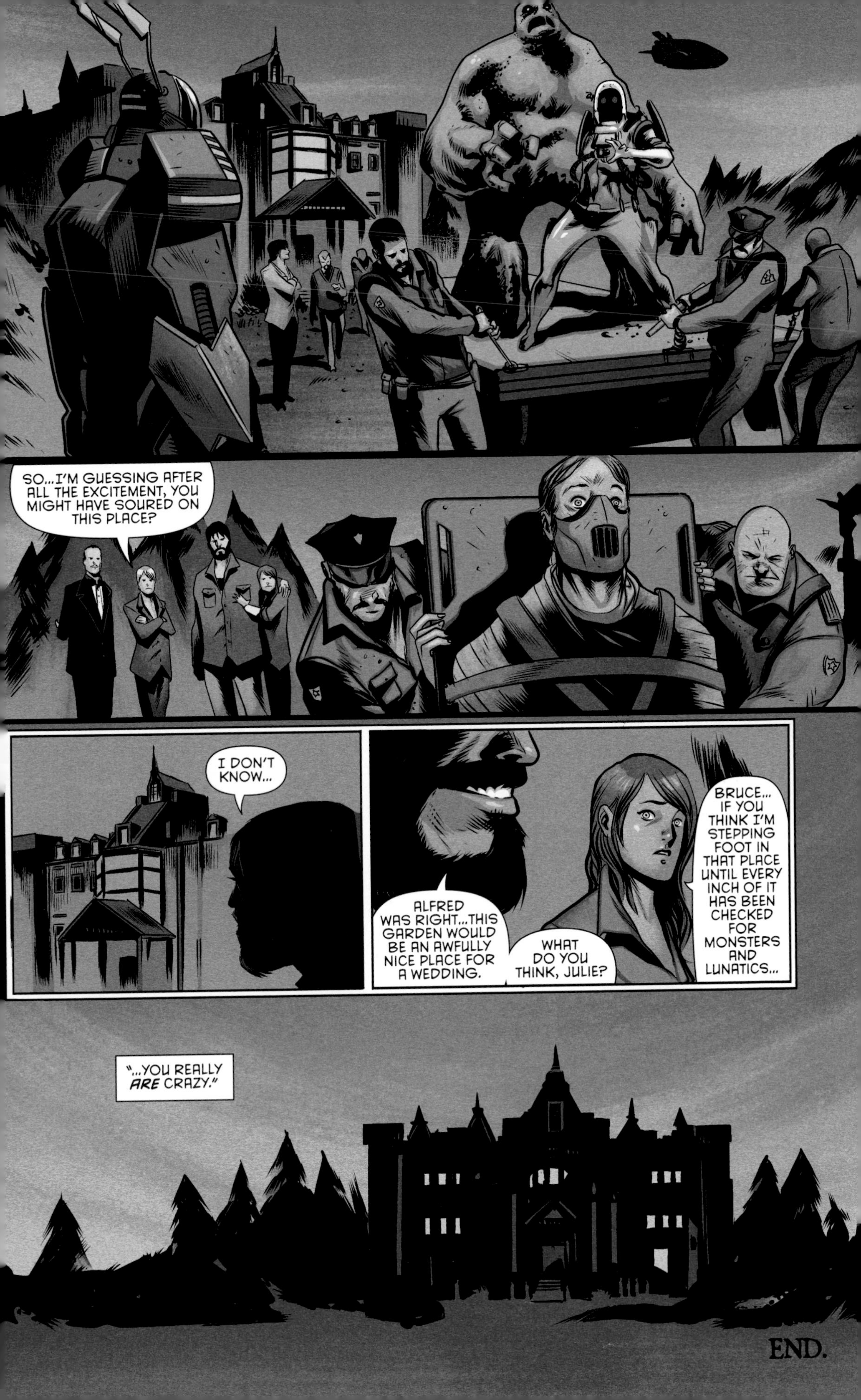
SO...I'M GUESSING AFTER ALL THE EXCITEMENT, YOU MIGHT HAVE SOURED ON THIS PLACE?
I DON'T KNOW...
ALFRED WAS RIGHT...THIS GARDEN WOULD BE AN AWFULLY NICE PLACE FOR A WEDDING.
WHAT DO YOU THINK, JULIE?
BRUCE... IF YOU THINK I'M STEPPING FOOT IN THAT PLACE UNTIL EVERY INCH OF IT HAS BEEN CHECKED FOR MONSTERS AND LUNATICS...
"...YOU REALLY ***ARE*** CRAZY."
END.

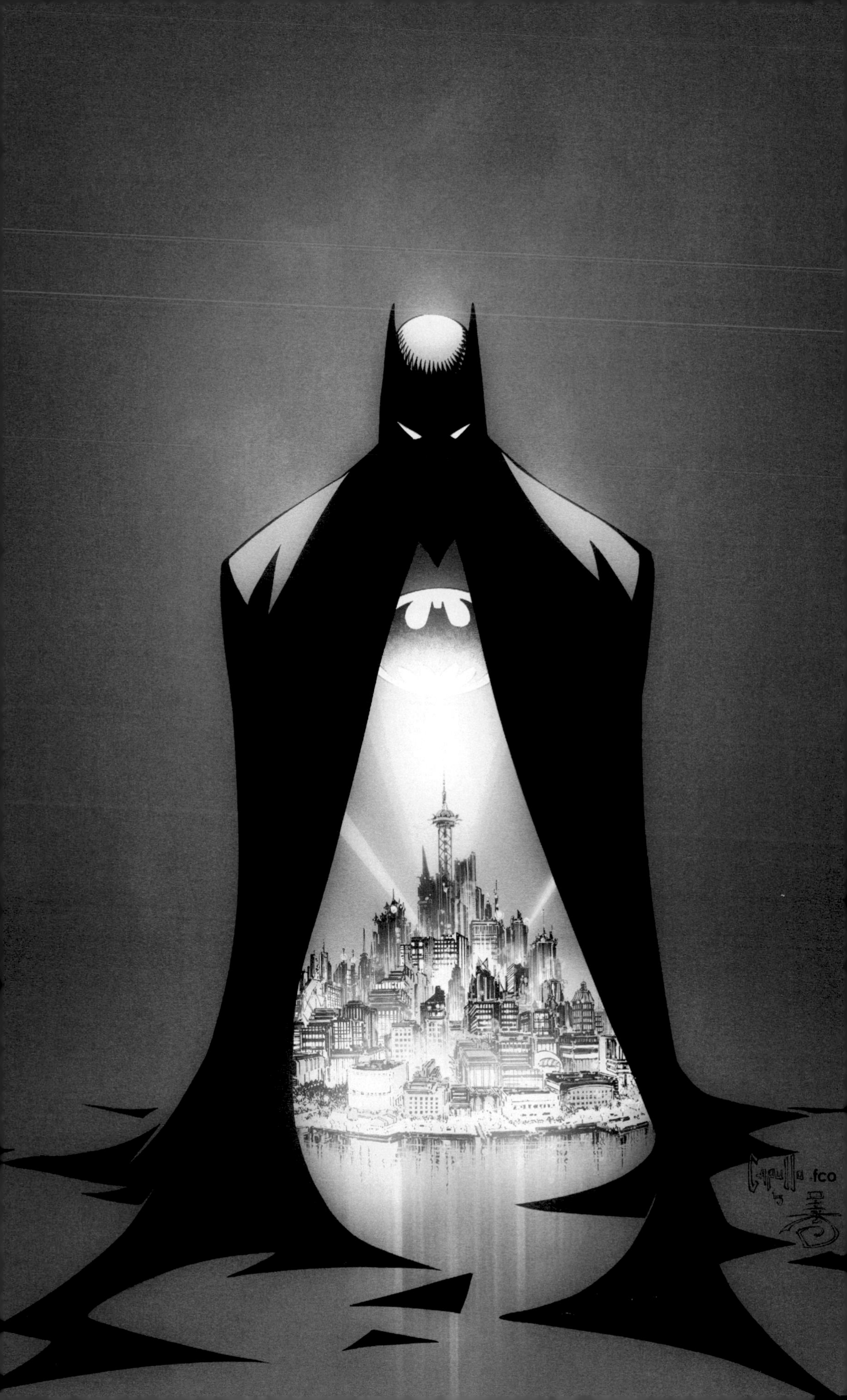

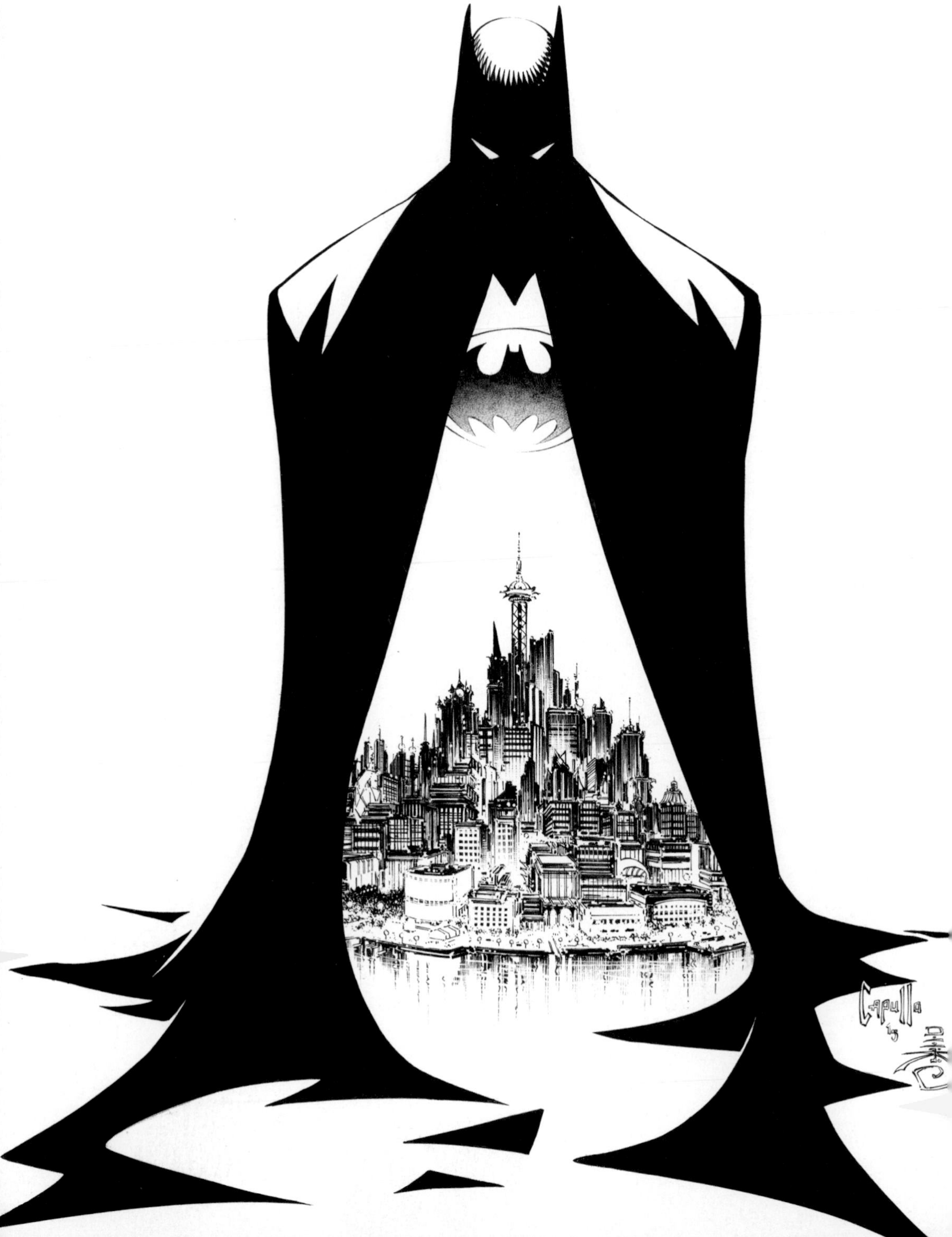
Capullo

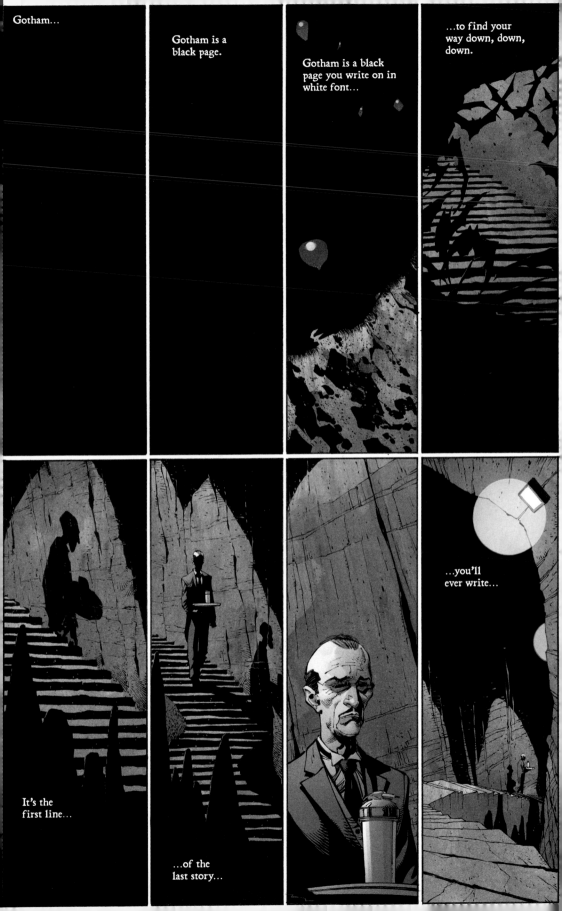

Gotham...

Gotham is a black page.

Gotham is a black page you write on in white font...

...to find your way down, down, down.

It's the first line...

...of the last story...

...you'll ever write...

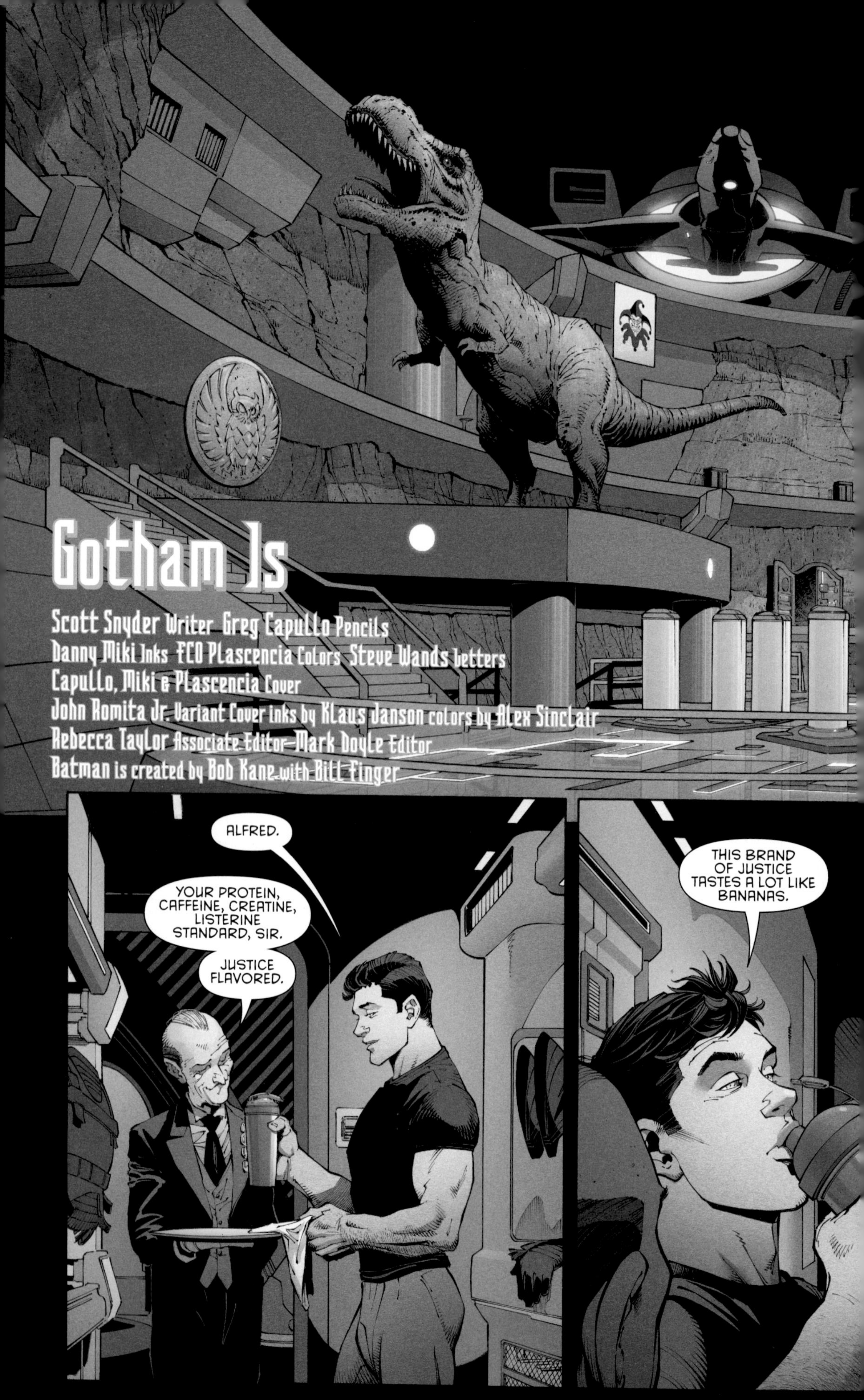
Gotham Is
Scott Snyder Writer Greg Capullo Pencils
Danny Miki Inks FCO Plascencia Colors Steve Wands Letters
Capullo, Miki & Plascencia Cover
John Romita Jr. Variant Cover inks by Klaus Janson colors by Alex Sinclair
Rebecca Taylor Associate Editor Mark Doyle Editor
Batman is created by Bob Kane with Bill Finger
ALFRED.
YOUR PROTEIN, CAFFEINE, CREATINE, LISTERINE STANDARD, SIR.
JUSTICE FLAVORED.
THIS BRAND OF JUSTICE TASTES A LOT LIKE BANANAS.

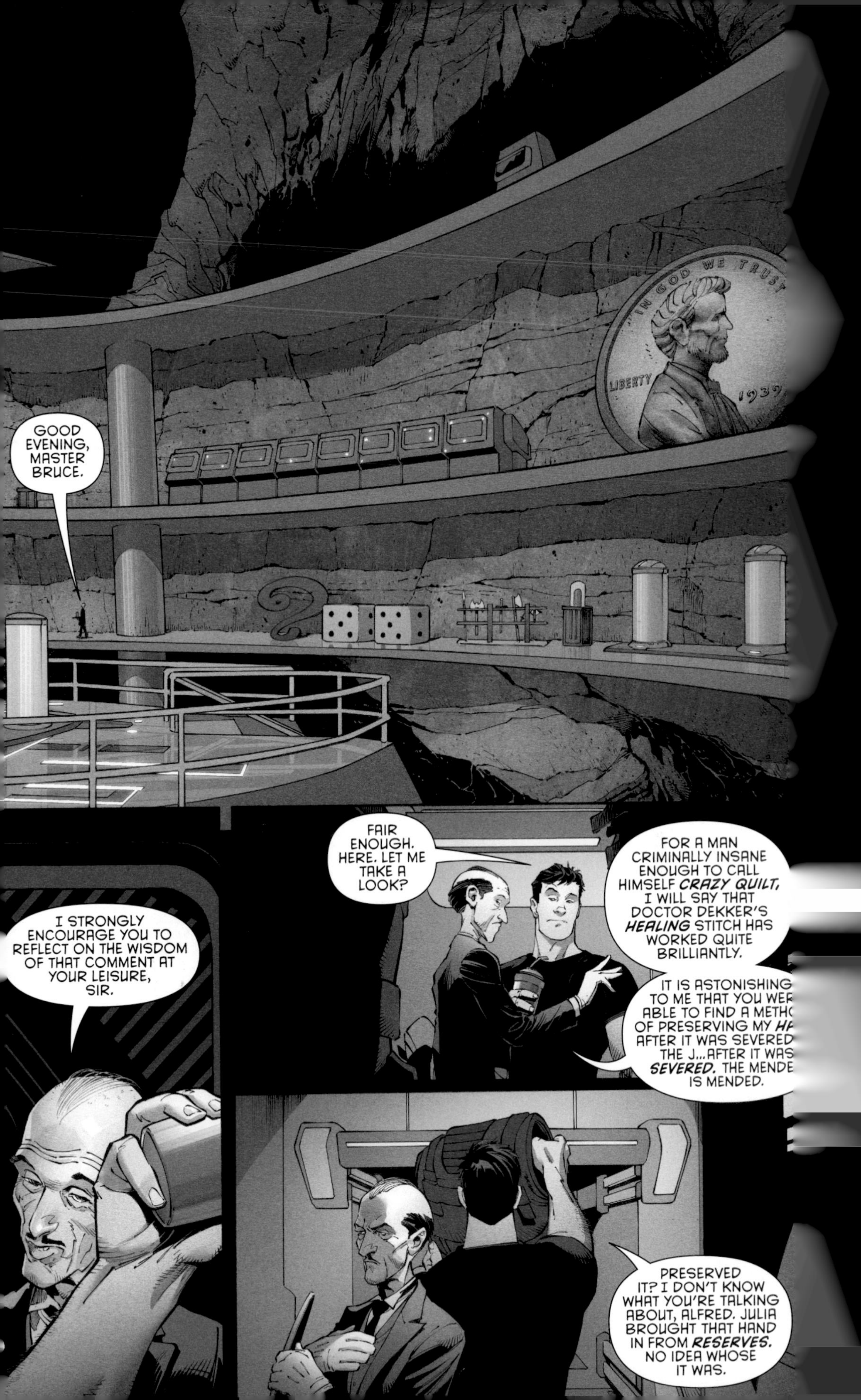
GOOD EVENING, MASTER BRUCE.
FAIR ENOUGH. HERE. LET ME TAKE A LOOK?
FOR A MAN CRIMINALLY INSANE ENOUGH TO CALL HIMSELF CRAZY QUILT, I WILL SAY THAT DOCTOR DEKKER'S HEALING STITCH HAS WORKED QUITE BRILLIANTLY.
IT IS ASTONISHING TO ME THAT YOU WER ABLE TO FIND A METHO OF PRESERVING MY HA AFTER IT WAS SEVERED THE J...AFTER IT WAS SEVERED. THE MENDE IS MENDED.
PRESERVED IT? I DON'T KNOW WHAT YOU'RE TALKING ABOUT, ALFRED. JULIA BROUGHT THAT HAND IN FROM RESERVES. NO IDEA WHOSE IT WAS.
I STRONGLY ENCOURAGE YOU TO REFLECT ON THE WISDOM OF THAT COMMENT AT YOUR LEISURE, SIR.

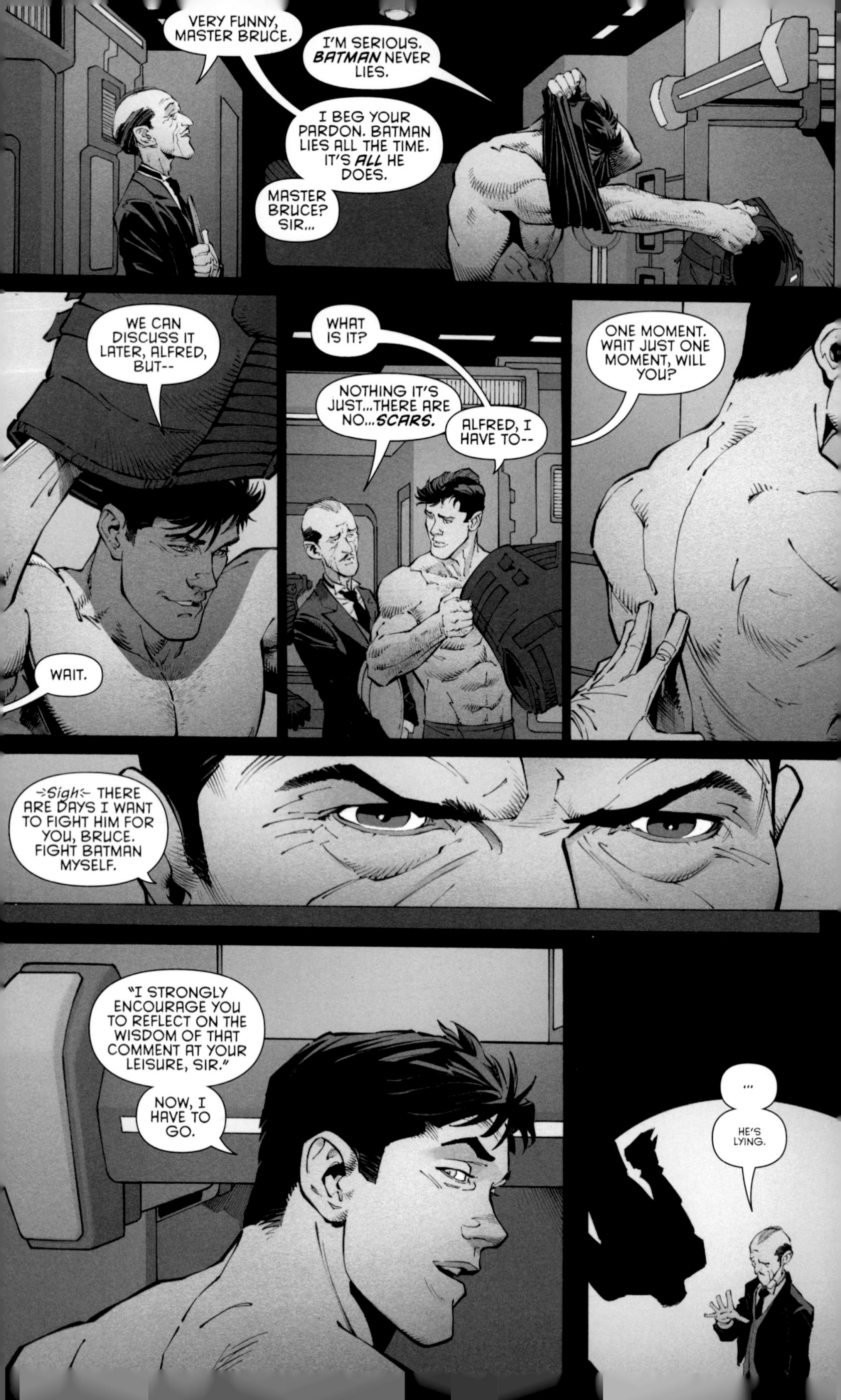
VERY FUNNY, MASTER BRUCE.
I'M SERIOUS. BATMAN NEVER LIES.
I BEG YOUR PARDON. BATMAN LIES ALL THE TIME. IT'S ALL HE DOES.
MASTER BRUCE? SIR...
WE CAN DISCUSS IT LATER, ALFRED, BUT--
WAIT.
WHAT IS IT?
NOTHING IT'S JUST...THERE ARE NO...SCARS.
ALFRED, I HAVE TO--
ONE MOMENT. WAIT JUST ONE MOMENT, WILL YOU?
-Sigh- THERE ARE DAYS I WANT TO FIGHT HIM FOR YOU, BRUCE. FIGHT BATMAN MYSELF.
"I STRONGLY ENCOURAGE YOU TO REFLECT ON THE WISDOM OF THAT COMMENT AT YOUR LEISURE, SIR."
NOW, I HAVE TO GO.
...
HE'S LYING.

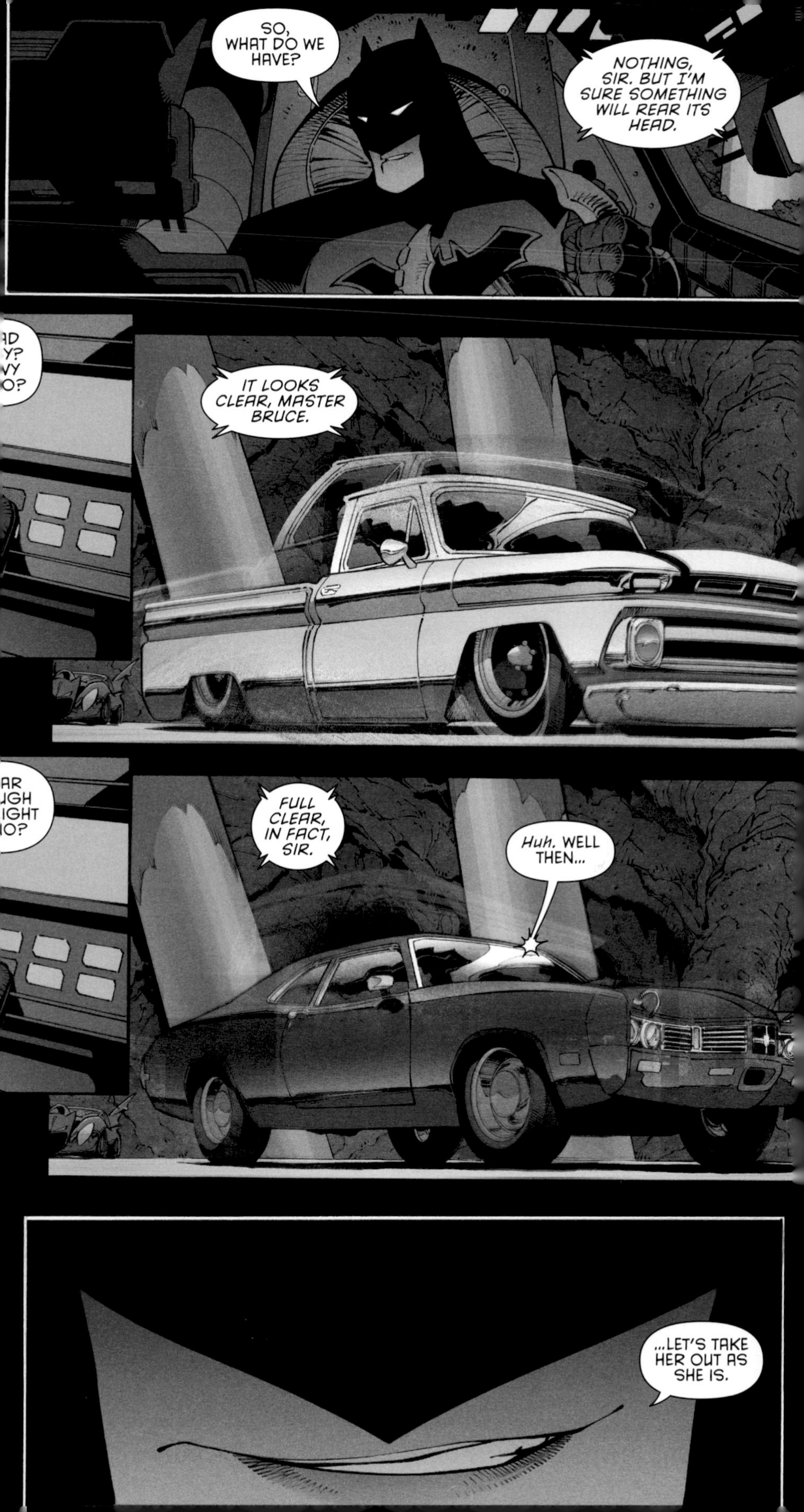
SO, WHAT DO WE HAVE?
NOTHING, SIR. BUT I'M SURE SOMETHING WILL REAR ITS HEAD.
IT LOOKS CLEAR, MASTER BRUCE.
FULL CLEAR, IN FACT, SIR.
Huh. WELL THEN...
...LET'S TAKE HER OUT AS SHE IS.

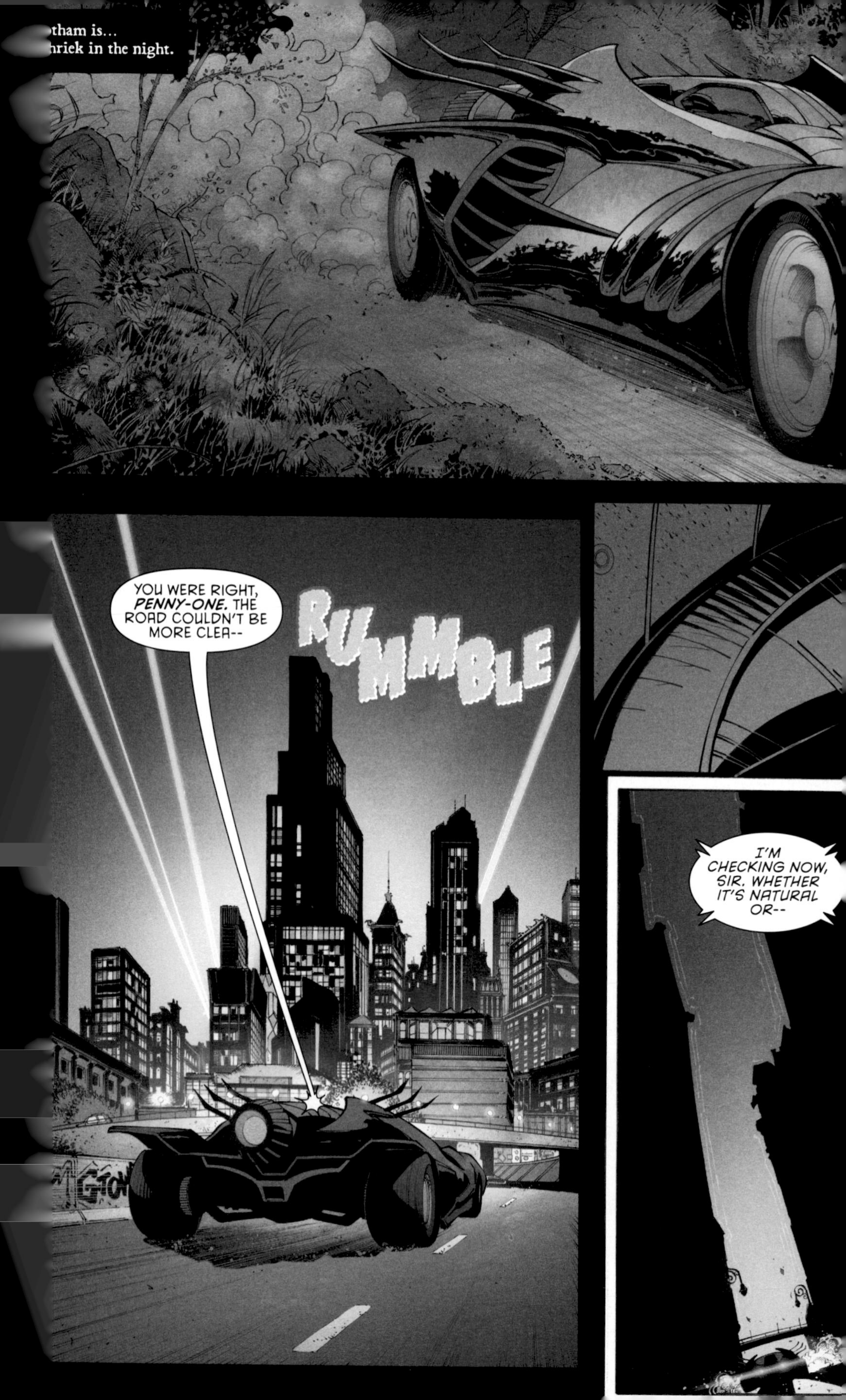
otham is…
hriek in the night.
YOU WERE RIGHT, PENNY-ONE. THE ROAD COULDN'T BE MORE CLEA--
RUMMBLE
I'M CHECKING NOW, SIR. WHETHER IT'S NATURAL OR--

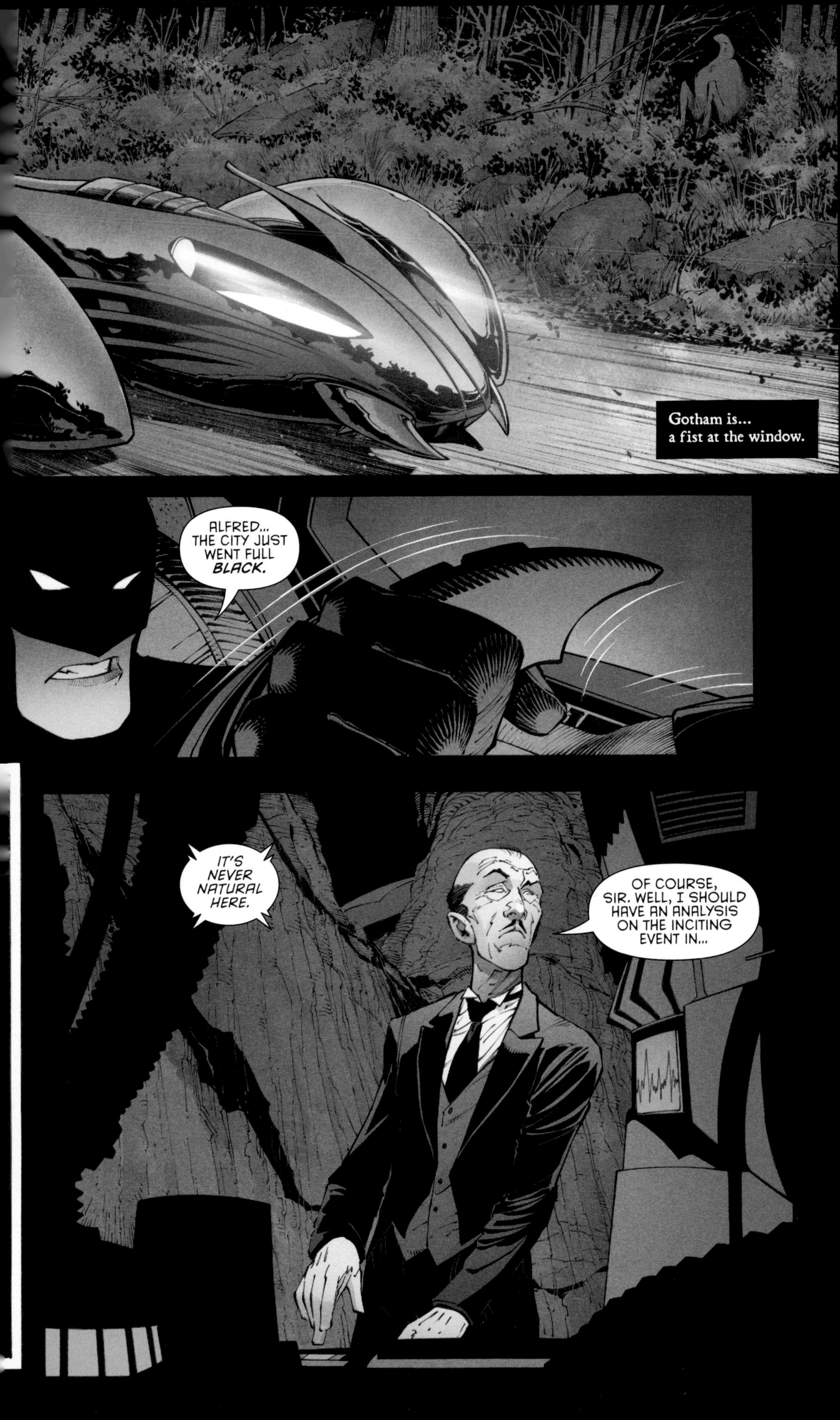
Gotham is...
a fist at the window.
ALFRED... THE CITY JUST WENT FULL BLACK.
IT'S NEVER NATURAL HERE.
OF COURSE, SIR. WELL, I SHOULD HAVE AN ANALYSIS ON THE INCITING EVENT IN...

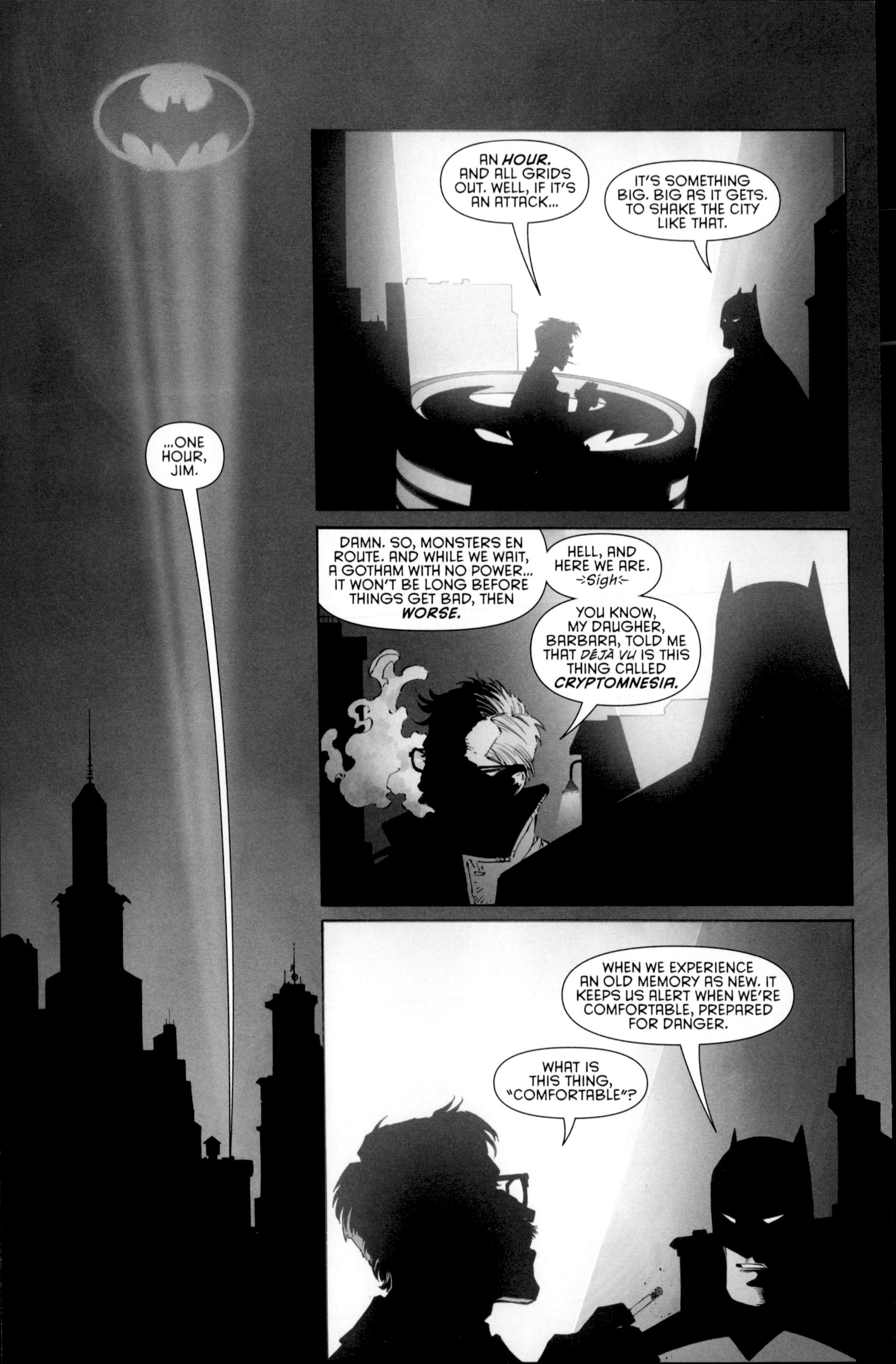
AN HOUR. AND ALL GRIDS OUT. WELL, IF IT'S AN ATTACK...
IT'S SOMETHING BIG. BIG AS IT GETS. TO SHAKE THE CITY LIKE THAT.
...ONE HOUR, JIM.
DAMN. SO, MONSTERS EN ROUTE. AND WHILE WE WAIT, A GOTHAM WITH NO POWER... IT WON'T BE LONG BEFORE THINGS GET BAD, THEN WORSE.
HELL, AND HERE WE ARE. *Sigh*
YOU KNOW, MY DAUGHER, BARBARA, TOLD ME THAT DÉJÀ VU IS THIS THING CALLED CRYPTOMNESIA.
WHEN WE EXPERIENCE AN OLD MEMORY AS NEW. IT KEEPS US ALERT WHEN WE'RE COMFORTABLE, PREPARED FOR DANGER.
WHAT IS THIS THING, "COMFORTABLE"?

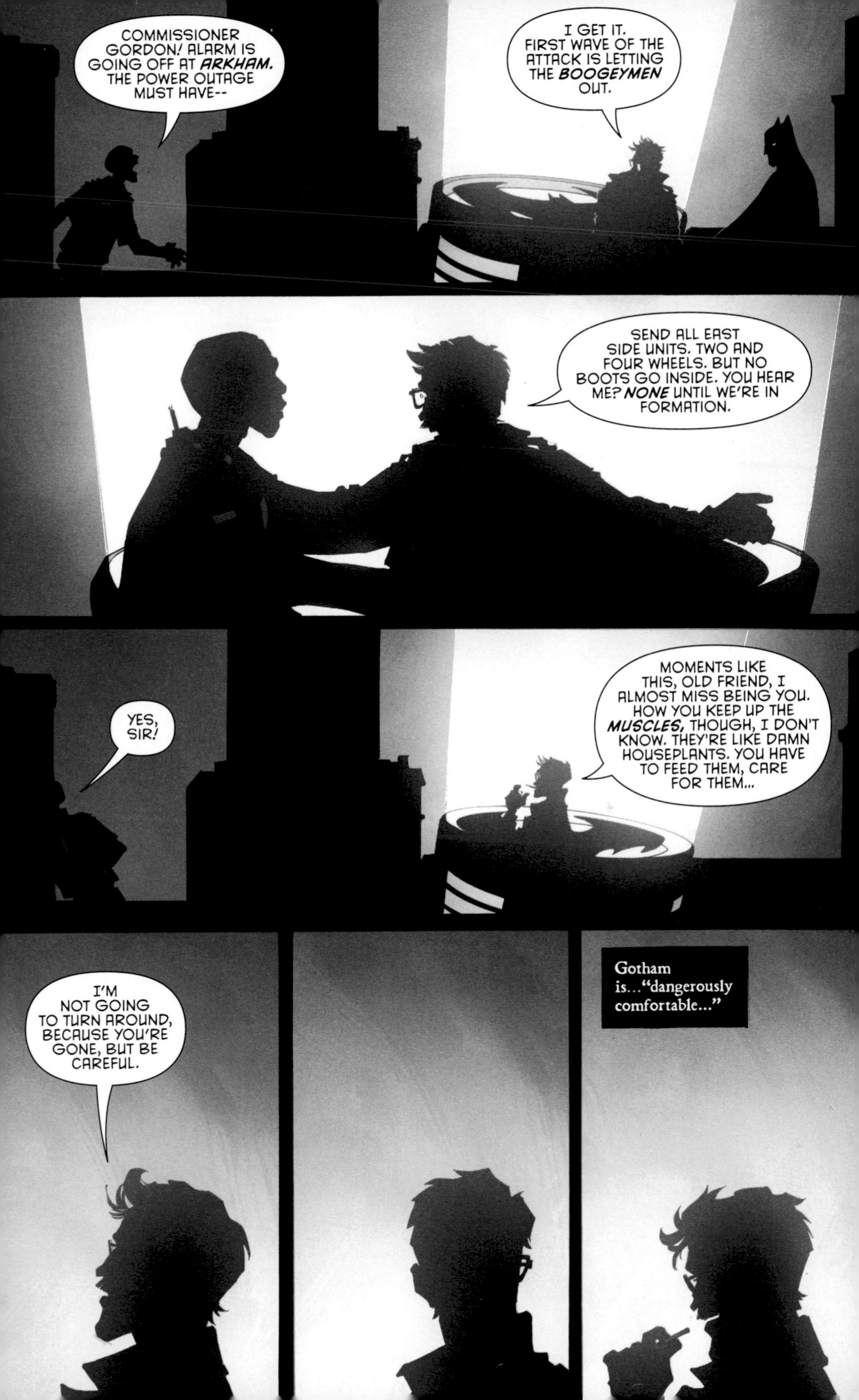
COMMISSIONER GORDON! ALARM IS GOING OFF AT ARKHAM. THE POWER OUTAGE MUST HAVE--
I GET IT. FIRST WAVE OF THE ATTACK IS LETTING THE BOOGEYMEN OUT.
SEND ALL EAST SIDE UNITS. TWO AND FOUR WHEELS. BUT NO BOOTS GO INSIDE. YOU HEAR ME? NONE UNTIL WE'RE IN FORMATION.
YES, SIR!
MOMENTS LIKE THIS, OLD FRIEND, I ALMOST MISS BEING YOU. HOW YOU KEEP UP THE MUSCLES, THOUGH, I DON'T KNOW. THEY'RE LIKE DAMN HOUSEPLANTS. YOU HAVE TO FEED THEM, CARE FOR THEM...
I'M NOT GOING TO TURN AROUND, BECAUSE YOU'RE GONE, BUT BE CAREFUL.
Gotham is..."dangerously comfortable..."

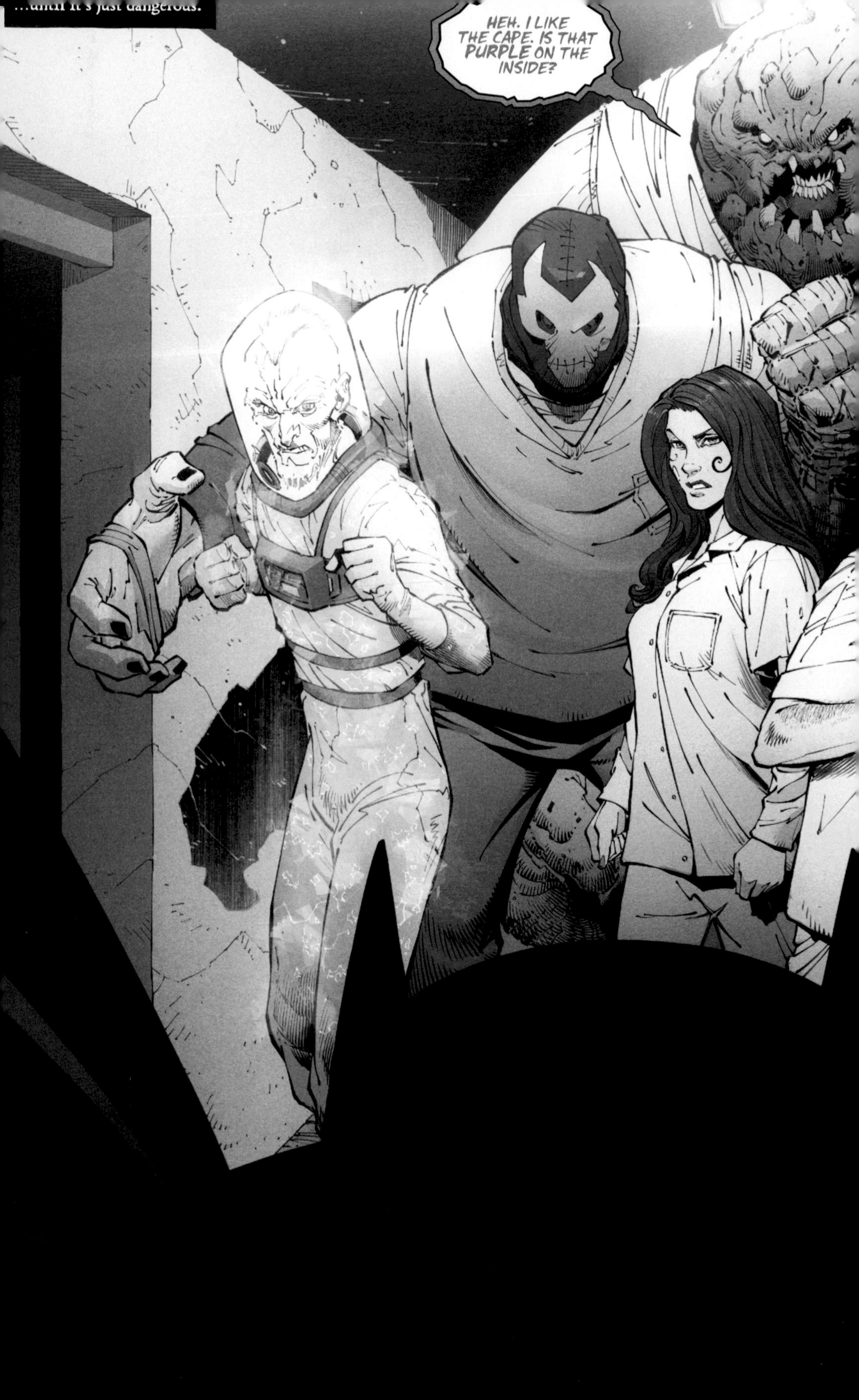
...until it's just dangerous.
HEH. I LIKE THE CAPE. IS THAT PURPLE ON THE INSIDE?

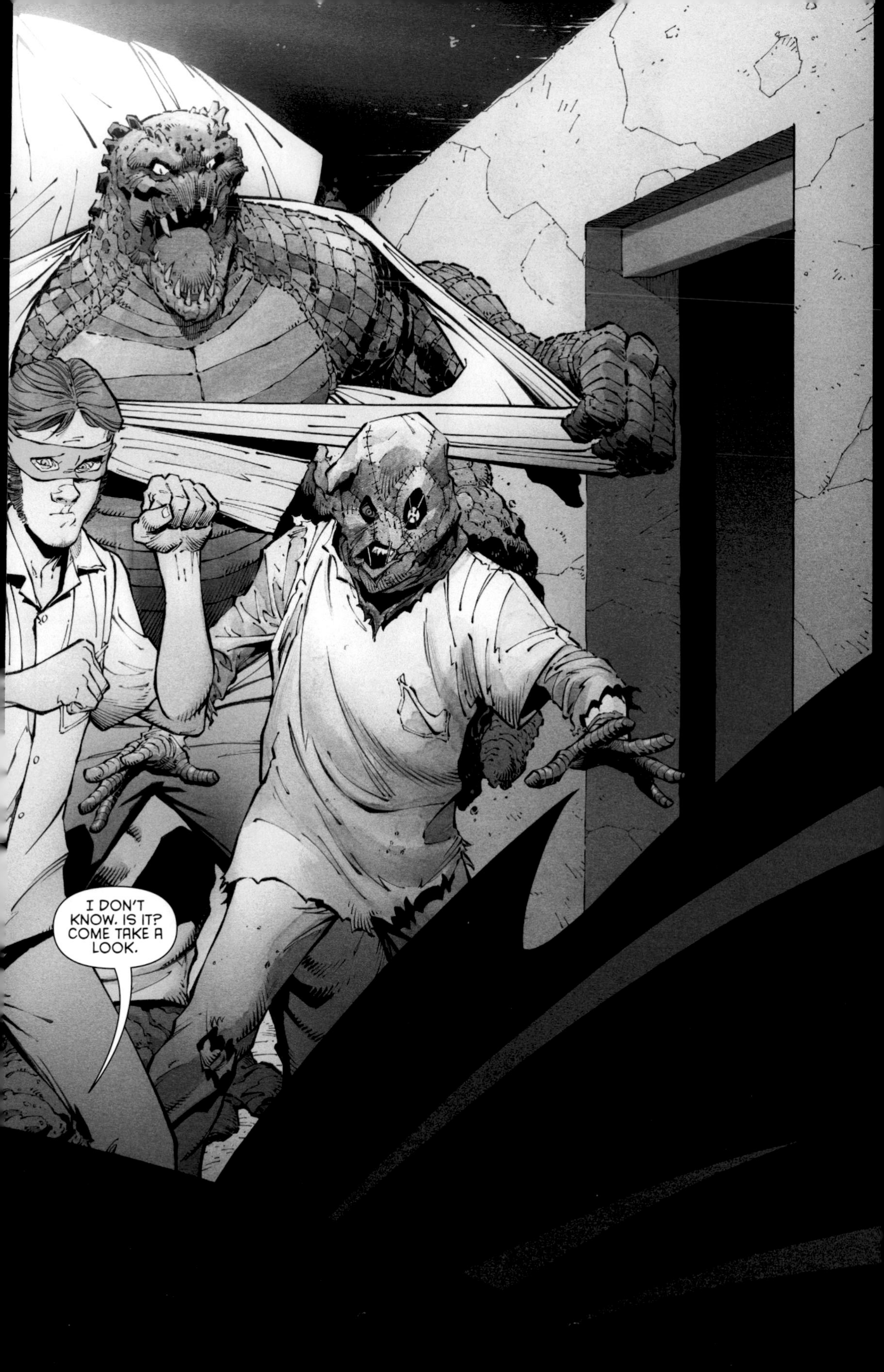
I DON'T KNOW. IS IT? COME TAKE A LOOK.

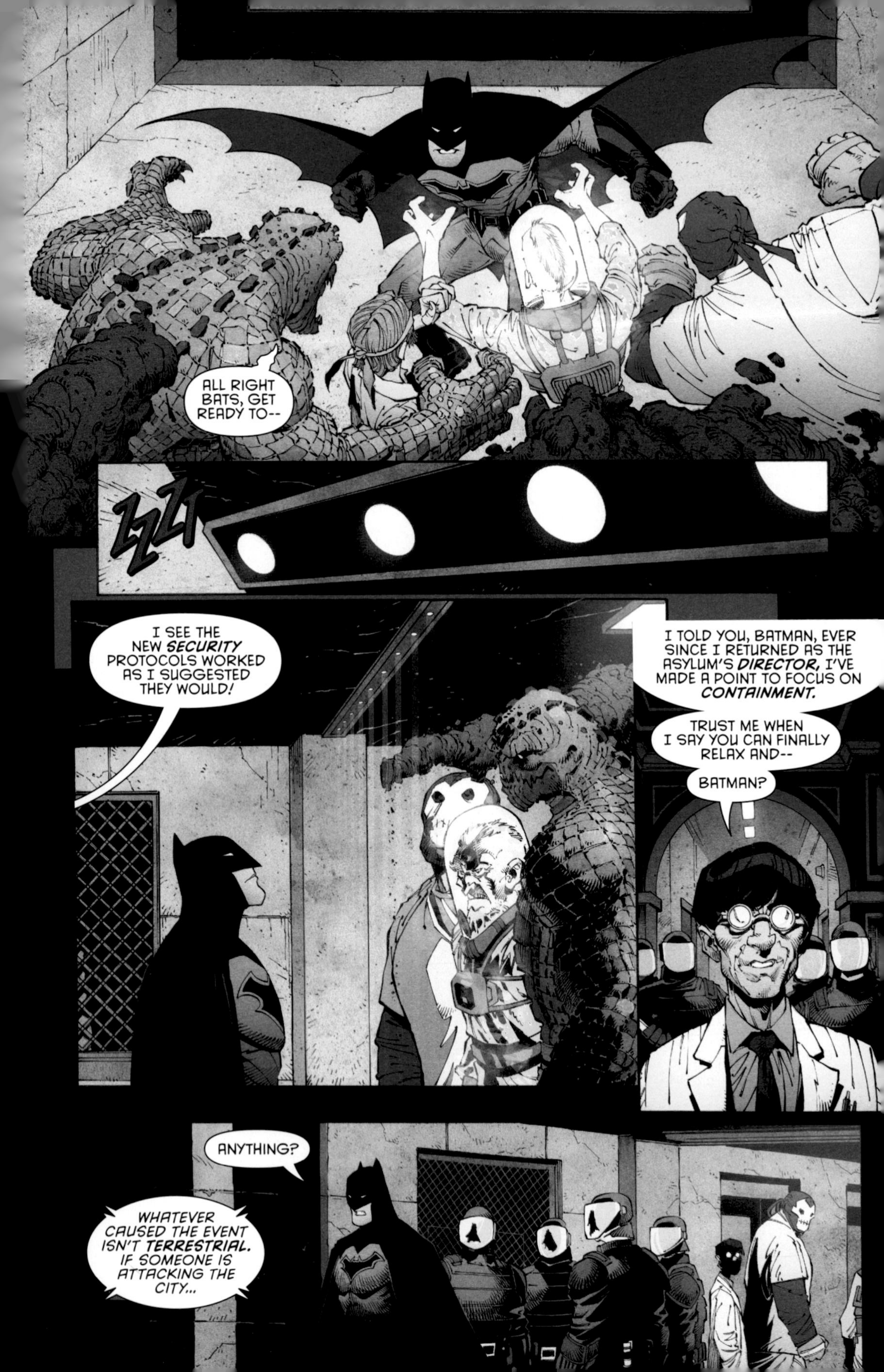
ALL RIGHT BATS, GET READY TO--
ZZZT
I SEE THE NEW *SECURITY* PROTOCOLS WORKED AS I SUGGESTED THEY WOULD!
I TOLD YOU, BATMAN, EVER SINCE I RETURNED AS THE ASYLUM'S *DIRECTOR,* I'VE MADE A POINT TO FOCUS ON ***CONTAINMENT.***
TRUST ME WHEN I SAY YOU CAN FINALLY RELAX AND--
BATMAN?
ANYTHING?
WHATEVER CAUSED THE EVENT ISN'T ***TERRESTRIAL.*** *IF SOMEONE IS ATTACKING THE CITY...*

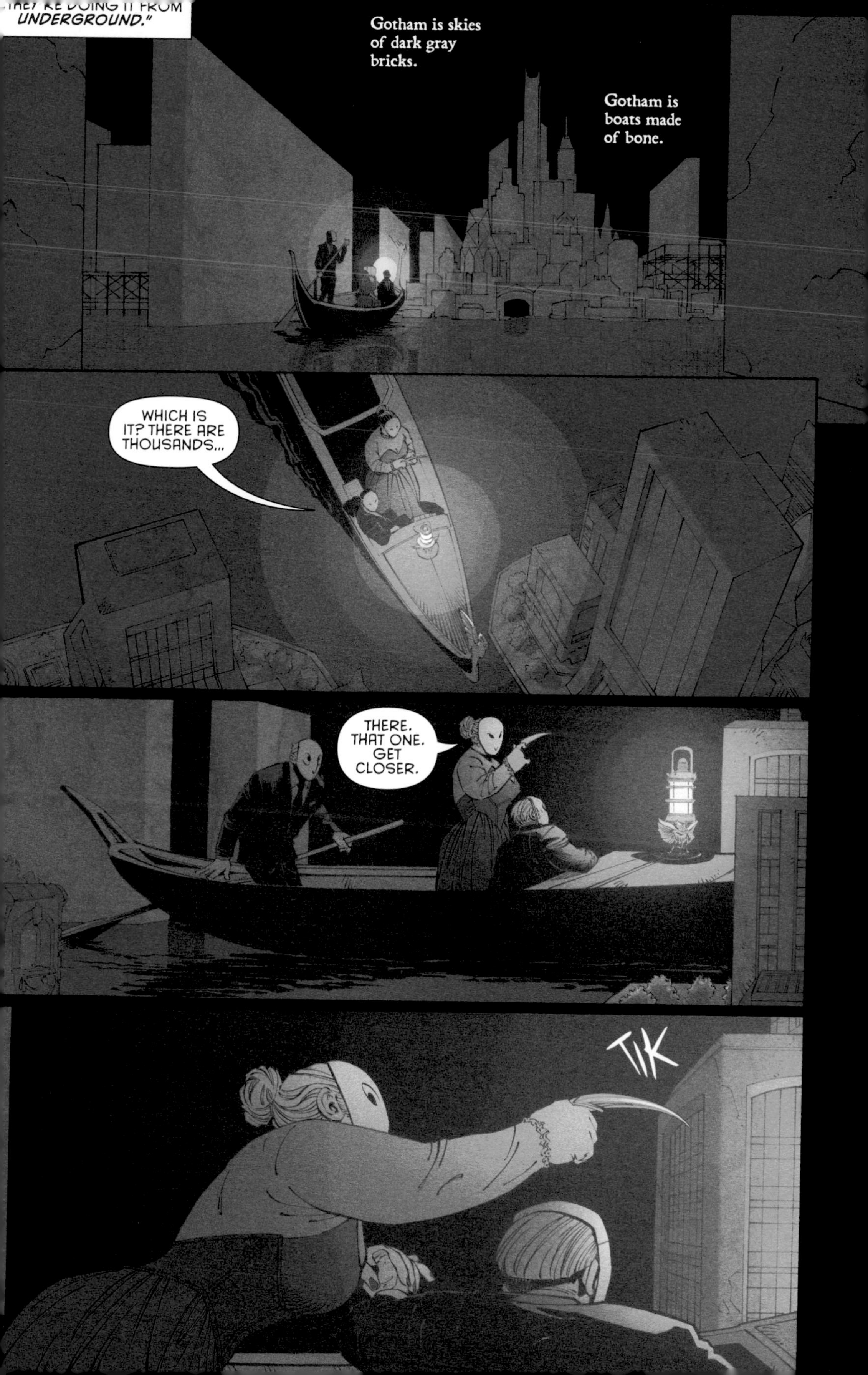
"THEY'RE DOING IT FROM UNDERGROUND."
Gotham is skies of dark gray bricks.
Gotham is boats made of bone.
WHICH IS IT? THERE ARE THOUSANDS...
THERE. THAT ONE. GET CLOSER.
TIK

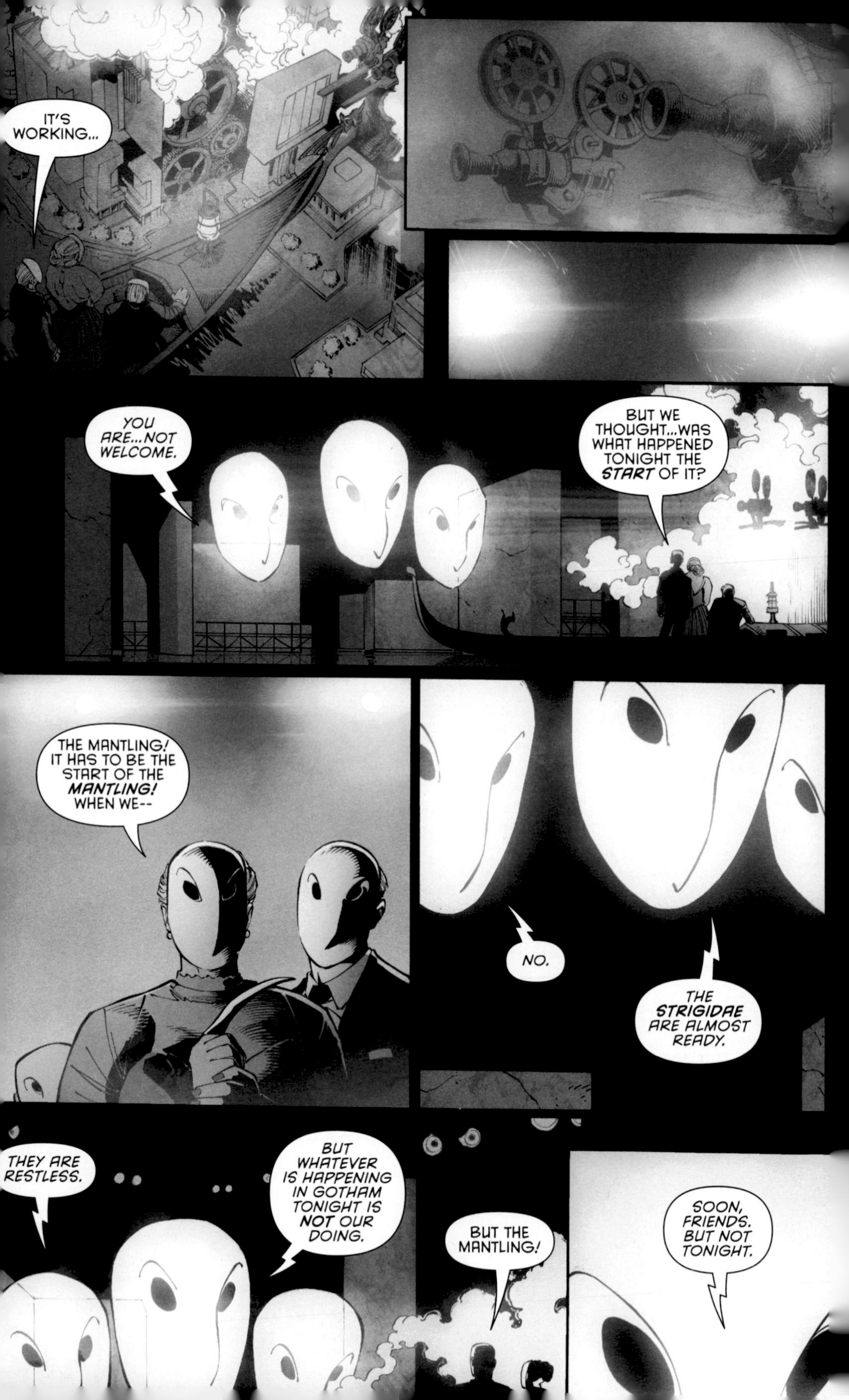
IT'S WORKING...
YOU ARE...NOT WELCOME.
BUT WE THOUGHT...WAS WHAT HAPPENED TONIGHT THE START OF IT?
THE MANTLING! IT HAS TO BE THE START OF THE MANTLING! WHEN WE--
NO.
THE STRIGIDAE ARE ALMOST READY.
THEY ARE RESTLESS.
BUT WHATEVER IS HAPPENING IN GOTHAM TONIGHT IS NOT OUR DOING.
BUT THE MANTLING!
SOON, FRIENDS. BUT NOT TONIGHT.

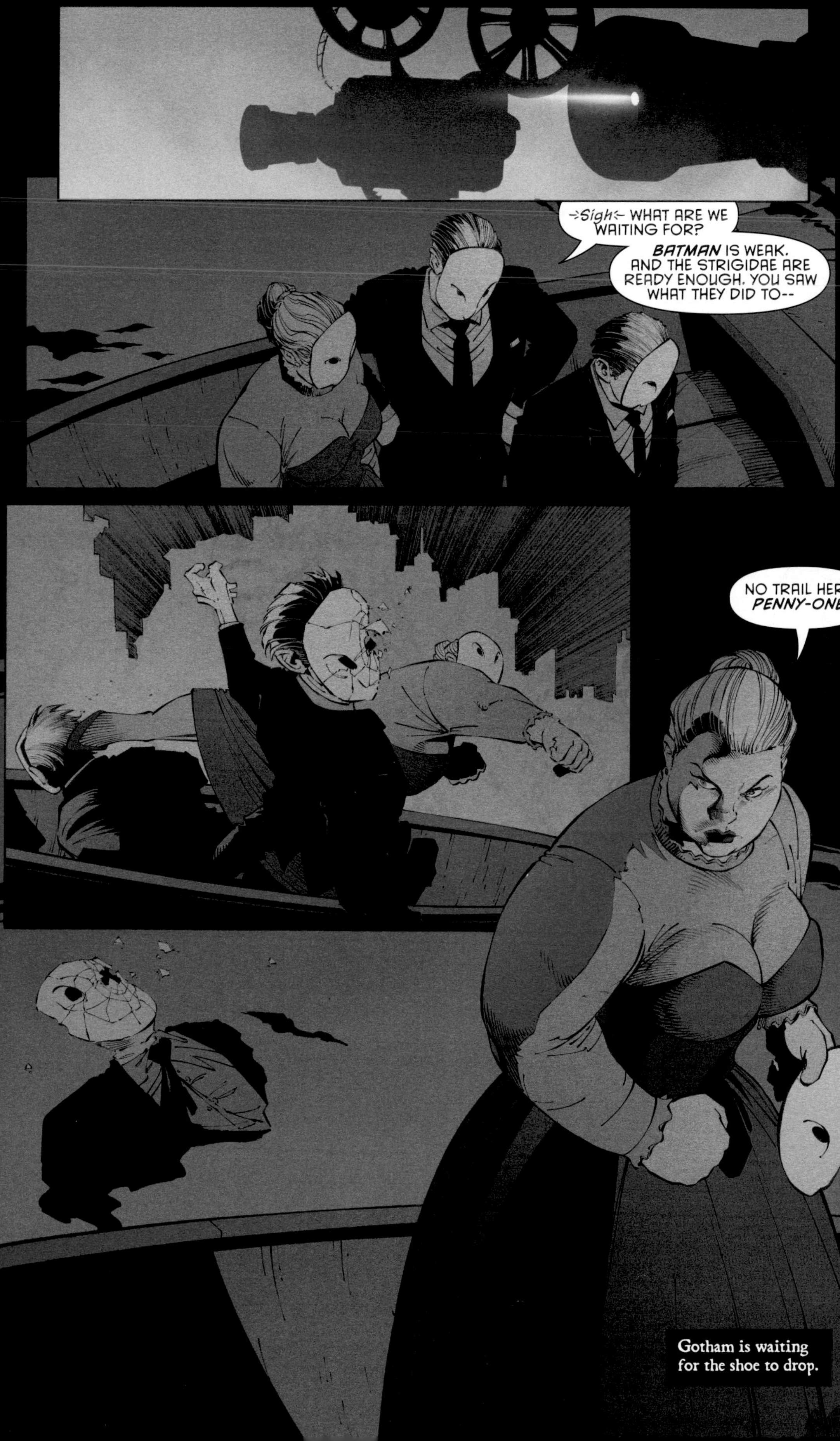

-Sigh- WHAT ARE WE WAITING FOR?
BATMAN IS WEAK. AND THE STRIGIDAE ARE READY ENOUGH. YOU SAW WHAT THEY DID TO--
NO TRAIL HERE, PENNY-ONE.
Gotham is waiting for the shoe to drop.

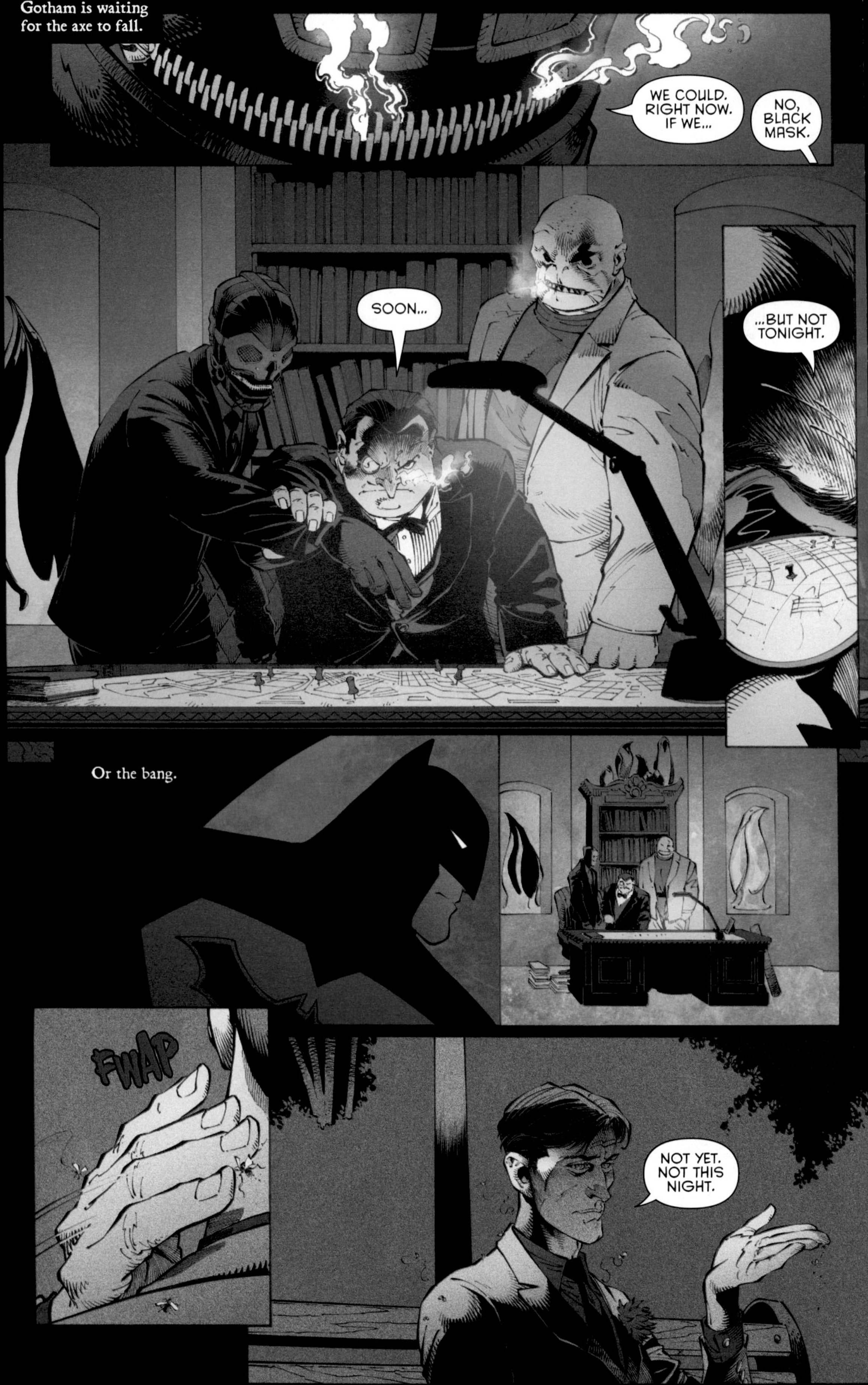
Gotham is waiting for the axe to fall.
WE COULD. RIGHT NOW. IF WE...
NO, BLACK MASK.
SOON...
...BUT NOT TONIGHT.
Or the bang.
FWAP
NOT YET. NOT THIS NIGHT.

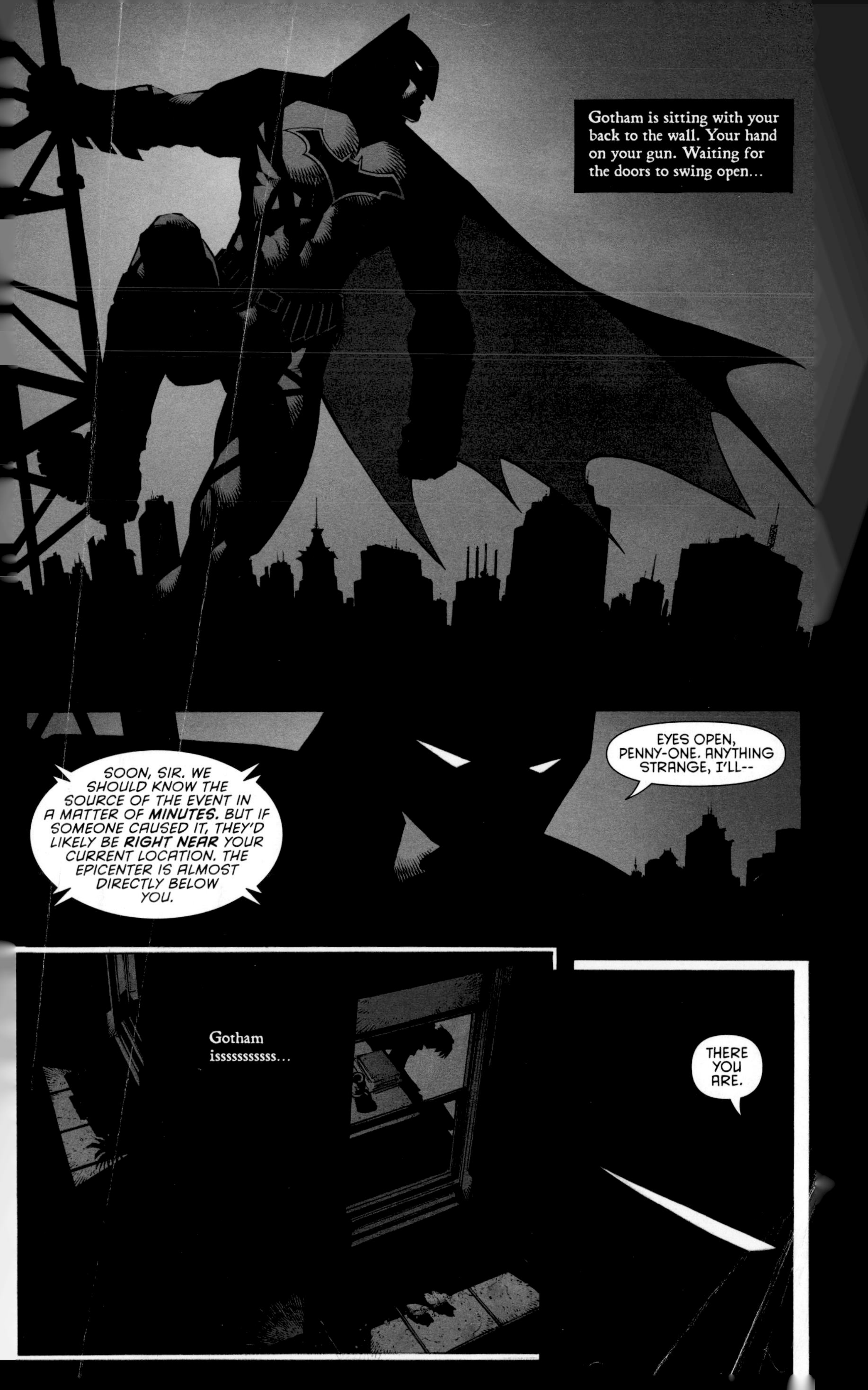

Gotham is sitting with your back to the wall. Your hand on your gun. Waiting for the doors to swing open...
SOON, SIR. WE SHOULD KNOW THE SOURCE OF THE EVENT IN A MATTER OF **MINUTES.** BUT IF SOMEONE CAUSED IT, THEY'D LIKELY BE **RIGHT NEAR** YOUR CURRENT LOCATION. THE EPICENTER IS ALMOST DIRECTLY BELOW YOU.
EYES OPEN, PENNY-ONE. ANYTHING STRANGE, I'LL--
Gotham isssssssssss...
THERE YOU ARE.

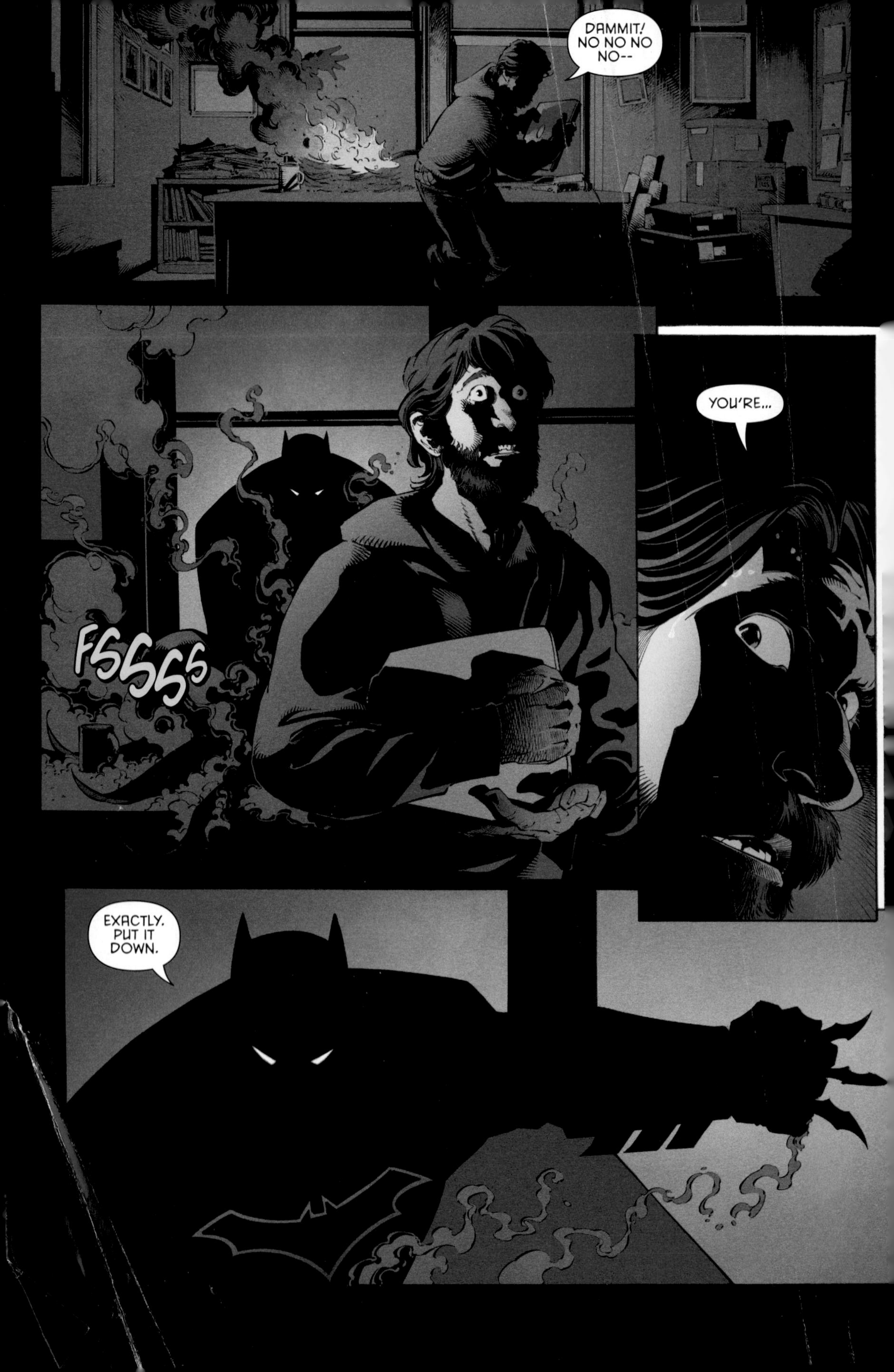
DAMMIT! NO NO NO NO--
FSSSSS
YOU'RE...
EXACTLY. PUT IT DOWN.

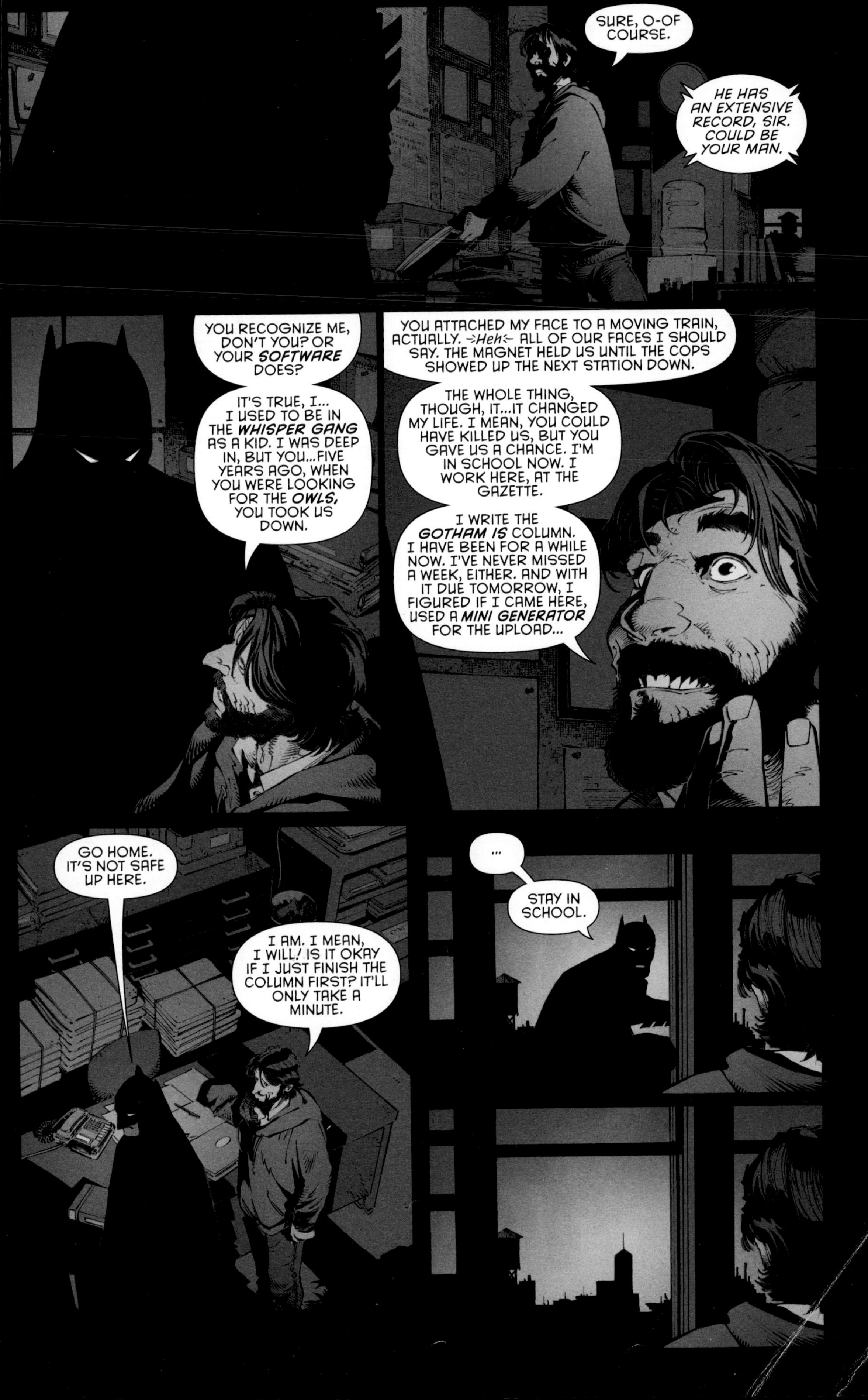
SURE, O-OF COURSE.
HE HAS AN EXTENSIVE RECORD, SIR. COULD BE YOUR MAN.
YOU RECOGNIZE ME, DON'T YOU? OR YOUR SOFTWARE DOES?
IT'S TRUE, I... I USED TO BE IN THE WHISPER GANG AS A KID. I WAS DEEP IN, BUT YOU...FIVE YEARS AGO, WHEN YOU WERE LOOKING FOR THE OWLS, YOU TOOK US DOWN.
YOU ATTACHED MY FACE TO A MOVING TRAIN, ACTUALLY. ⇒Heh⇐ ALL OF OUR FACES I SHOULD SAY. THE MAGNET HELD US UNTIL THE COPS SHOWED UP THE NEXT STATION DOWN.
THE WHOLE THING, THOUGH, IT...IT CHANGED MY LIFE. I MEAN, YOU COULD HAVE KILLED US, BUT YOU GAVE US A CHANCE. I'M IN SCHOOL NOW. I WORK HERE, AT THE GAZETTE.
I WRITE THE GOTHAM IS COLUMN. I HAVE BEEN FOR A WHILE NOW. I'VE NEVER MISSED A WEEK, EITHER. AND WITH IT DUE TOMORROW, I FIGURED IF I CAME HERE, USED A MINI GENERATOR FOR THE UPLOAD...
GO HOME. IT'S NOT SAFE UP HERE.
I AM. I MEAN, I WILL! IS IT OKAY IF I JUST FINISH THE COLUMN FIRST? IT'LL ONLY TAKE A MINUTE.
...
STAY IN SCHOOL.

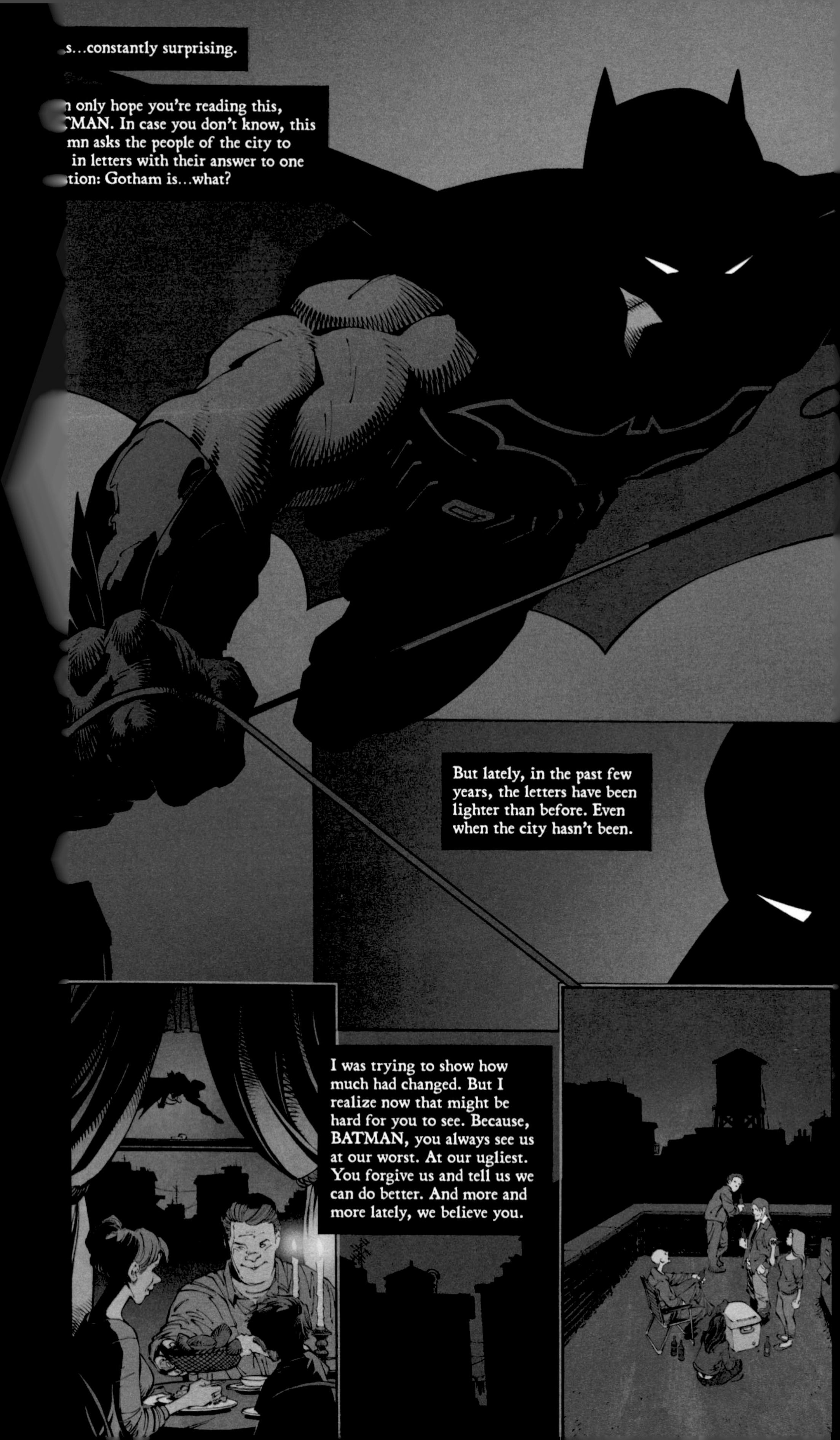
s...constantly surprising.
n only hope you're reading this, MAN. In case you don't know, this mn asks the people of the city to in letters with their answer to one tion: Gotham is...what?
But lately, in the past few years, the letters have been lighter than before. Even when the city hasn't been.
I was trying to show how much had changed. But I realize now that might be hard for you to see. Because, BATMAN, you always see us at our worst. At our ugliest. You forgive us and tell us we can do better. And more and more lately, we believe you.

These letters, they come in every week, and then the column's official writer talks about how the times are reflected in them. It's one of the oldest columns at the paper, and better writers than me have worked on it.

But what I like about it is that as much as it's written by a single person, it's really created by the people who send in letters--everyone out there.

And when I started here? The letters coming in were pretty dark, pretty hopeless. Tonight, I've been listing old ones here.

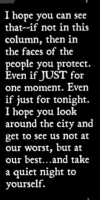

I hope you can see that--if not in this column, then in the faces of the people you protect. Even if JUST for one moment. Even if just for tonight. I hope you look around the city and get to see us not at our worst, but at our best...and take a quiet night to yourself.

A night off.

YOU'RE NOT GOING TO BELIEVE THIS, SIR, BUT THE TREMOR WAS JUST A *NATURAL OCCURRENCE*, AND THE POWER SHOULD COME ON AT ANY...

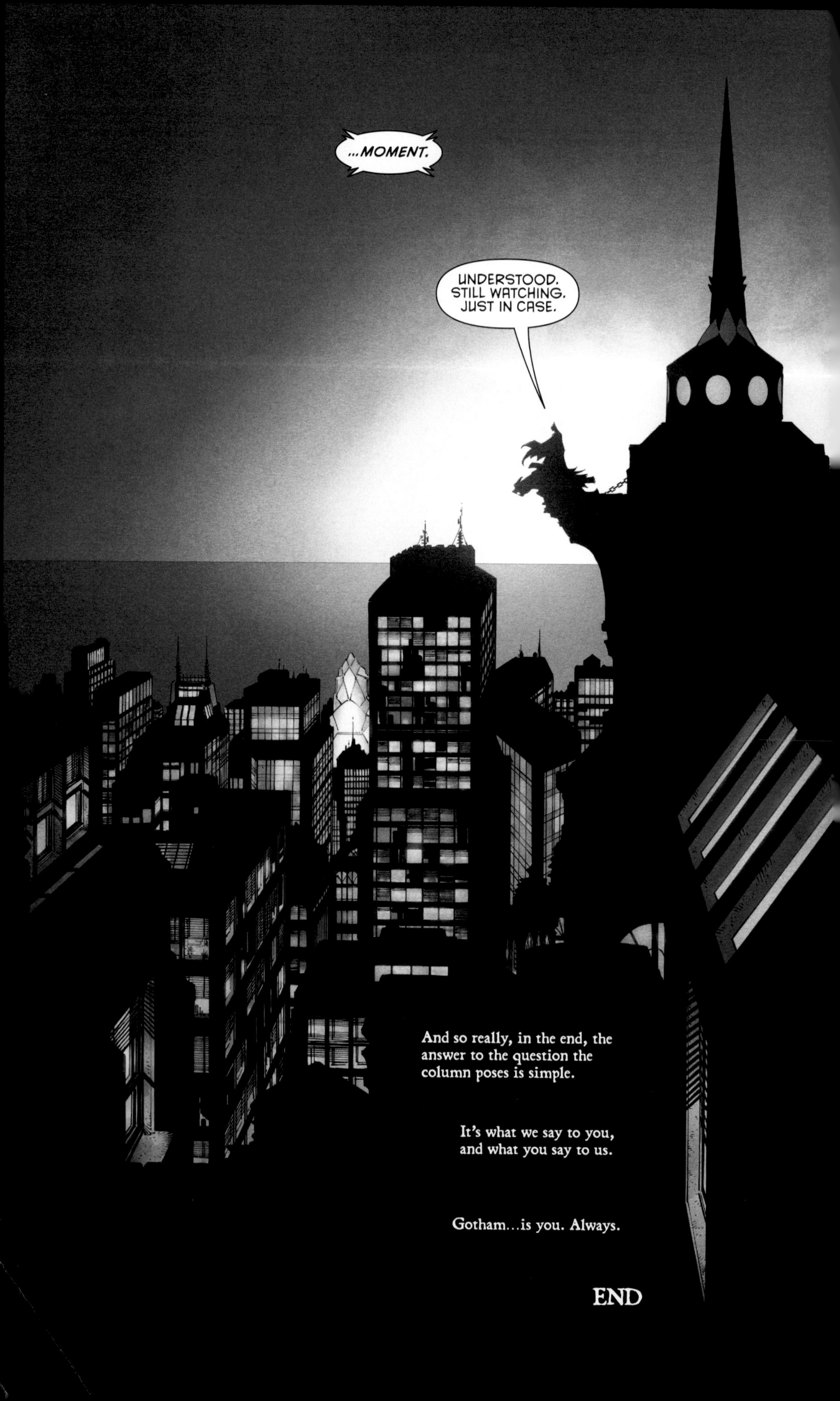
...MOMENT.
UNDERSTOOD. STILL WATCHING. JUST IN CASE.
And so really, in the end, the answer to the question the column poses is simple.
It's what we say to you, and what you say to us.
Gotham...is you. Always.
END

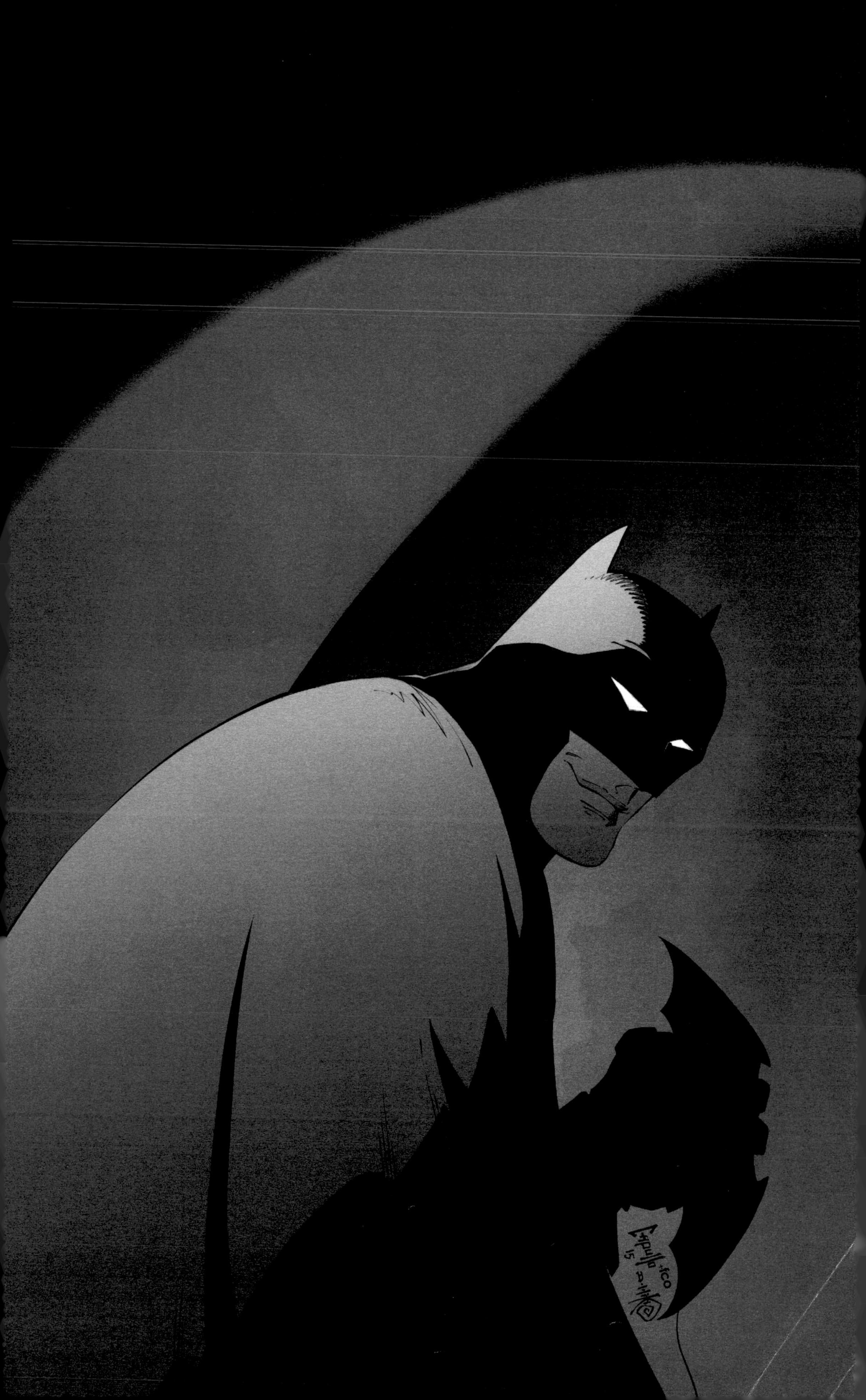

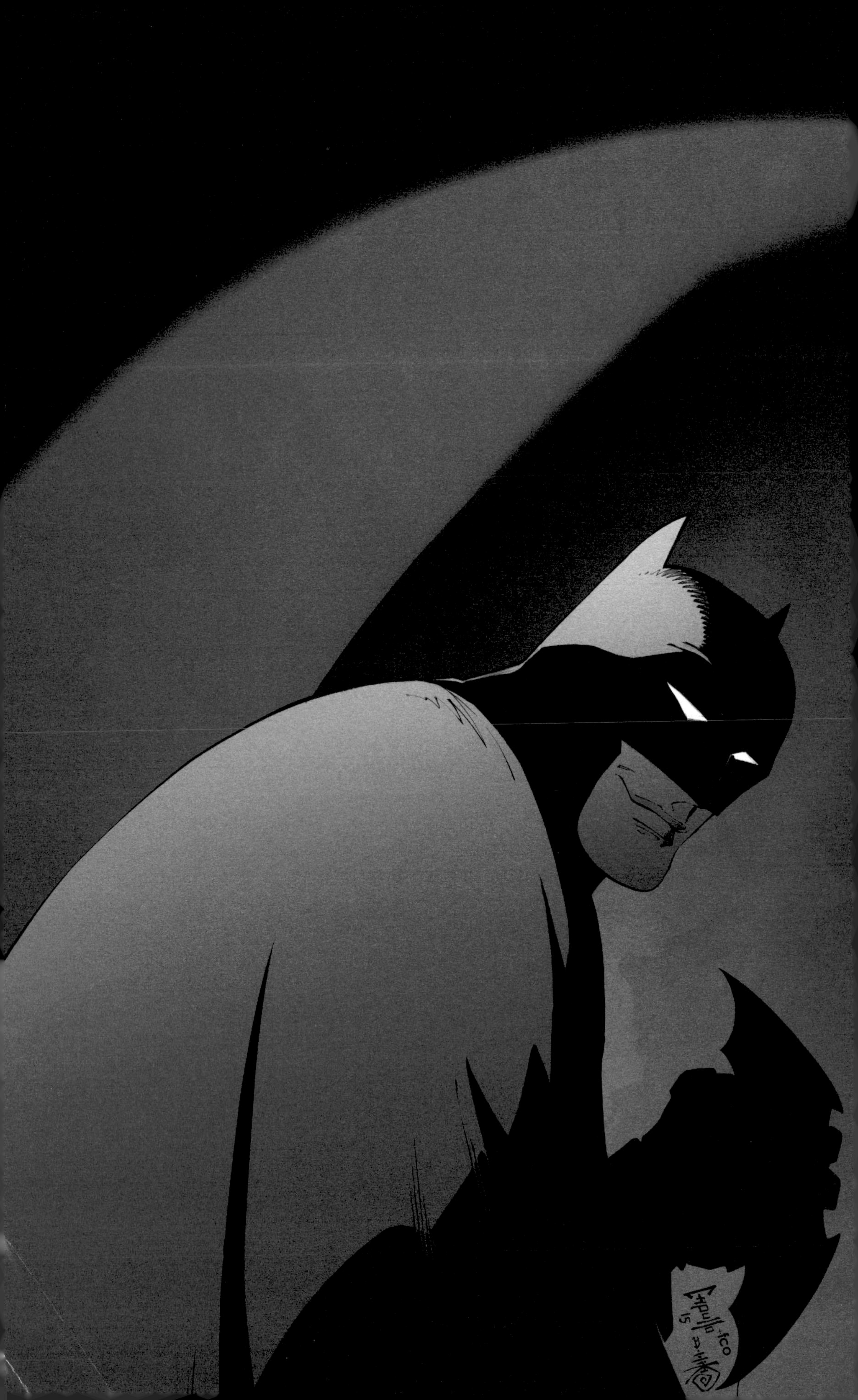

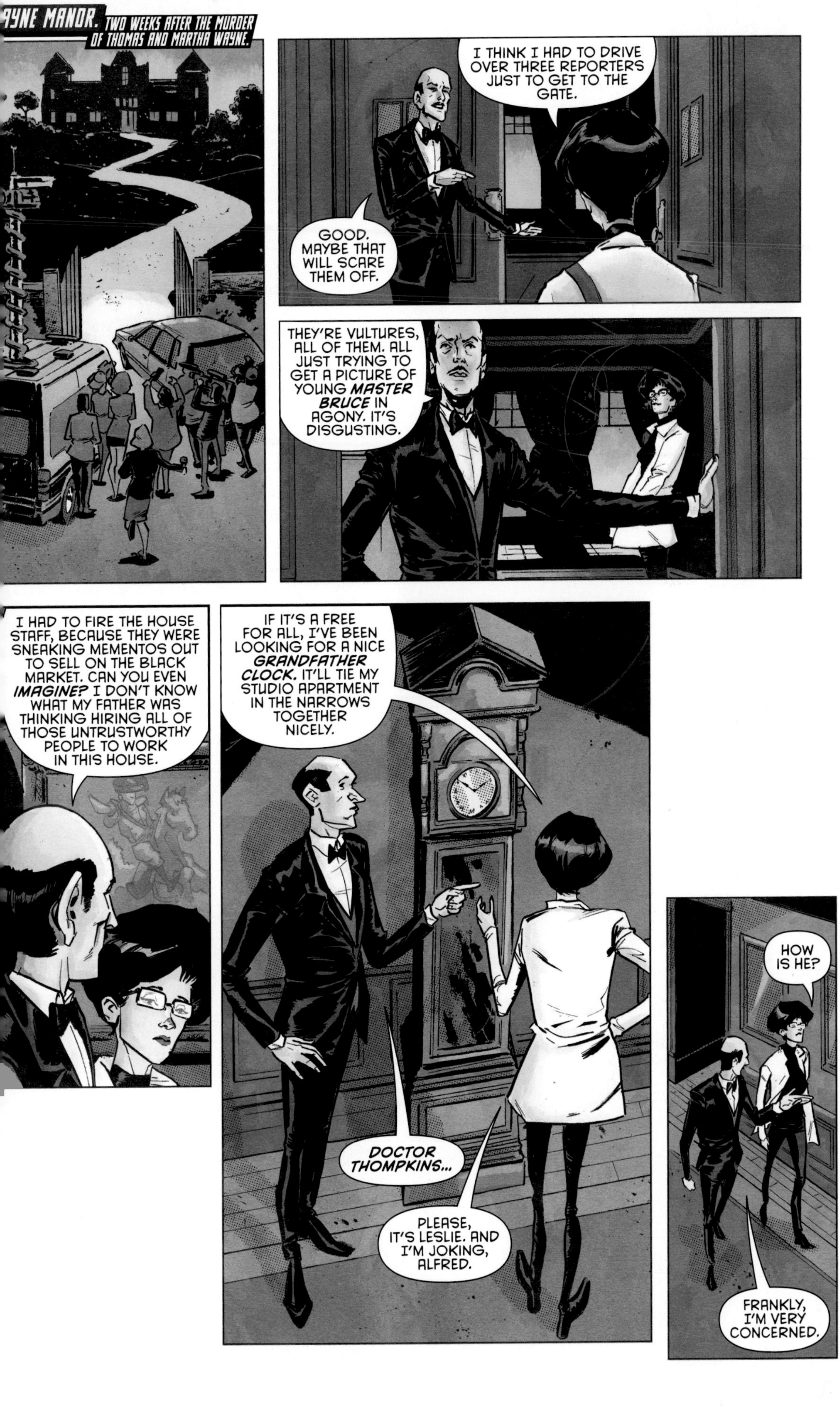
AYNE MANOR. TWO WEEKS AFTER THE MURDER OF THOMAS AND MARTHA WAYNE.
I THINK I HAD TO DRIVE OVER THREE REPORTERS JUST TO GET TO THE GATE.
GOOD. MAYBE THAT WILL SCARE THEM OFF.
THEY'RE VULTURES, ALL OF THEM. ALL JUST TRYING TO GET A PICTURE OF YOUNG MASTER BRUCE IN AGONY. IT'S DISGUSTING.
I HAD TO FIRE THE HOUSE STAFF, BECAUSE THEY WERE SNEAKING MEMENTOS OUT TO SELL ON THE BLACK MARKET. CAN YOU EVEN IMAGINE? I DON'T KNOW WHAT MY FATHER WAS THINKING HIRING ALL OF THOSE UNTRUSTWORTHY PEOPLE TO WORK IN THIS HOUSE.
IF IT'S A FREE FOR ALL, I'VE BEEN LOOKING FOR A NICE GRANDFATHER CLOCK. IT'LL TIE MY STUDIO APARTMENT IN THE NARROWS TOGETHER NICELY.
DOCTOR THOMPKINS...
PLEASE, IT'S LESLIE. AND I'M JOKING, ALFRED.
HOW IS HE?
FRANKLY, I'M VERY CONCERNED.

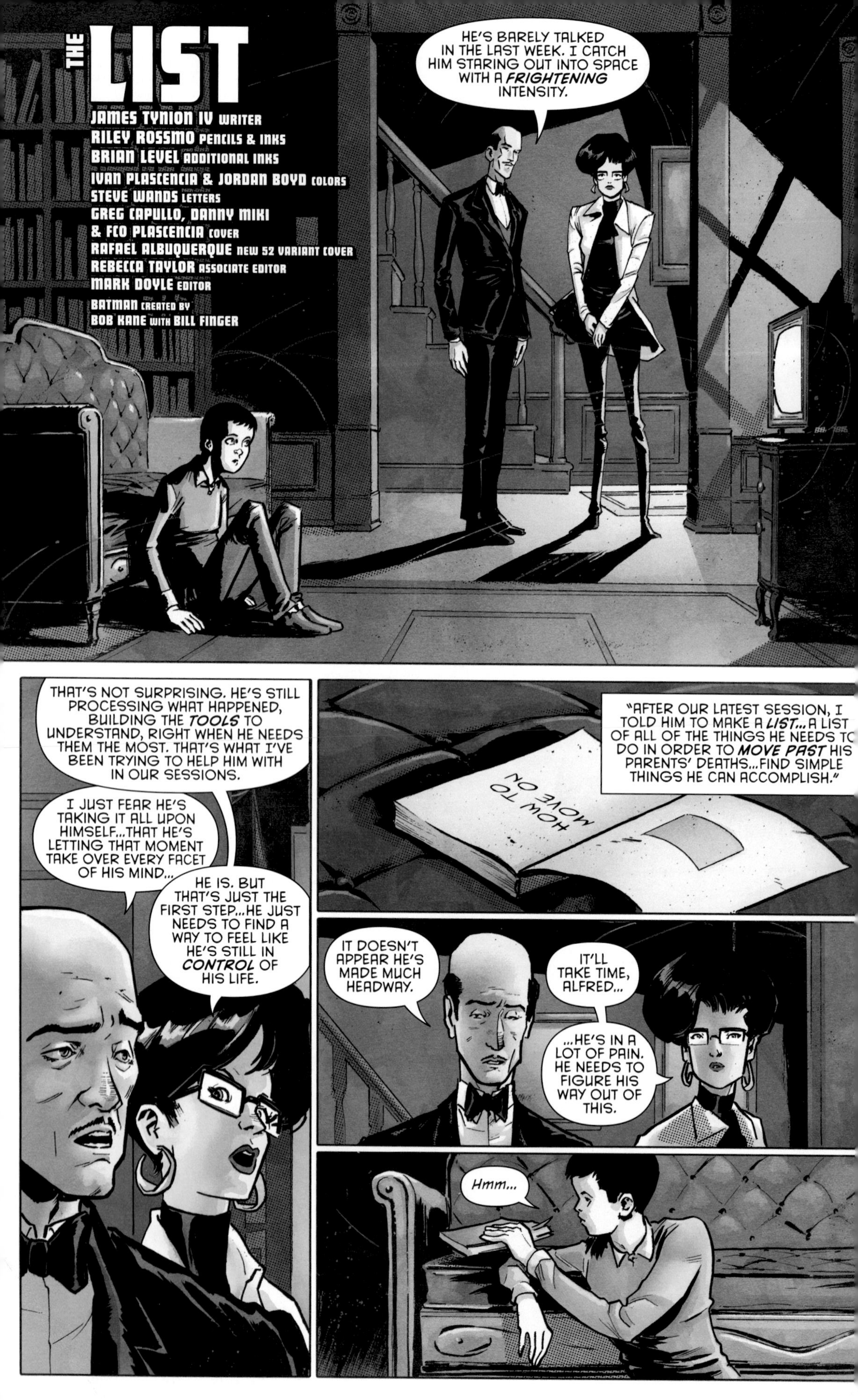

THE LIST
JAMES TYNION IV WRITER
RILEY ROSSMO PENCILS & INKS
BRIAN LEVEL ADDITIONAL INKS
IVAN PLASCENCIA & JORDAN BOYD COLORS
STEVE WANDS LETTERS
GREG CAPULLO, DANNY MIKI & FCO PLASCENCIA COVER
RAFAEL ALBUQUERQUE NEW 52 VARIANT COVER
REBECCA TAYLOR ASSOCIATE EDITOR
MARK DOYLE EDITOR
BATMAN CREATED BY BOB KANE WITH BILL FINGER
HE'S BARELY TALKED IN THE LAST WEEK. I CATCH HIM STARING OUT INTO SPACE WITH A FRIGHTENING INTENSITY.
THAT'S NOT SURPRISING. HE'S STILL PROCESSING WHAT HAPPENED, BUILDING THE TOOLS TO UNDERSTAND, RIGHT WHEN HE NEEDS THEM THE MOST. THAT'S WHAT I'VE BEEN TRYING TO HELP HIM WITH IN OUR SESSIONS.
I JUST FEAR HE'S TAKING IT ALL UPON HIMSELF...THAT HE'S LETTING THAT MOMENT TAKE OVER EVERY FACET OF HIS MIND...
HE IS. BUT THAT'S JUST THE FIRST STEP...HE JUST NEEDS TO FIND A WAY TO FEEL LIKE HE'S STILL IN CONTROL OF HIS LIFE.
"AFTER OUR LATEST SESSION, I TOLD HIM TO MAKE A LIST...A LIST OF ALL OF THE THINGS HE NEEDS TO DO IN ORDER TO MOVE PAST HIS PARENTS' DEATHS...FIND SIMPLE THINGS HE CAN ACCOMPLISH."
HOW TO MOVE ON
IT DOESN'T APPEAR HE'S MADE MUCH HEADWAY.
IT'LL TAKE TIME, ALFRED...
...HE'S IN A LOT OF PAIN. HE NEEDS TO FIGURE HIS WAY OUT OF THIS.
Hmm...

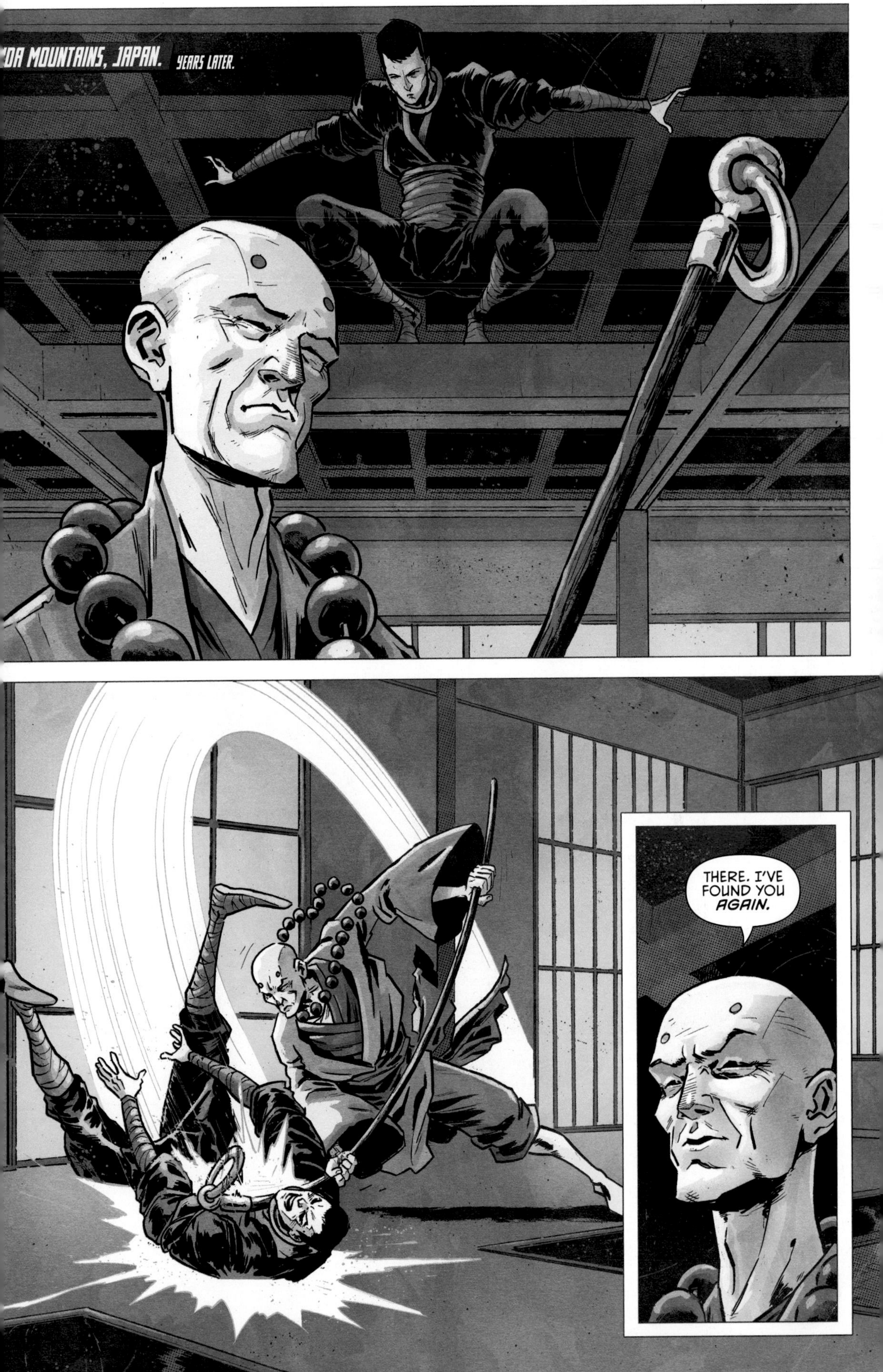
OA MOUNTAINS, JAPAN. YEARS LATER.
THERE. I'VE FOUND YOU AGAIN.

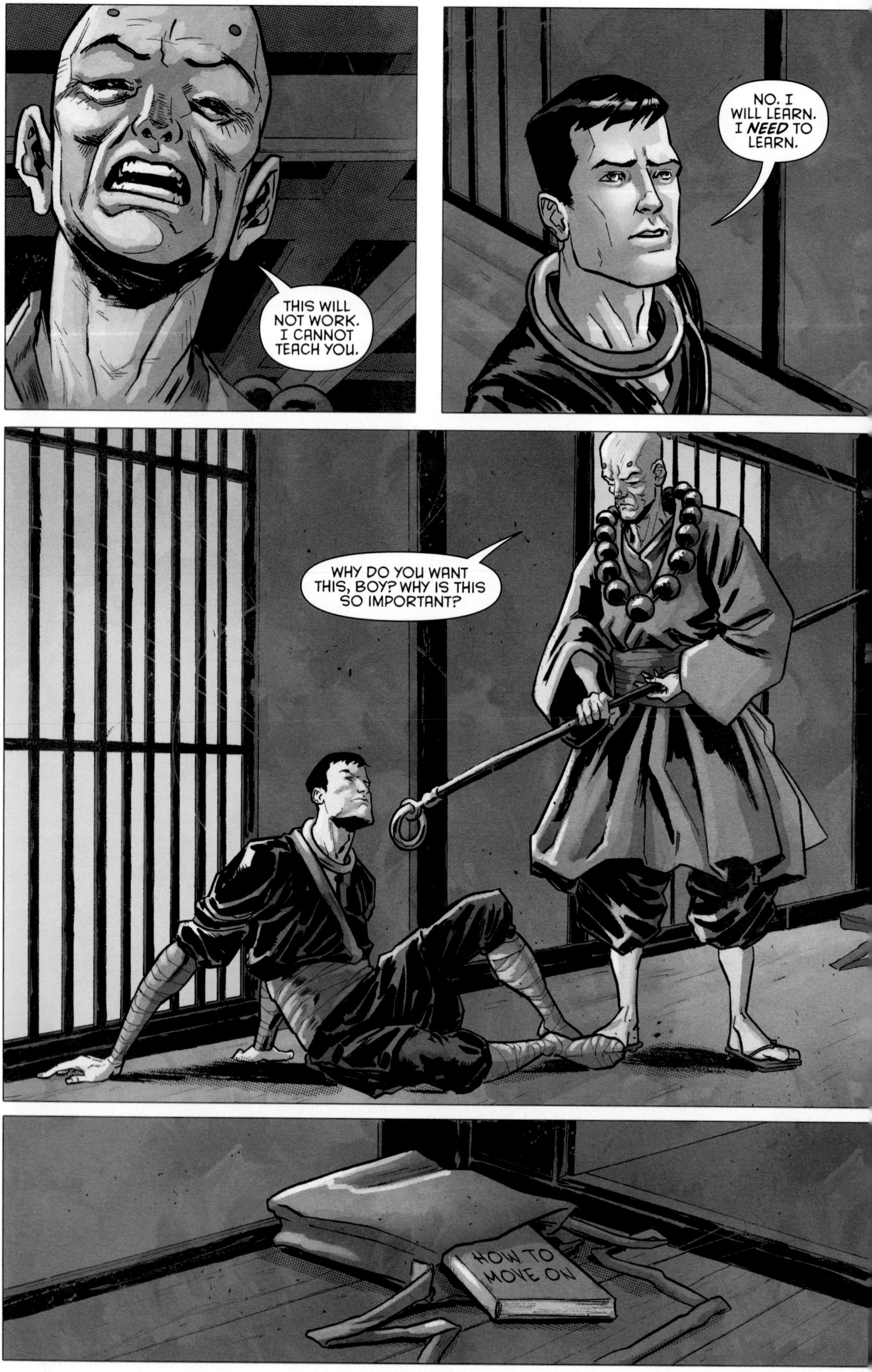
THIS WILL NOT WORK. I CANNOT TEACH YOU.
NO. I WILL LEARN. I *NEED* TO LEARN.
WHY DO YOU WANT THIS, BOY? WHY IS THIS SO IMPORTANT?
HOW TO MOVE ON

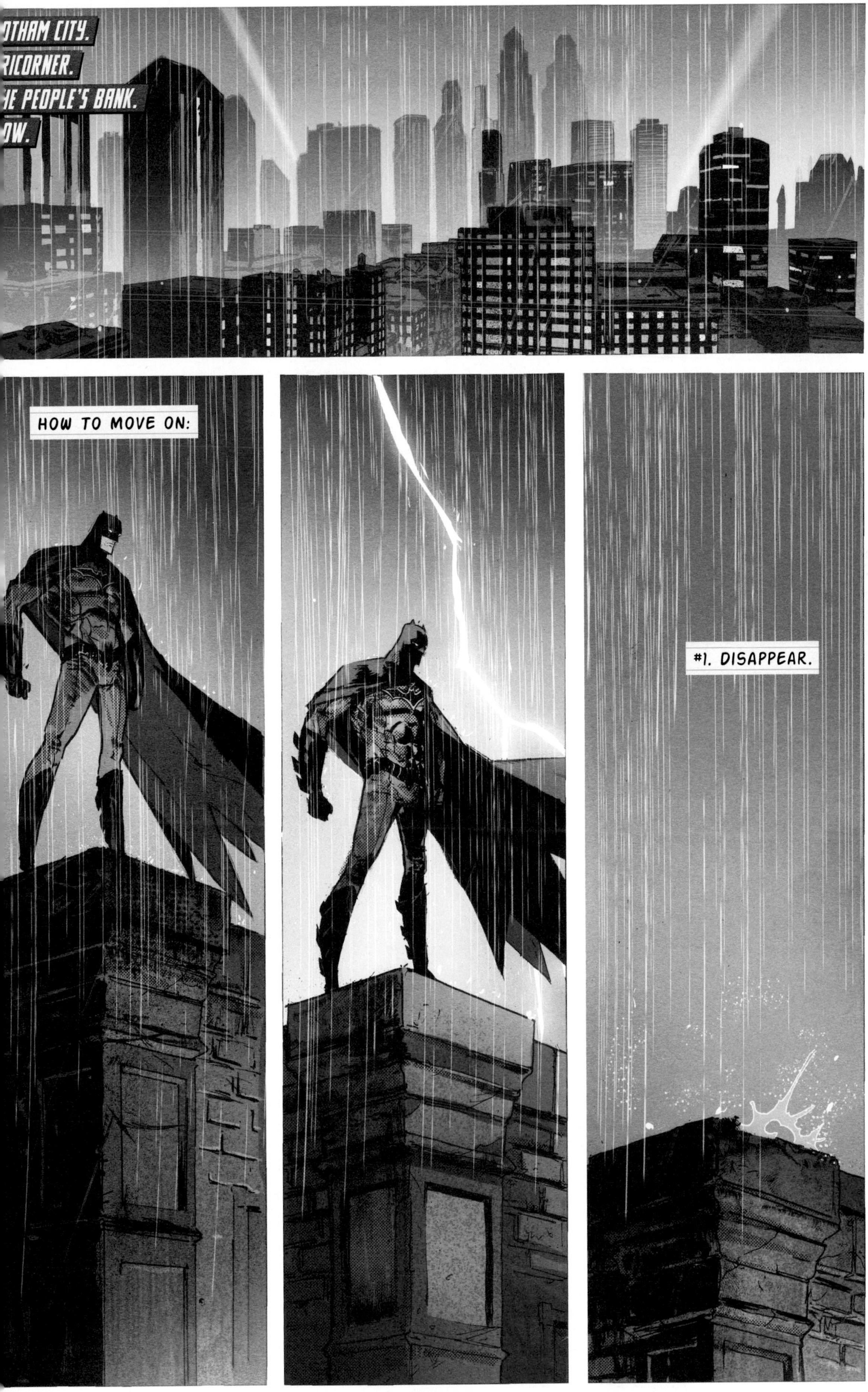
OTHAM CITY.
RICORNER.
HE PEOPLE'S BANK.
OW.
HOW TO MOVE ON:
#1. DISAPPEAR.

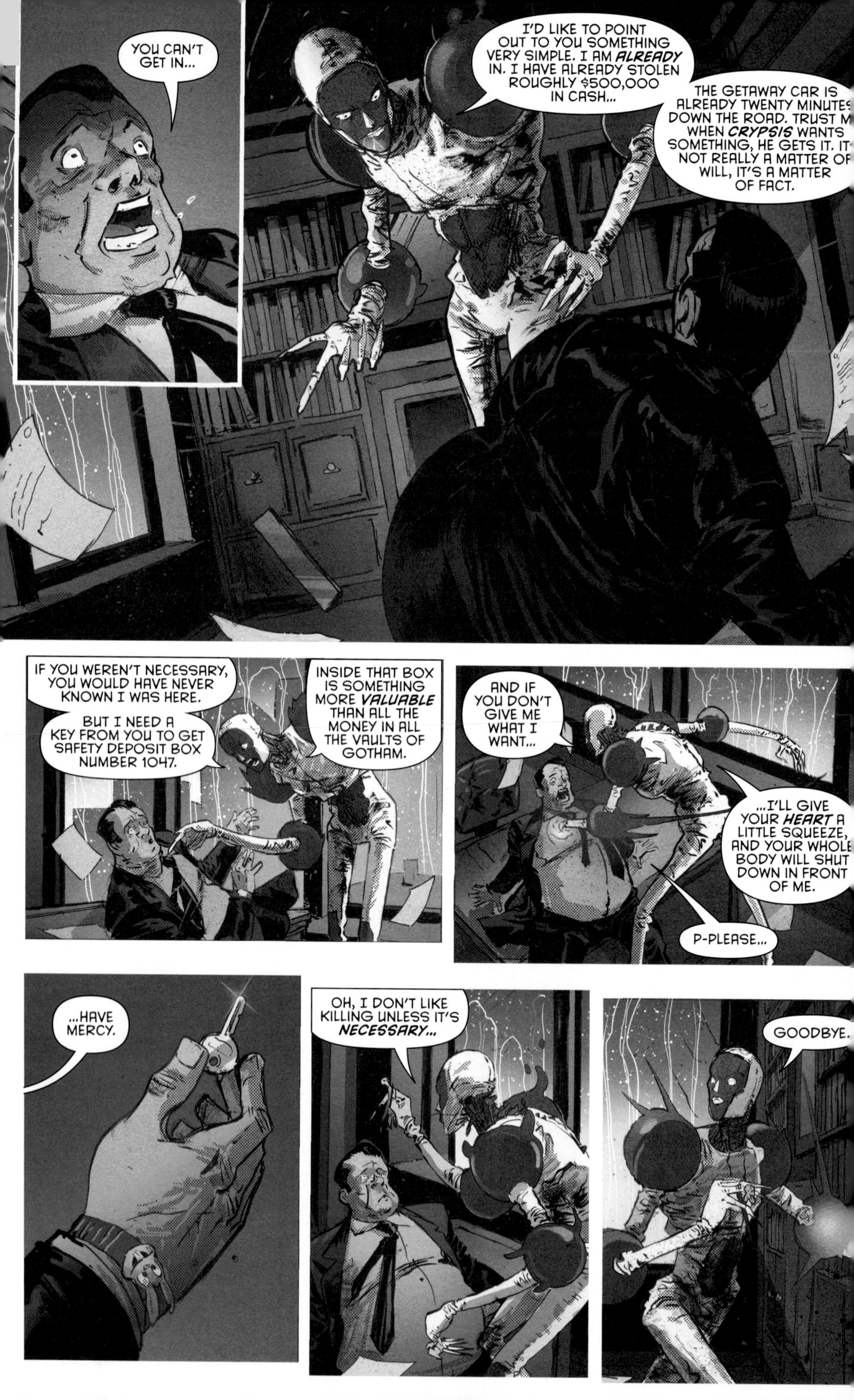
YOU CAN'T GET IN...
I'D LIKE TO POINT OUT TO YOU SOMETHING VERY SIMPLE. I AM *ALREADY* IN. I HAVE ALREADY STOLEN ROUGHLY $500,000 IN CASH...
THE GETAWAY CAR IS ALREADY TWENTY MINUTES DOWN THE ROAD. TRUST ME WHEN *CRYPSIS* WANTS SOMETHING, HE GETS IT. IT'S NOT REALLY A MATTER OF WILL, IT'S A MATTER OF FACT.
IF YOU WEREN'T NECESSARY, YOU WOULD HAVE NEVER KNOWN I WAS HERE.
BUT I NEED A KEY FROM YOU TO GET SAFETY DEPOSIT BOX NUMBER 1047.
INSIDE THAT BOX IS SOMETHING MORE *VALUABLE* THAN ALL THE MONEY IN ALL THE VAULTS OF GOTHAM.
AND IF YOU DON'T GIVE ME WHAT I WANT...
...I'LL GIVE YOUR *HEART* A LITTLE SQUEEZE, AND YOUR WHOLE BODY WILL SHUT DOWN IN FRONT OF ME.
P-PLEASE...
...HAVE MERCY.
OH, I DON'T LIKE KILLING UNLESS IT'S *NECESSARY*...
GOODBYE.

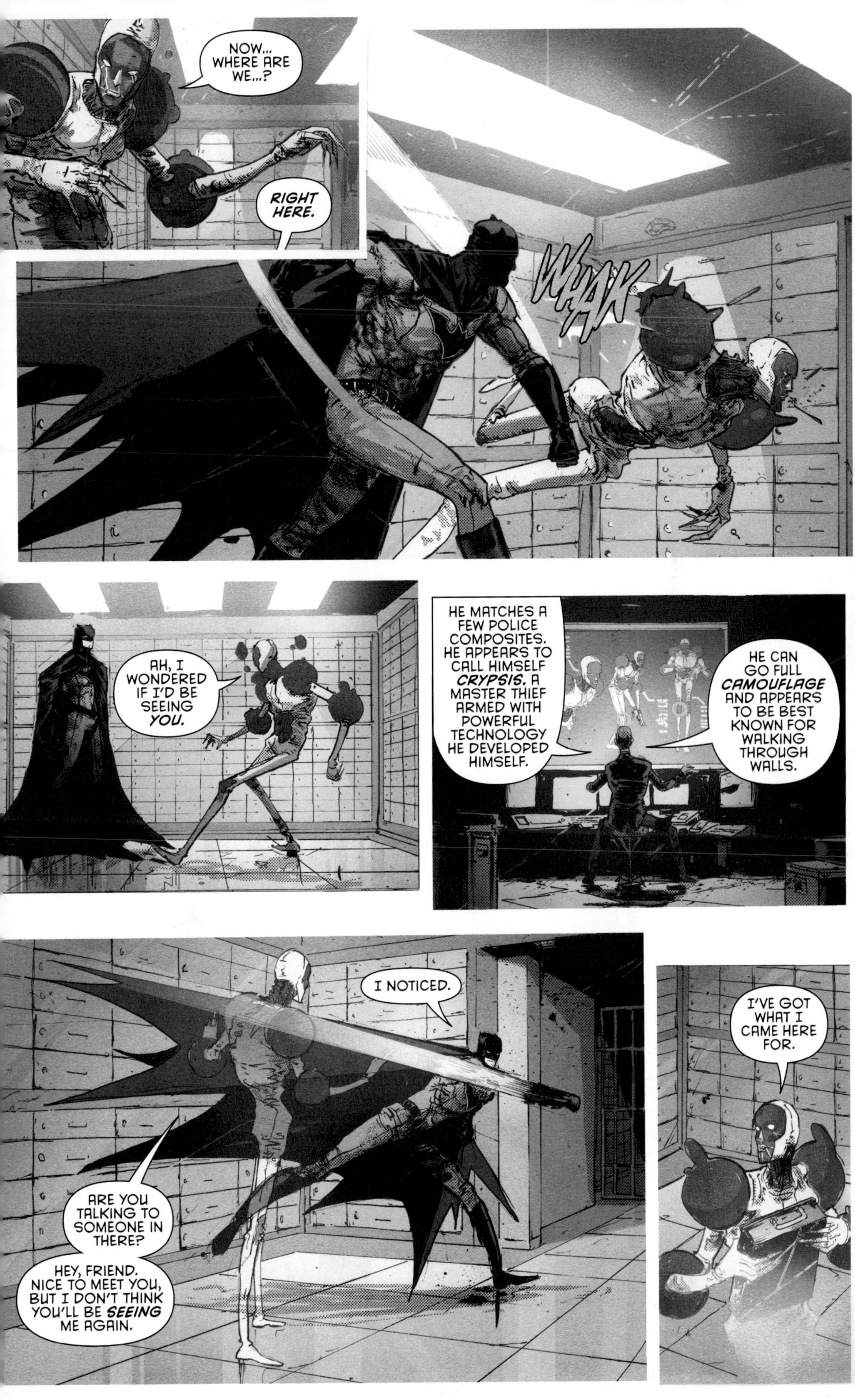
NOW... WHERE ARE WE...?
RIGHT HERE.
WHAK
AH, I WONDERED IF I'D BE SEEING YOU.
HE MATCHES A FEW POLICE COMPOSITES. HE APPEARS TO CALL HIMSELF CRYPSIS. A MASTER THIEF ARMED WITH POWERFUL TECHNOLOGY HE DEVELOPED HIMSELF.
HE CAN GO FULL CAMOUFLAGE AND APPEARS TO BE BEST KNOWN FOR WALKING THROUGH WALLS.
I NOTICED.
ARE YOU TALKING TO SOMEONE IN THERE?
HEY, FRIEND. NICE TO MEET YOU, BUT I DON'T THINK YOU'LL BE SEEING ME AGAIN.
I'VE GOT WHAT I CAME HERE FOR.

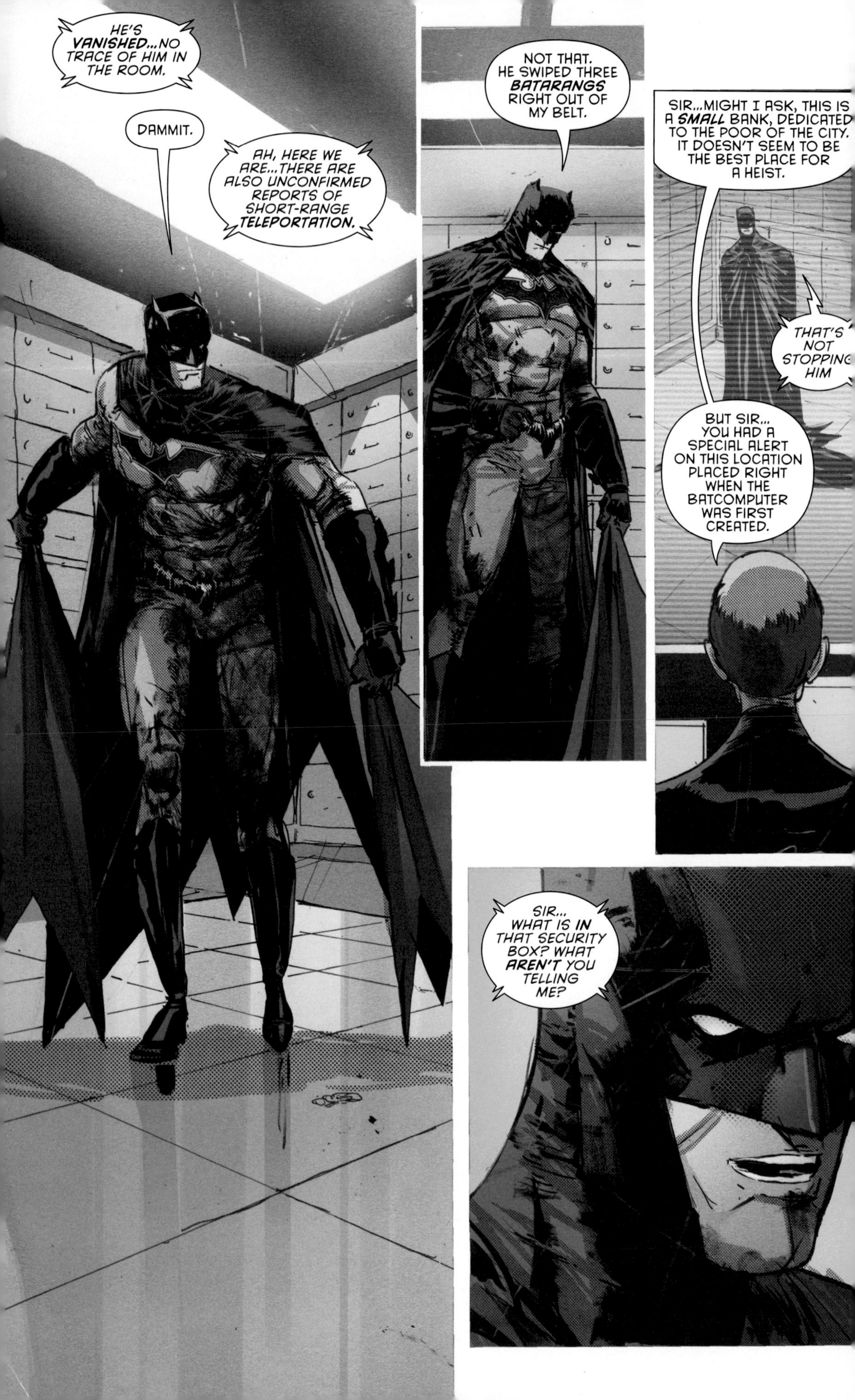
HE'S VANISHED...NO TRACE OF HIM IN THE ROOM.
DAMMIT.
AH, HERE WE ARE...THERE ARE ALSO UNCONFIRMED REPORTS OF SHORT-RANGE TELEPORTATION.
NOT THAT. HE SWIPED THREE BATARANGS RIGHT OUT OF MY BELT.
SIR...MIGHT I ASK, THIS IS A SMALL BANK, DEDICATED TO THE POOR OF THE CITY. IT DOESN'T SEEM TO BE THE BEST PLACE FOR A HEIST.
THAT'S NOT STOPPING HIM
BUT SIR... YOU HAD A SPECIAL ALERT ON THIS LOCATION PLACED RIGHT WHEN THE BATCOMPUTER WAS FIRST CREATED.
SIR... WHAT IS IN THAT SECURITY BOX? WHAT AREN'T YOU TELLING ME?

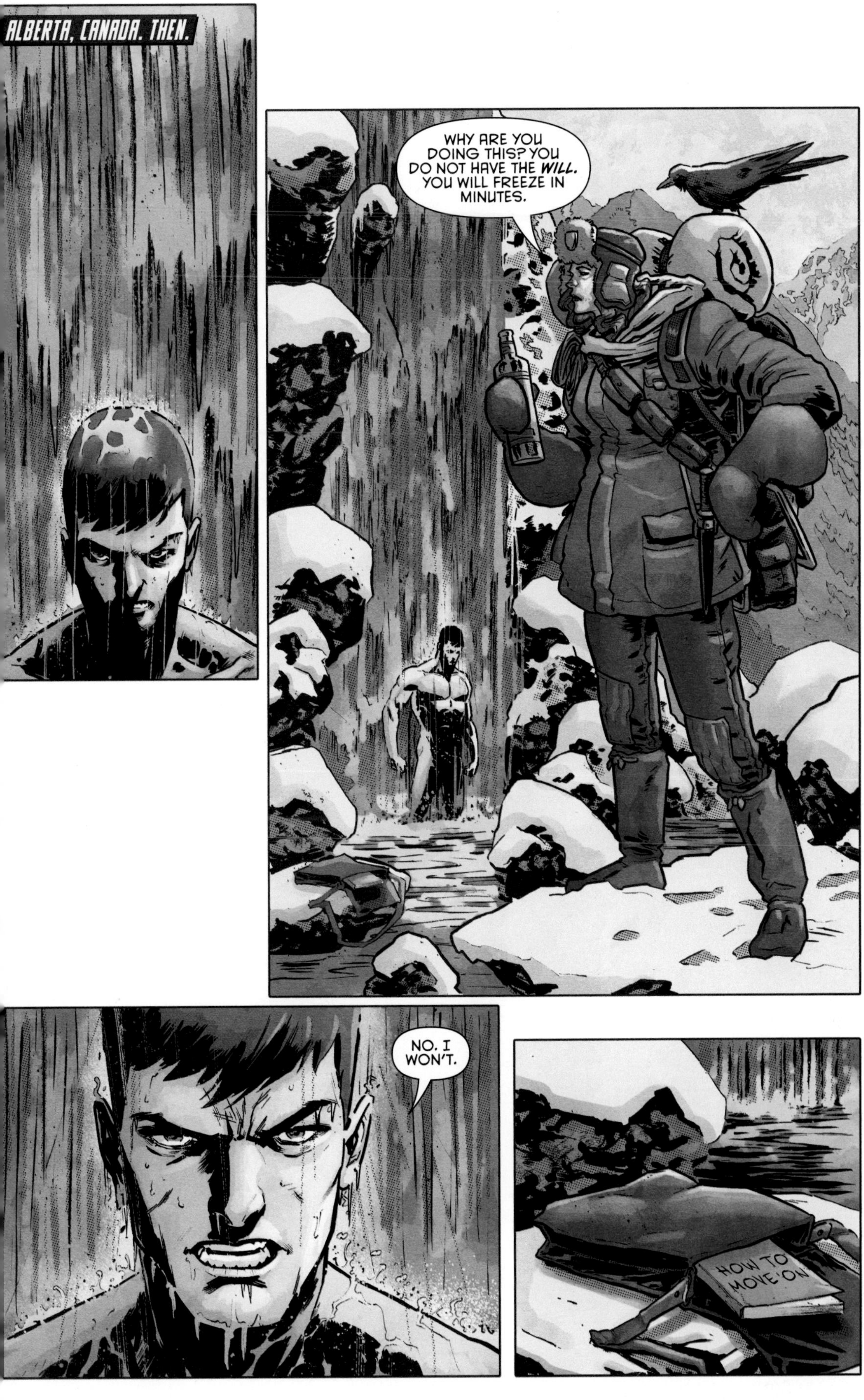
ALBERTA, CANADA. THEN.
WHY ARE YOU DOING THIS? YOU DO NOT HAVE THE *WILL.* YOU WILL FREEZE IN MINUTES.
NO. I WON'T.
HOW TO MOVE ON

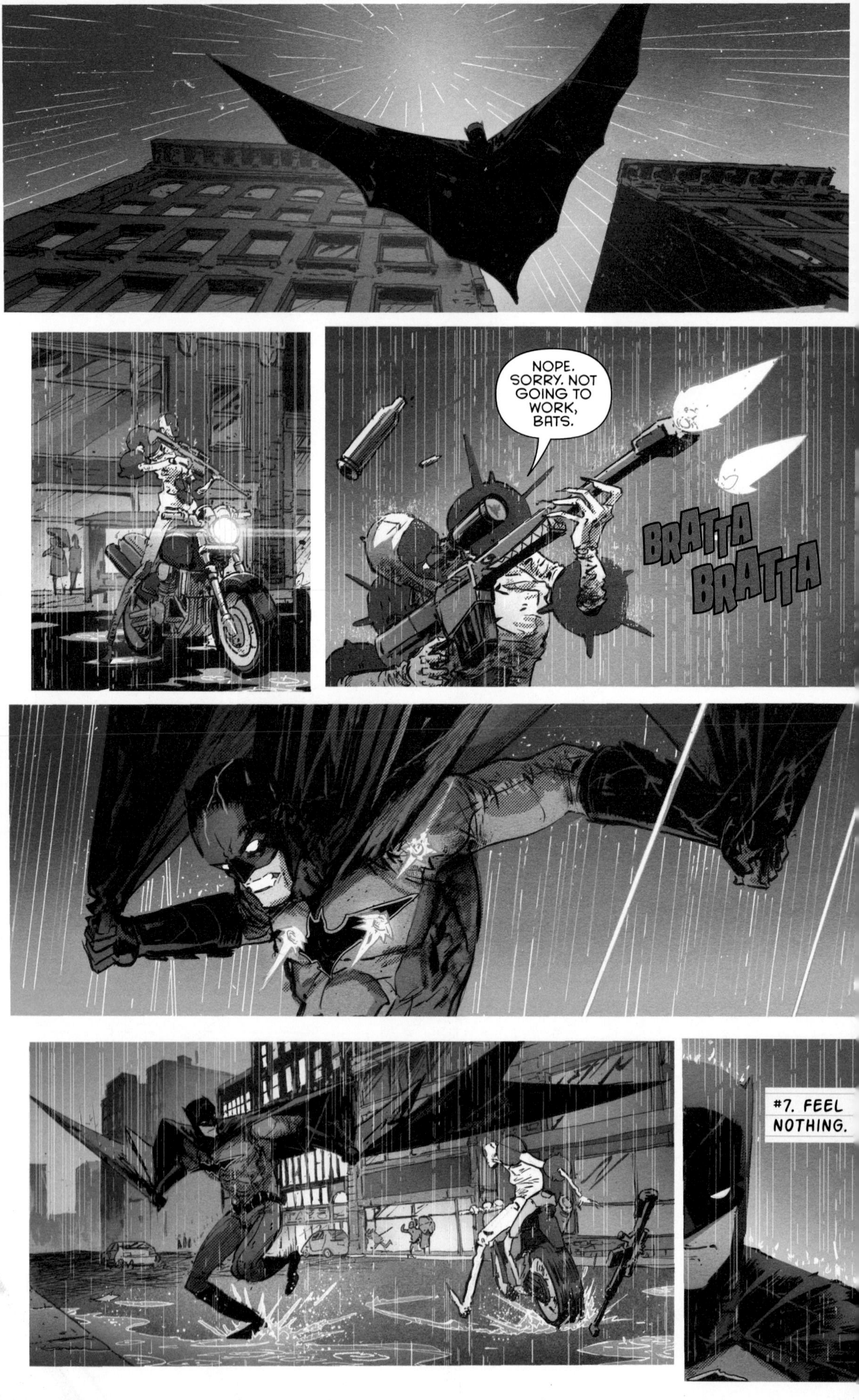
NOPE. SORRY. NOT GOING TO WORK, BATS.
BRATTA BRATTA
#7. FEEL NOTHING.

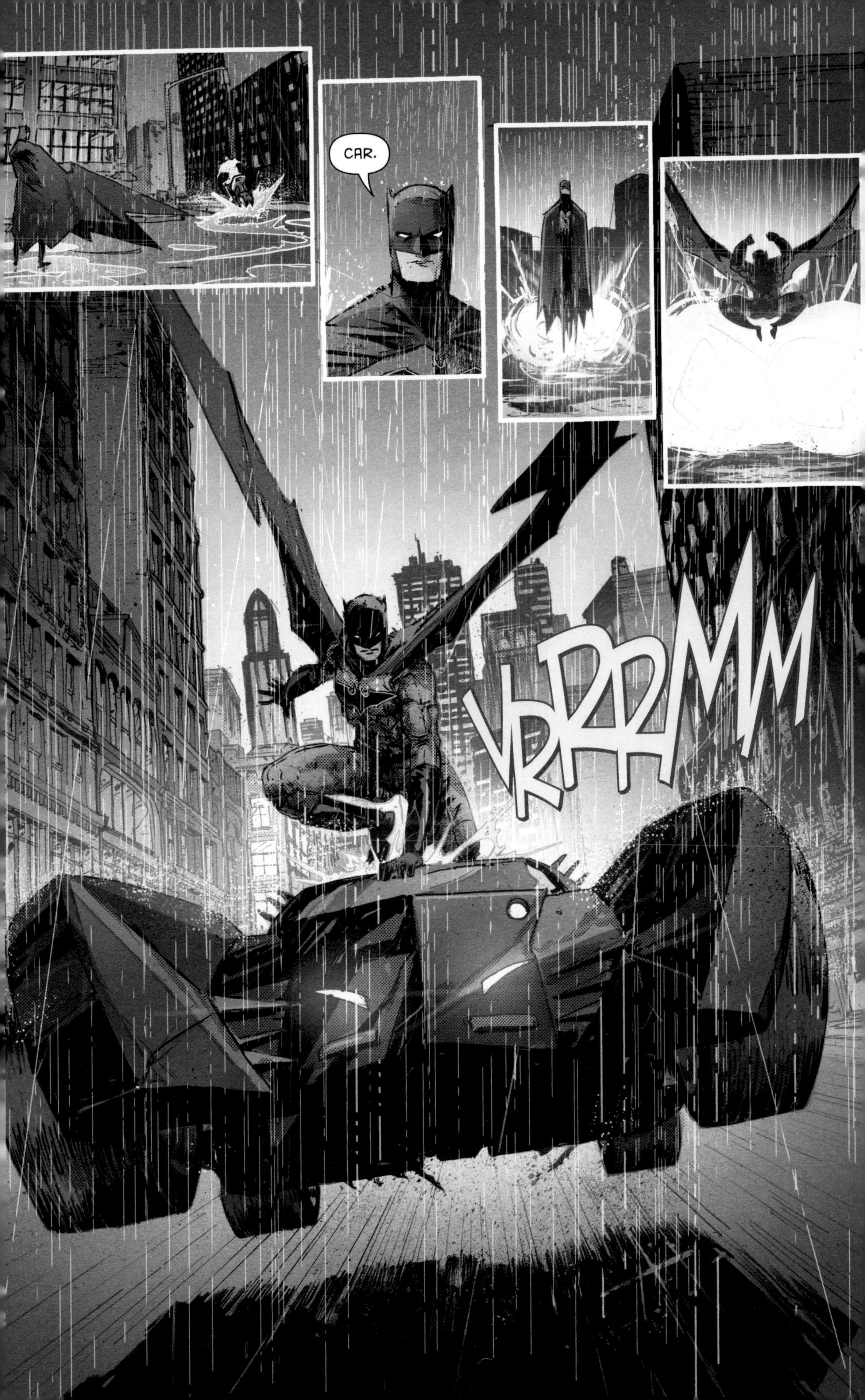
CAR.
VRRRMM

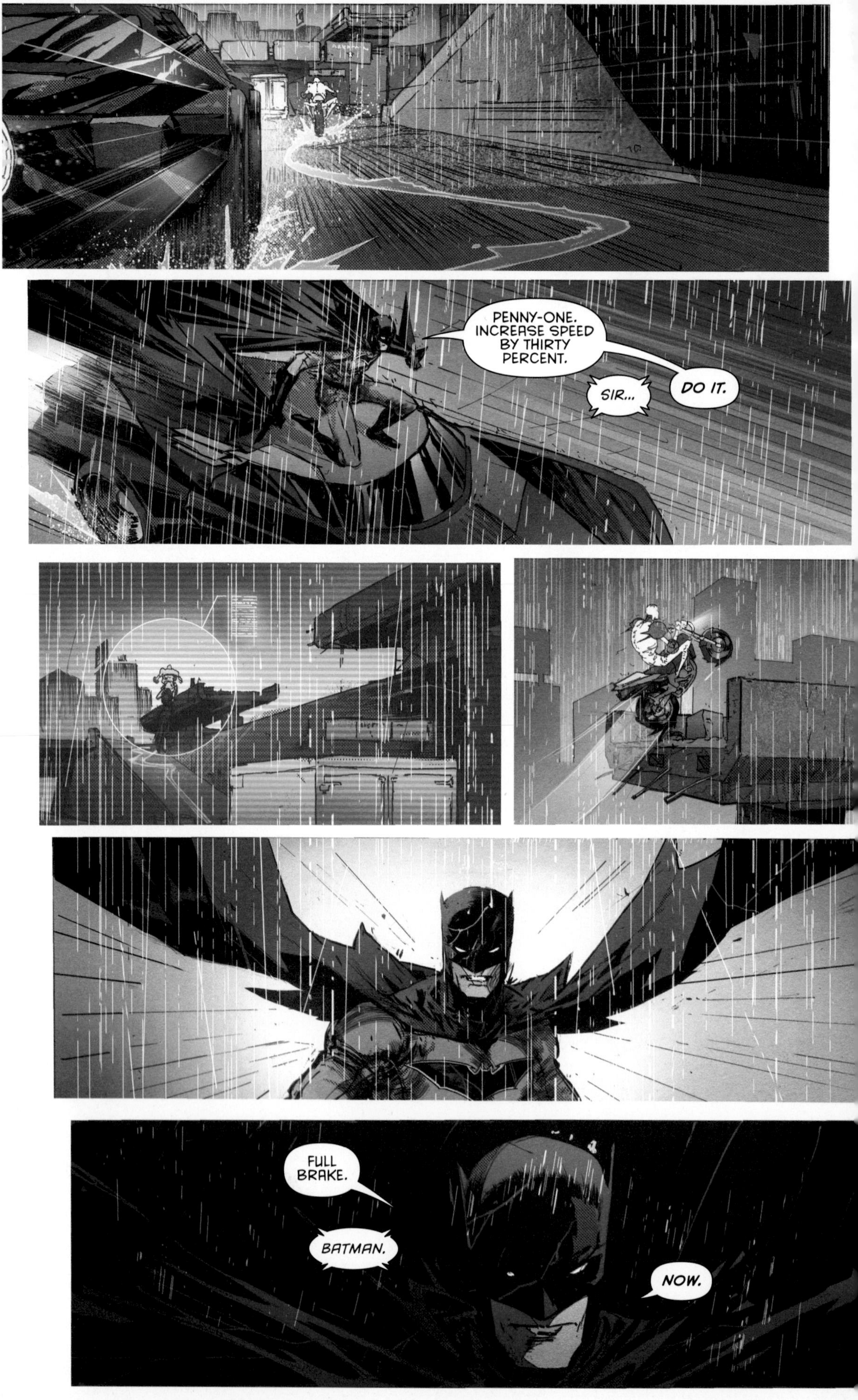
PENNY-ONE. INCREASE SPEED BY THIRTY PERCENT.
SIR...
DO IT.
FULL BRAKE.
BATMAN.
NOW.

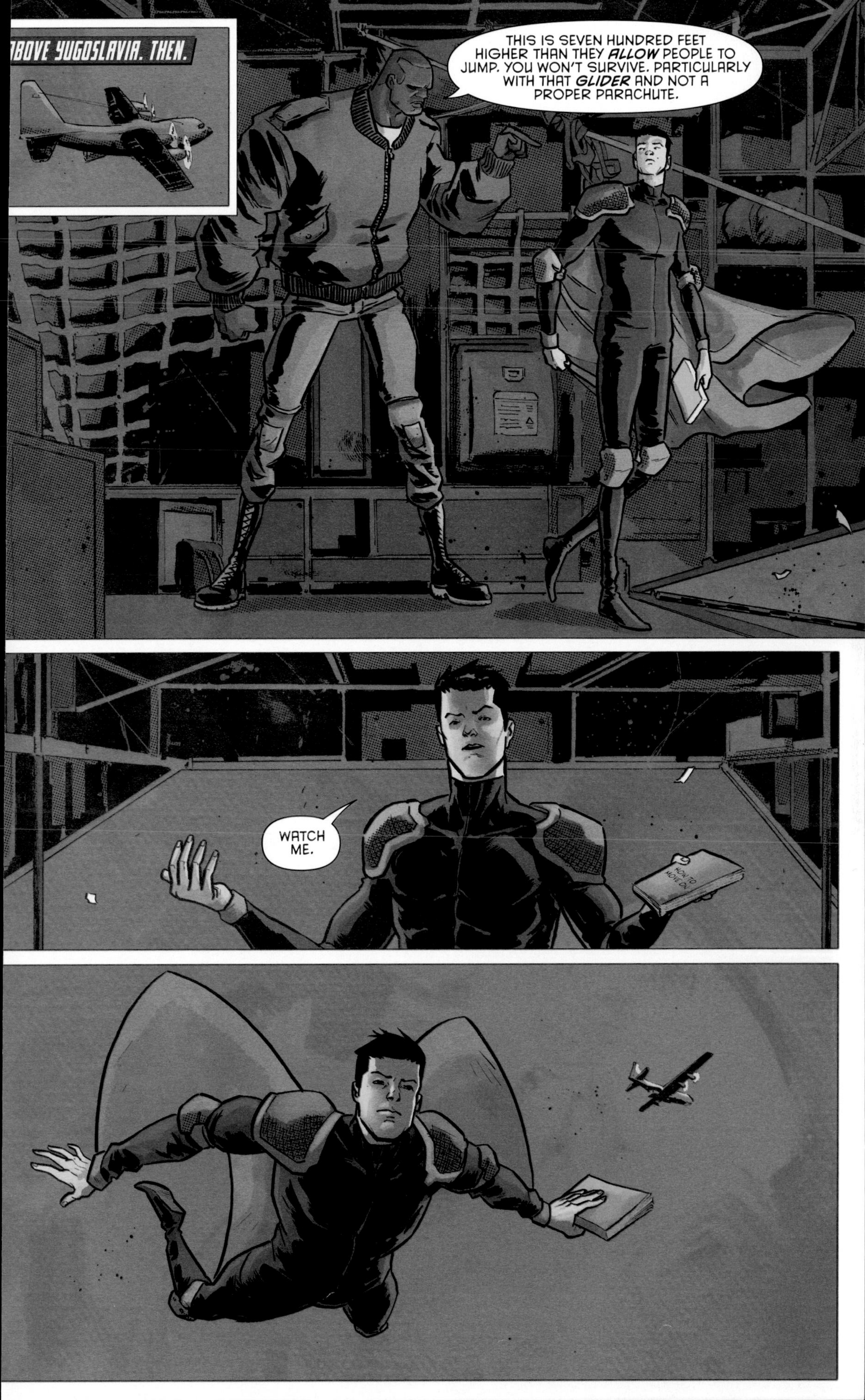
ABOVE YUGOSLAVIA. THEN.
THIS IS SEVEN HUNDRED FEET HIGHER THAN THEY ALLOW PEOPLE TO JUMP. YOU WON'T SURVIVE. PARTICULARLY WITH THAT GLIDER AND NOT A PROPER PARACHUTE.
WATCH ME.

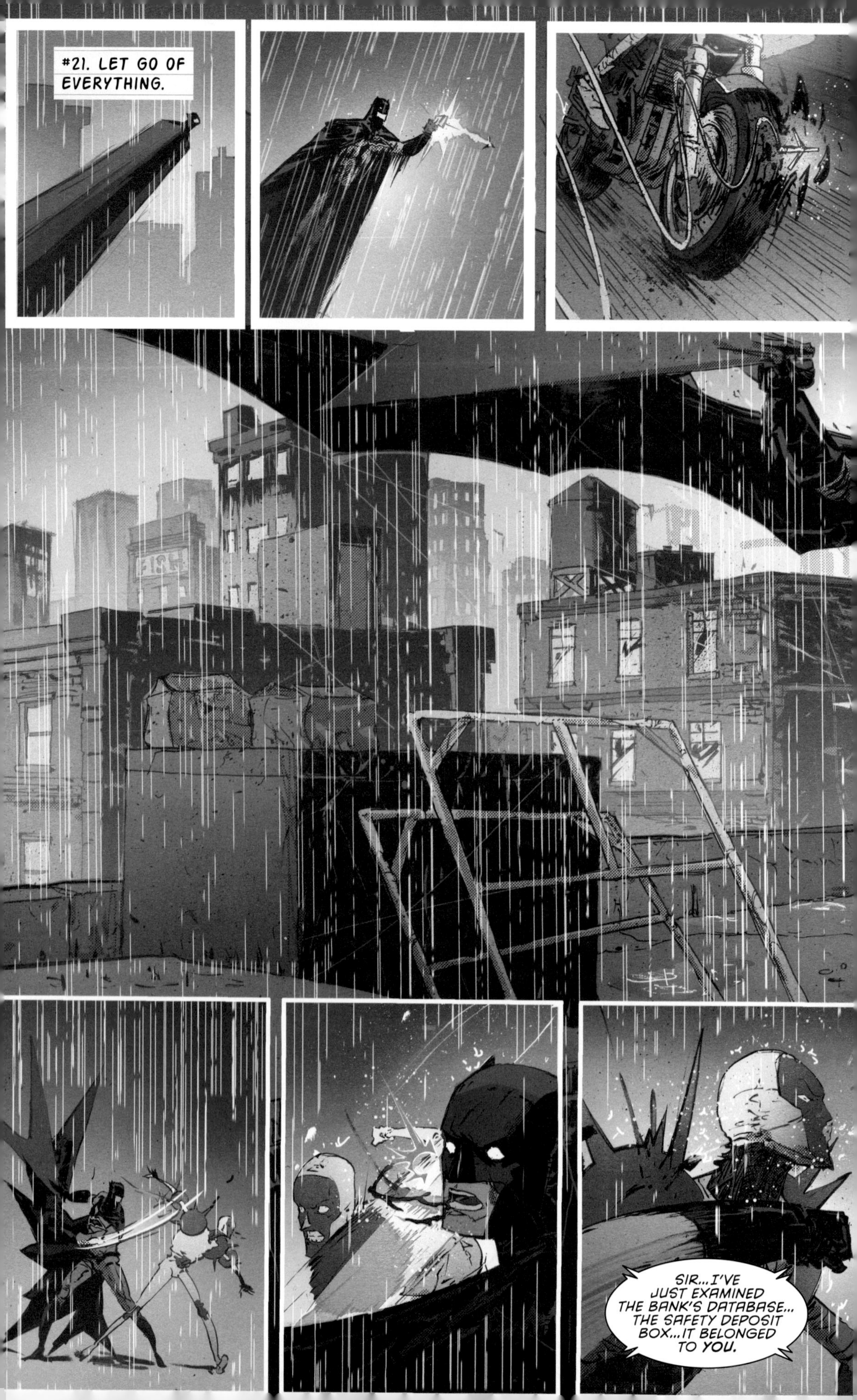
#21. LET GO OF EVERYTHING.
SIR...I'VE JUST EXAMINED THE BANK'S DATABASE... THE SAFETY DEPOSIT BOX...IT BELONGED TO YOU.

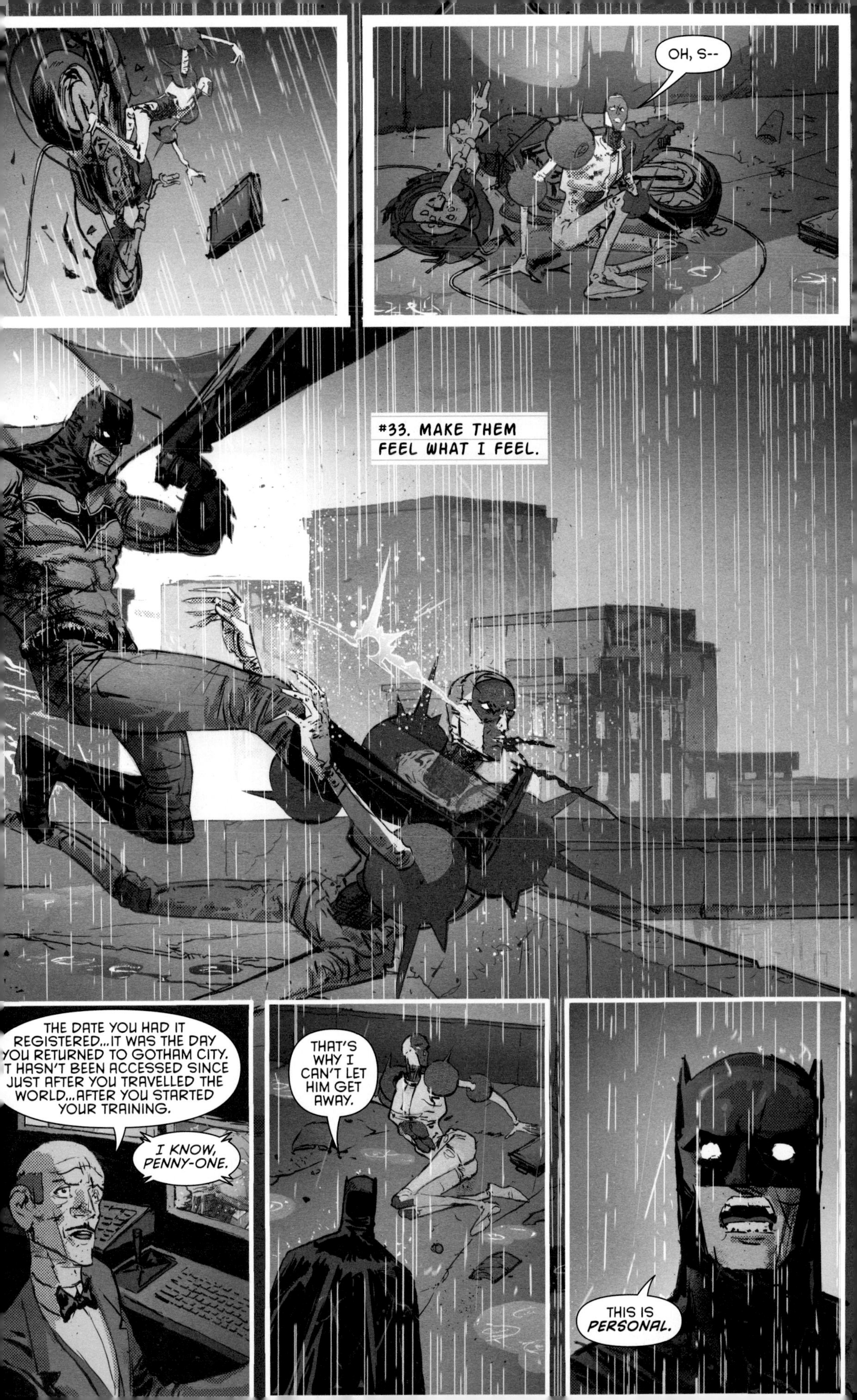

OH, S--
#33. MAKE THEM FEEL WHAT I FEEL.
THE DATE YOU HAD IT REGISTERED...IT WAS THE DAY YOU RETURNED TO GOTHAM CITY. IT HASN'T BEEN ACCESSED SINCE JUST AFTER YOU TRAVELLED THE WORLD...AFTER YOU STARTED YOUR TRAINING.
I KNOW, PENNY-ONE.
THAT'S WHY I CAN'T LET HIM GET AWAY.
THIS IS PERSONAL.

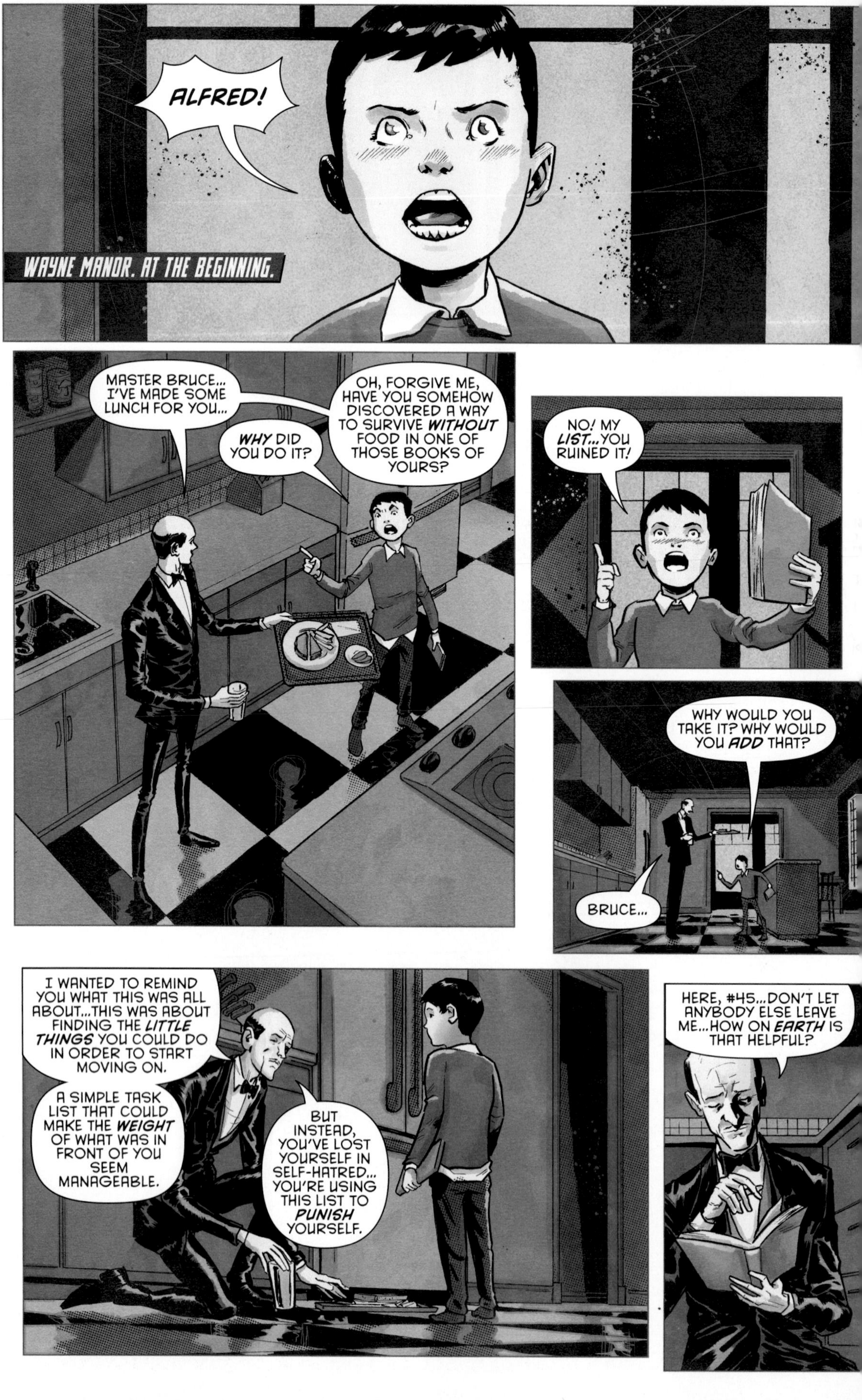
ALFRED!
WAYNE MANOR. AT THE BEGINNING.
MASTER BRUCE... I'VE MADE SOME LUNCH FOR YOU...
WHY DID YOU DO IT?
OH, FORGIVE ME, HAVE YOU SOMEHOW DISCOVERED A WAY TO SURVIVE WITHOUT FOOD IN ONE OF THOSE BOOKS OF YOURS?
NO! MY LIST...YOU RUINED IT!
WHY WOULD YOU TAKE IT? WHY WOULD YOU ADD THAT?
BRUCE...
I WANTED TO REMIND YOU WHAT THIS WAS ALL ABOUT...THIS WAS ABOUT FINDING THE LITTLE THINGS YOU COULD DO IN ORDER TO START MOVING ON.
A SIMPLE TASK LIST THAT COULD MAKE THE WEIGHT OF WHAT WAS IN FRONT OF YOU SEEM MANAGEABLE.
BUT INSTEAD, YOU'VE LOST YOURSELF IN SELF-HATRED... YOU'RE USING THIS LIST TO PUNISH YOURSELF.
HERE, #45...DON'T LET ANYBODY ELSE LEAVE ME...HOW ON EARTH IS THAT HELPFUL?

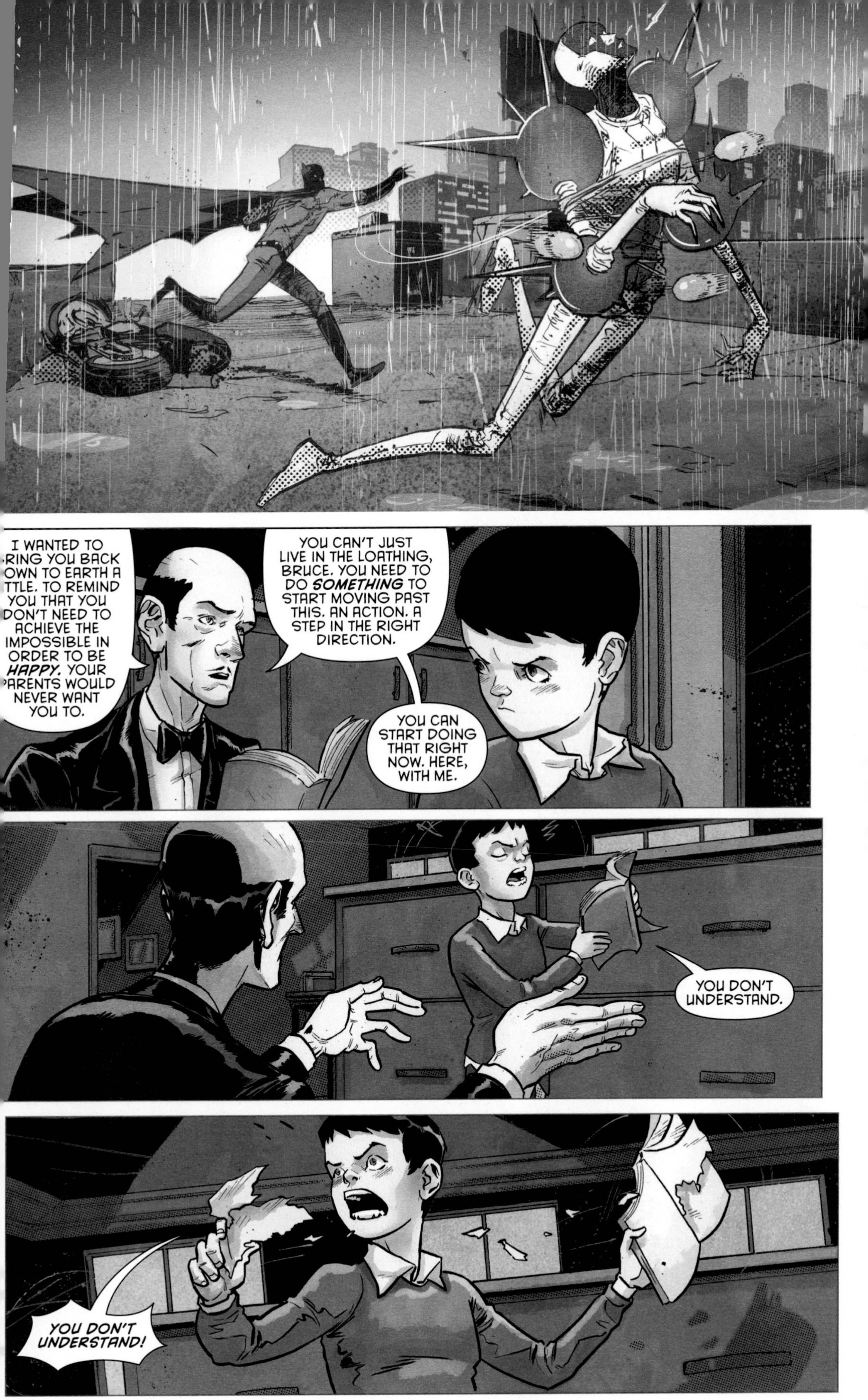
I WANTED TO RING YOU BACK OWN TO EARTH A TTLE. TO REMIND YOU THAT YOU DON'T NEED TO ACHIEVE THE IMPOSSIBLE IN ORDER TO BE *HAPPY.* YOUR ARENTS WOULD NEVER WANT YOU TO.
YOU CAN'T JUST LIVE IN THE LOATHING, BRUCE. YOU NEED TO DO *SOMETHING* TO START MOVING PAST THIS. AN ACTION. A STEP IN THE RIGHT DIRECTION.
YOU CAN START DOING THAT RIGHT NOW. HERE, WITH ME.
YOU DON'T UNDERSTAND.
YOU DON'T UNDERSTAND!

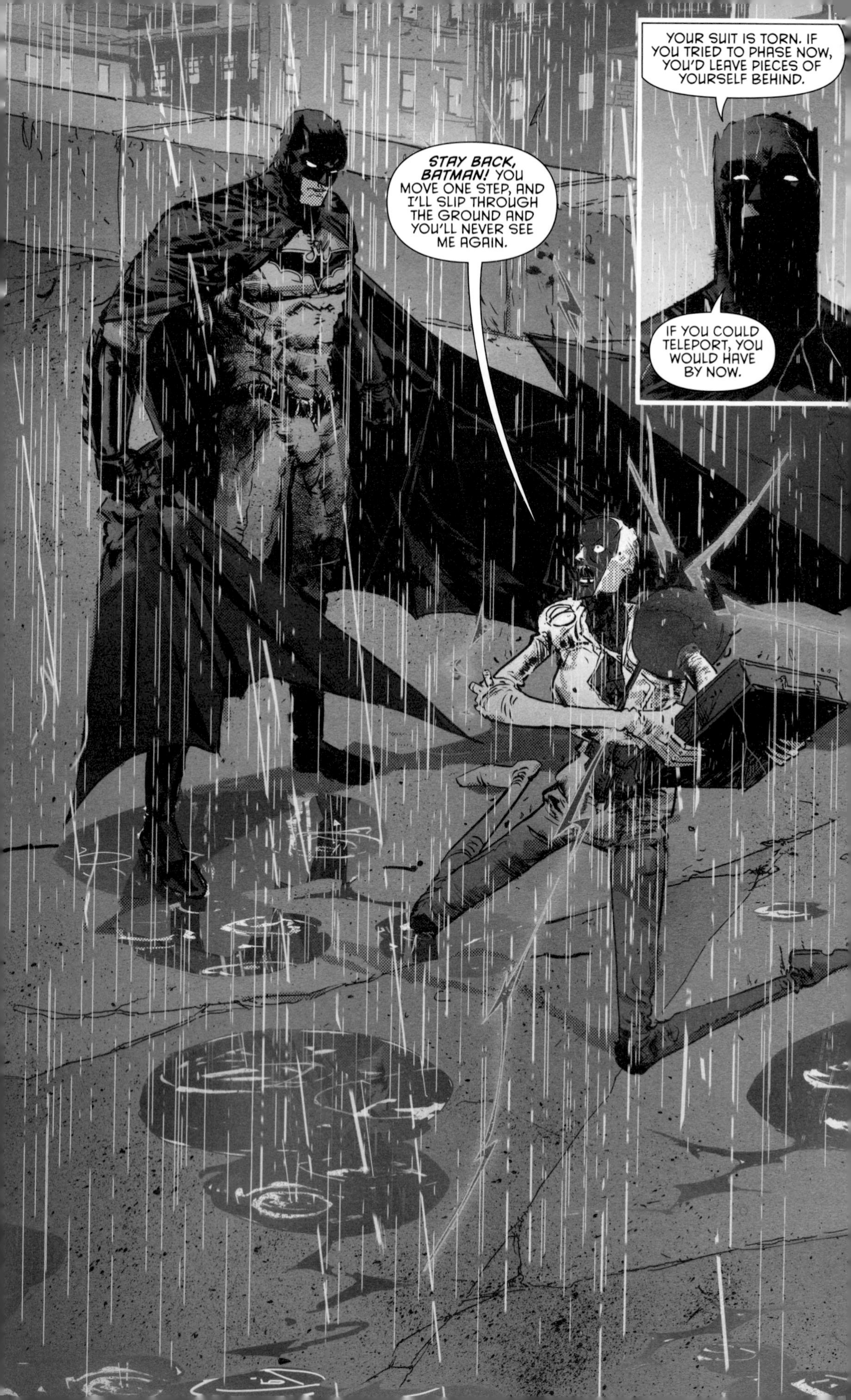
STAY BACK, BATMAN! YOU MOVE ONE STEP, AND I'LL SLIP THROUGH THE GROUND AND YOU'LL NEVER SEE ME AGAIN.
YOUR SUIT IS TORN. IF YOU TRIED TO PHASE NOW, YOU'D LEAVE PIECES OF YOURSELF BEHIND.
IF YOU COULD TELEPORT, YOU WOULD HAVE BY NOW.

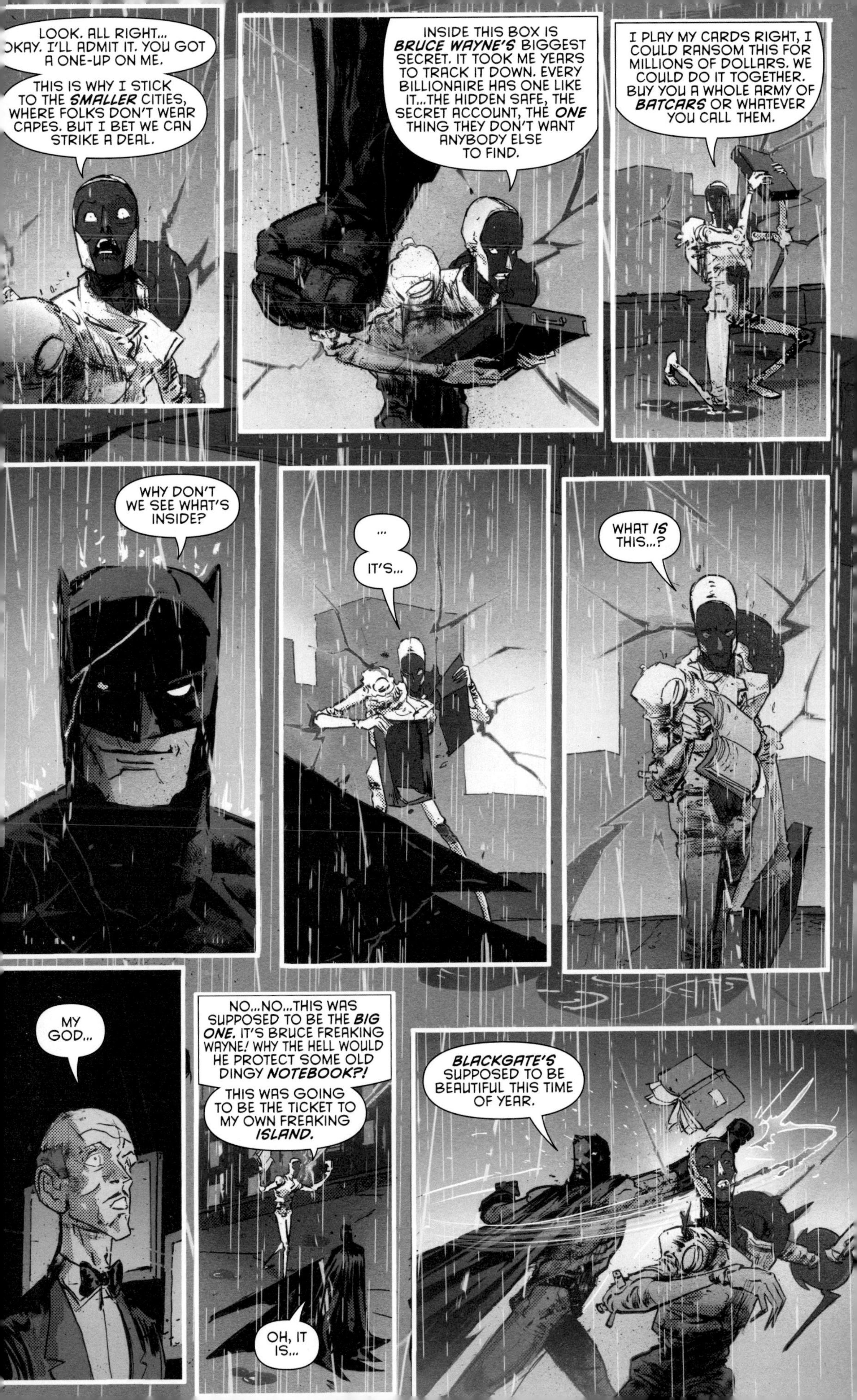

LOOK. ALL RIGHT... OKAY. I'LL ADMIT IT. YOU GOT A ONE-UP ON ME.
THIS IS WHY I STICK TO THE *SMALLER* CITIES, WHERE FOLKS DON'T WEAR CAPES. BUT I BET WE CAN STRIKE A DEAL.
INSIDE THIS BOX IS *BRUCE WAYNE'S* BIGGEST SECRET. IT TOOK ME YEARS TO TRACK IT DOWN. EVERY BILLIONAIRE HAS ONE LIKE IT...THE HIDDEN SAFE, THE SECRET ACCOUNT, THE *ONE* THING THEY DON'T WANT ANYBODY ELSE TO FIND.
I PLAY MY CARDS RIGHT, I COULD RANSOM THIS FOR MILLIONS OF DOLLARS. WE COULD DO IT TOGETHER. BUY YOU A WHOLE ARMY OF *BATCARS* OR WHATEVER YOU CALL THEM.
WHY DON'T WE SEE WHAT'S INSIDE?
...
IT'S...
WHAT *IS* THIS...?
MY GOD...
NO...NO...THIS WAS SUPPOSED TO BE THE *BIG ONE.* IT'S BRUCE FREAKING WAYNE! WHY THE HELL WOULD HE PROTECT SOME OLD DINGY *NOTEBOOK?!*
THIS WAS GOING TO BE THE TICKET TO MY OWN FREAKING *ISLAND.*
OH, IT IS...
BLACKGATE'S SUPPOSED TO BE BEAUTIFUL THIS TIME OF YEAR.

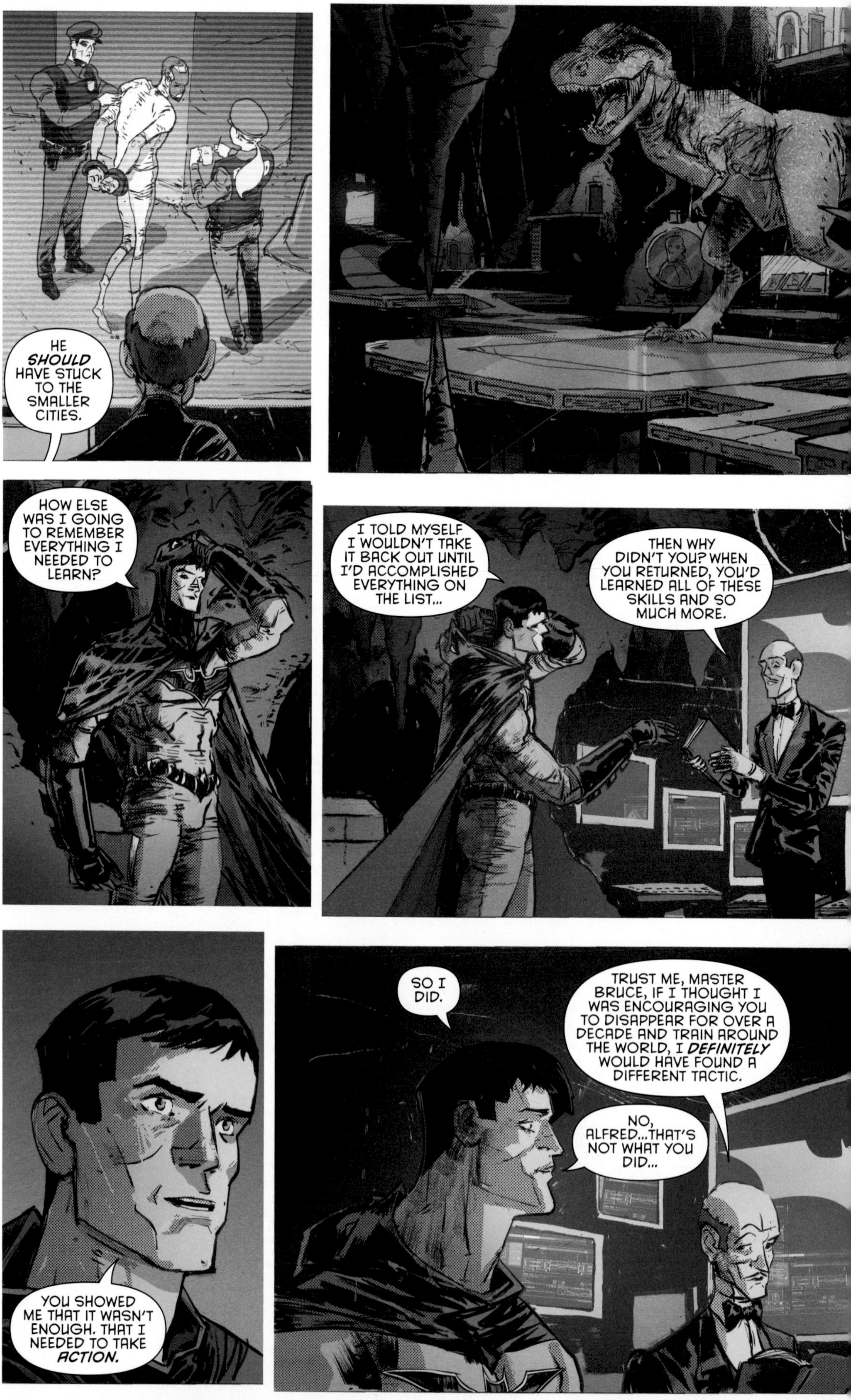
HE *SHOULD* HAVE STUCK TO THE SMALLER CITIES.
HOW ELSE WAS I GOING TO REMEMBER EVERYTHING I NEEDED TO LEARN?
I TOLD MYSELF I WOULDN'T TAKE IT BACK OUT UNTIL I'D ACCOMPLISHED EVERYTHING ON THE LIST...
THEN WHY DIDN'T YOU? WHEN YOU RETURNED, YOU'D LEARNED ALL OF THESE SKILLS AND SO MUCH MORE.
YOU SHOWED ME THAT IT WASN'T ENOUGH. THAT I NEEDED TO TAKE *ACTION.*
SO I DID.
TRUST ME, MASTER BRUCE, IF I THOUGHT I WAS ENCOURAGING YOU TO DISAPPEAR FOR OVER A DECADE AND TRAIN AROUND THE WORLD, I *DEFINITELY* WOULD HAVE FOUND A DIFFERENT TACTIC.
NO, ALFRED...THAT'S NOT WHAT YOU DID...

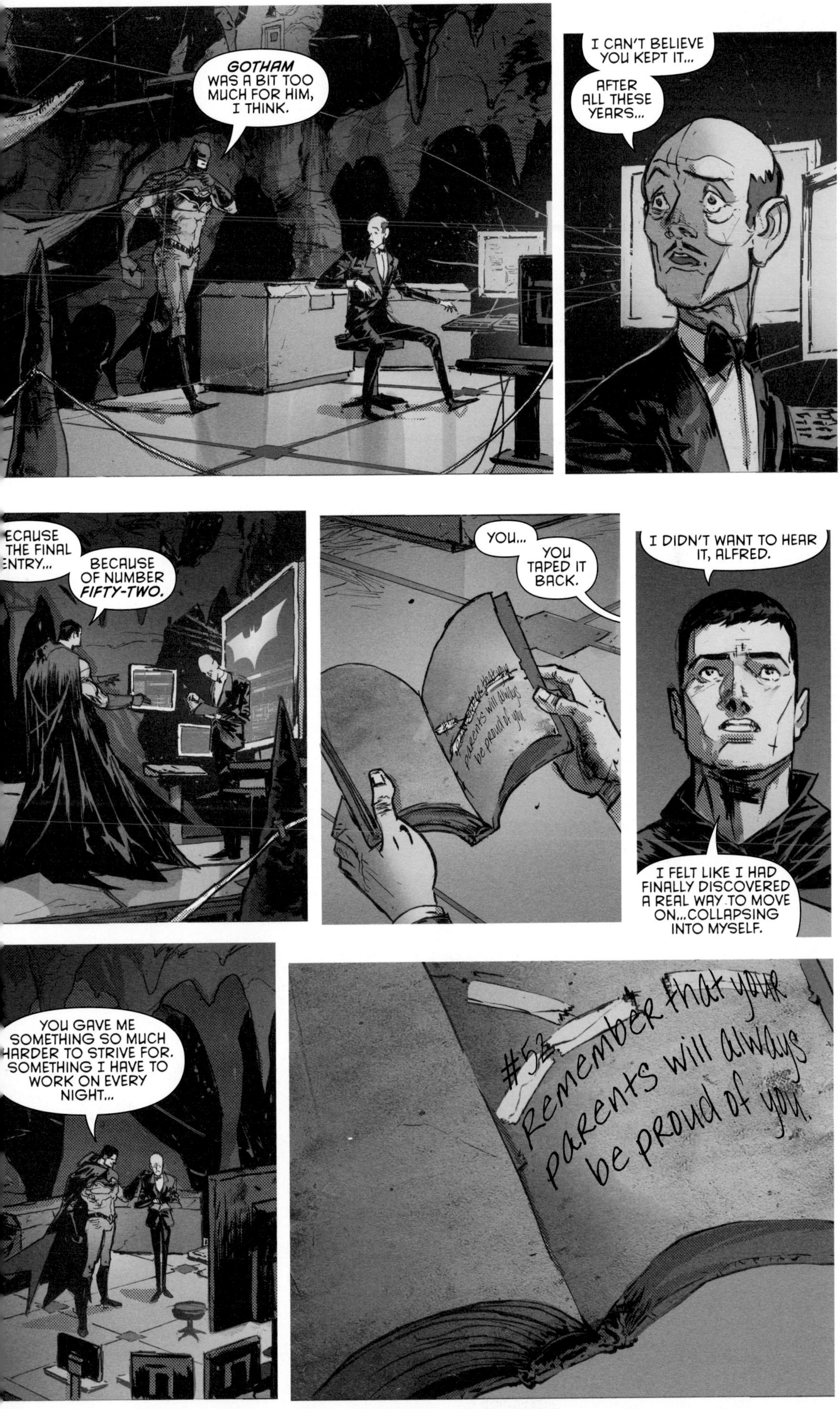
GOTHAM WAS A BIT TOO MUCH FOR HIM, I THINK.
I CAN'T BELIEVE YOU KEPT IT...
AFTER ALL THESE YEARS...
ECAUSE THE FINAL ENTRY...
BECAUSE OF NUMBER *FIFTY-TWO.*
YOU...
YOU TAPED IT BACK.
I DIDN'T WANT TO HEAR IT, ALFRED.
I FELT LIKE I HAD FINALLY DISCOVERED A REAL WAY TO MOVE ON...COLLAPSING INTO MYSELF.
YOU GAVE ME SOMETHING SO MUCH HARDER TO STRIVE FOR. SOMETHING I HAVE TO WORK ON EVERY NIGHT...
#52 Remember that your parents will always be proud of you.

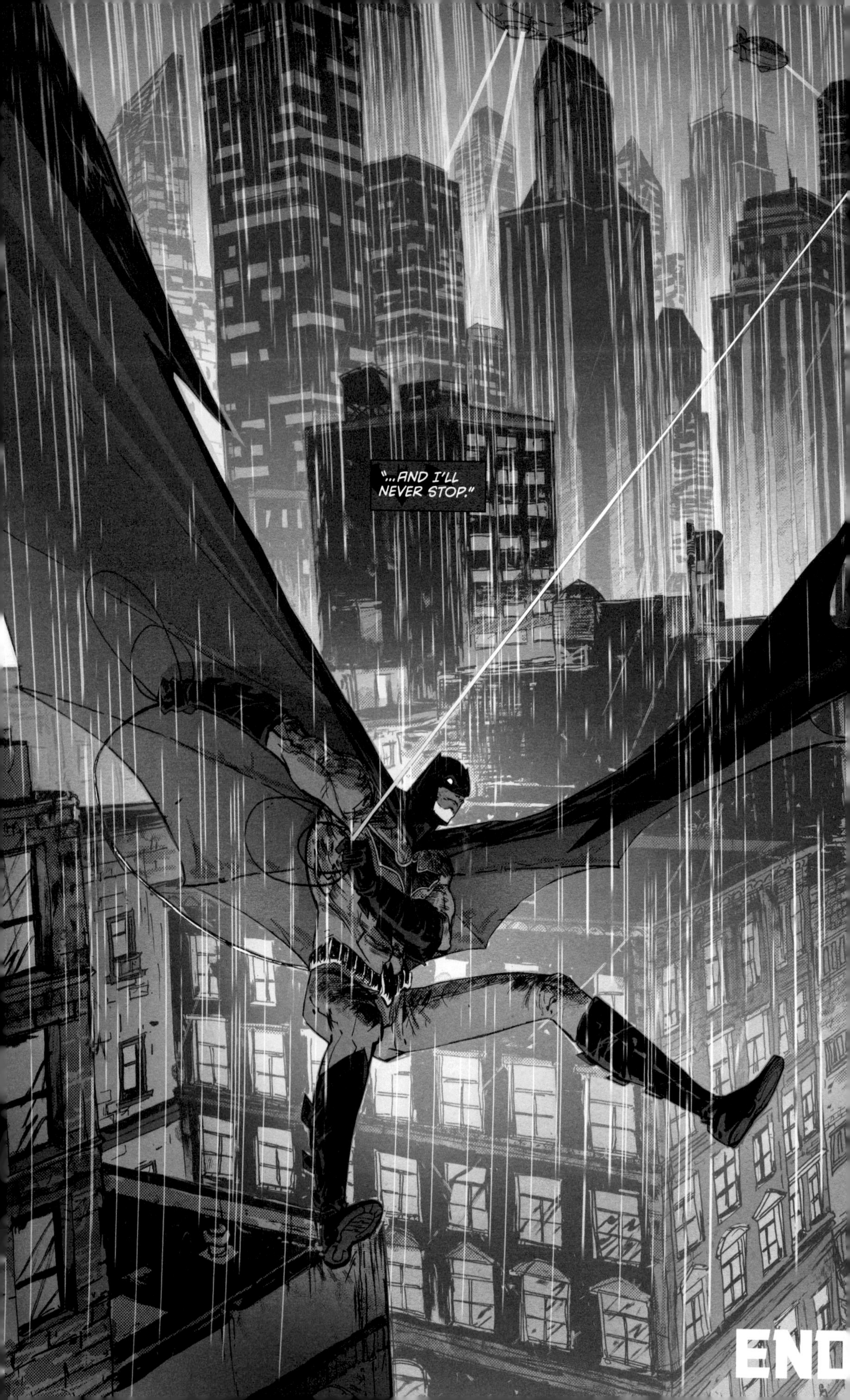
"...AND I'LL NEVER STOP."
END

BATMAN: FUTURES END #1
ALTERNATIVE COVER BY JASON FABOK & BRAD ANDERSON

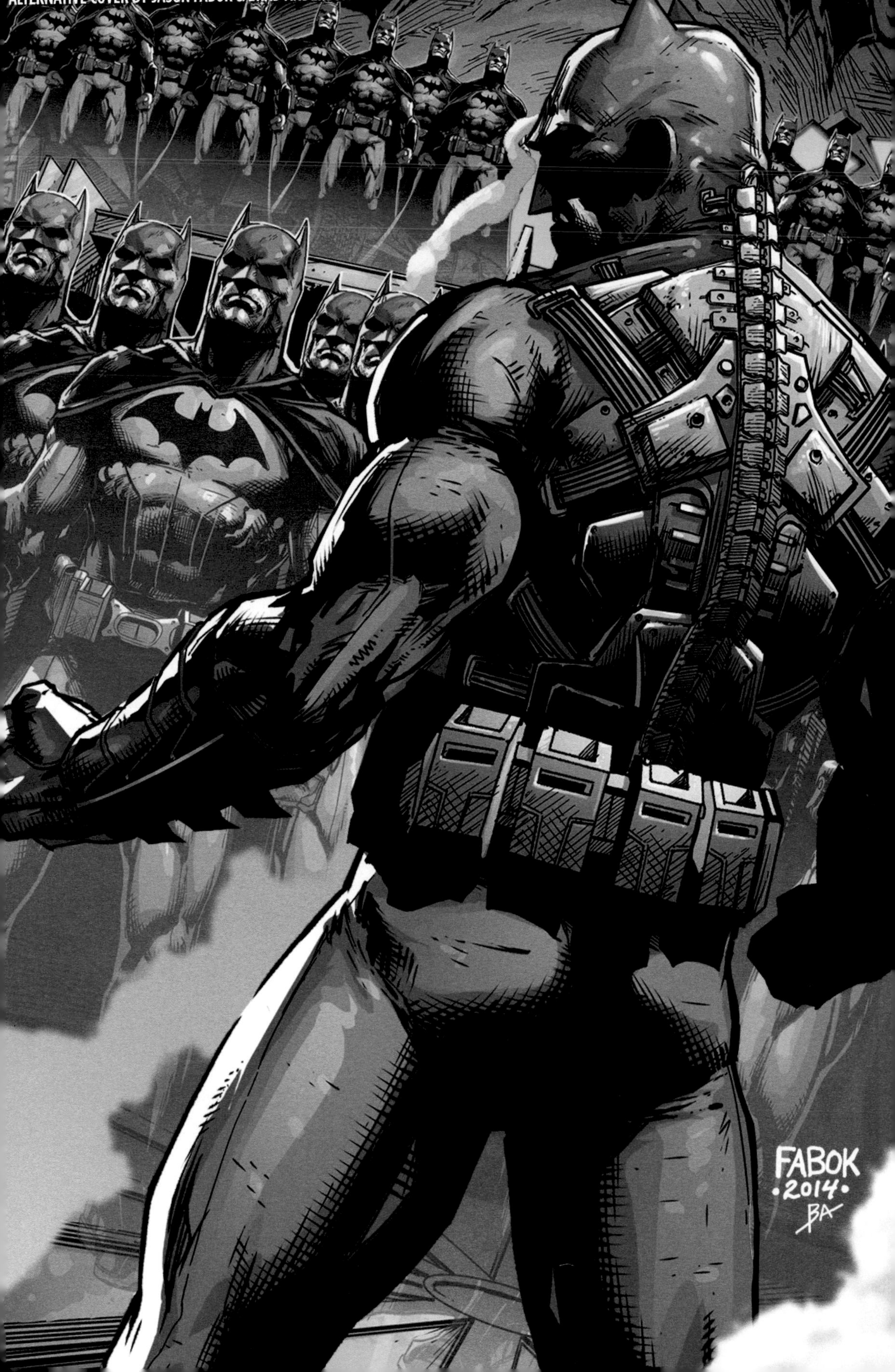

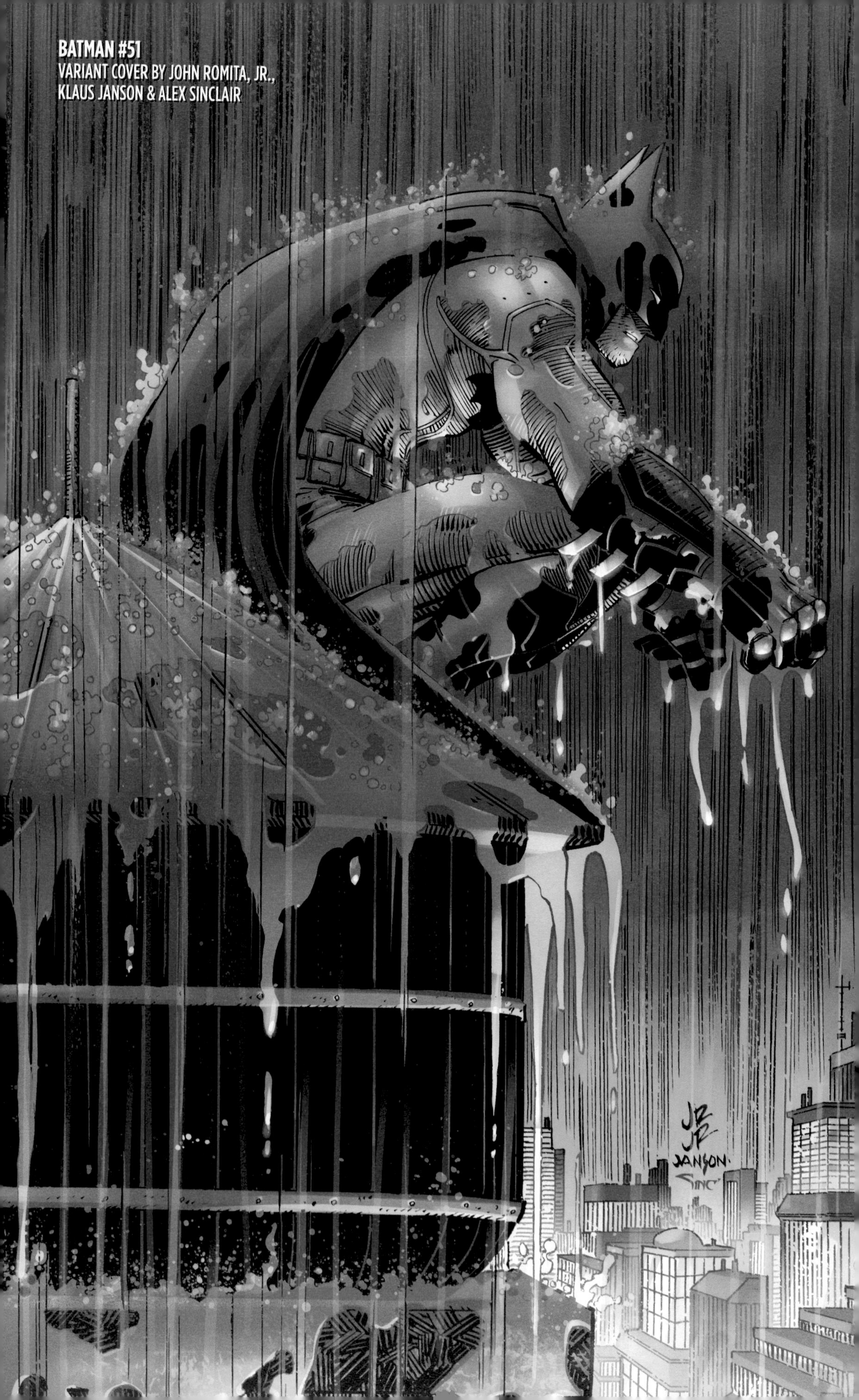

BATMAN #51
VARIANT COVER BY JOHN ROMITA, JR., KLAUS JANSON & ALEX SINCLAIR

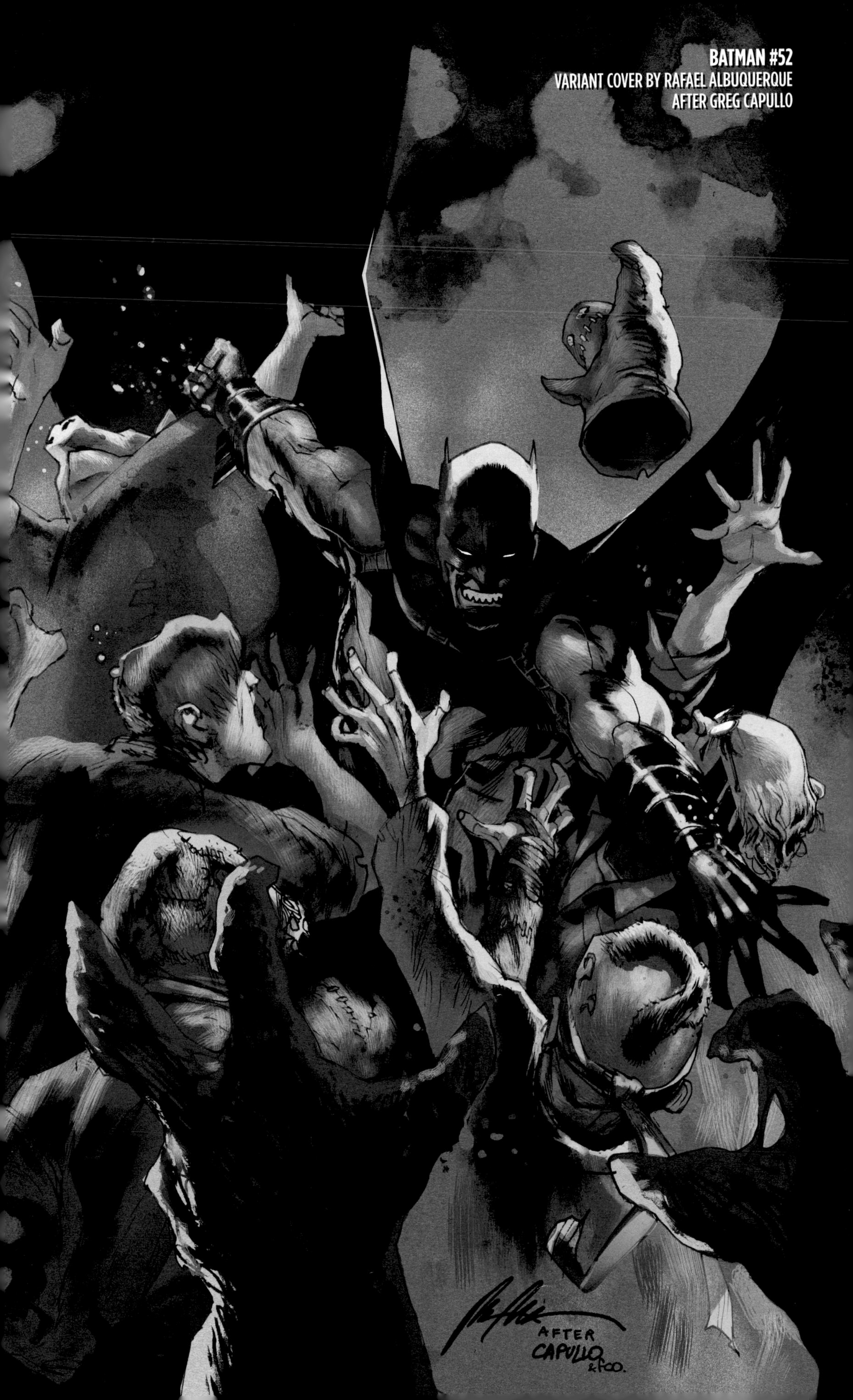
AFTER
CAPULLO
&FCO.

BATMAN #52
VARIANT COVER BY RAFAEL ALBUQUERQUE
AFTER GREG CAPULLO

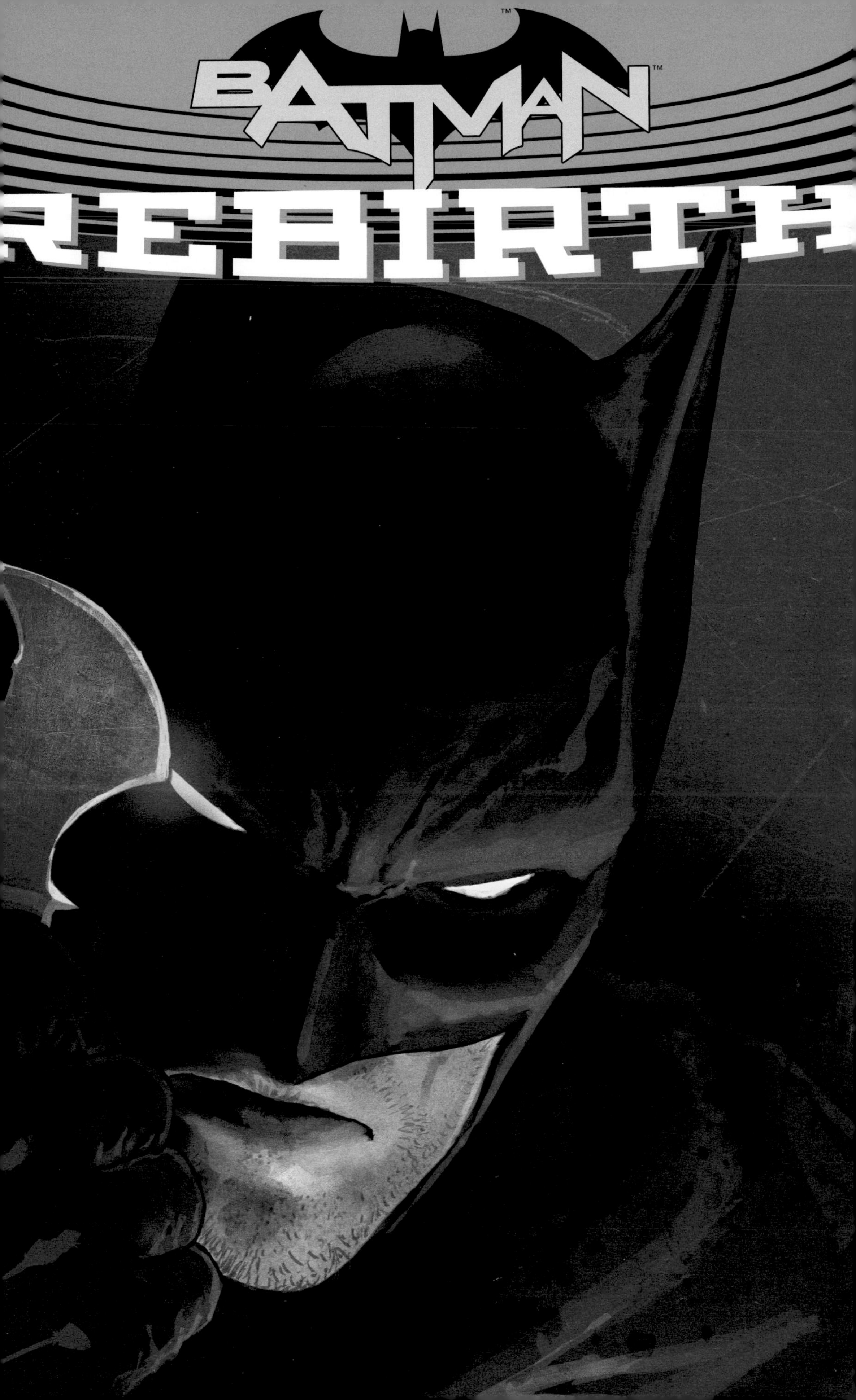
BATMAN

The future (and past) of the DC Universe starts with DC UNIVERSE: REBIRTH!

Explore the changing world of Batman in this special bonus preview of **BATMAN: REBIRTH #1.**

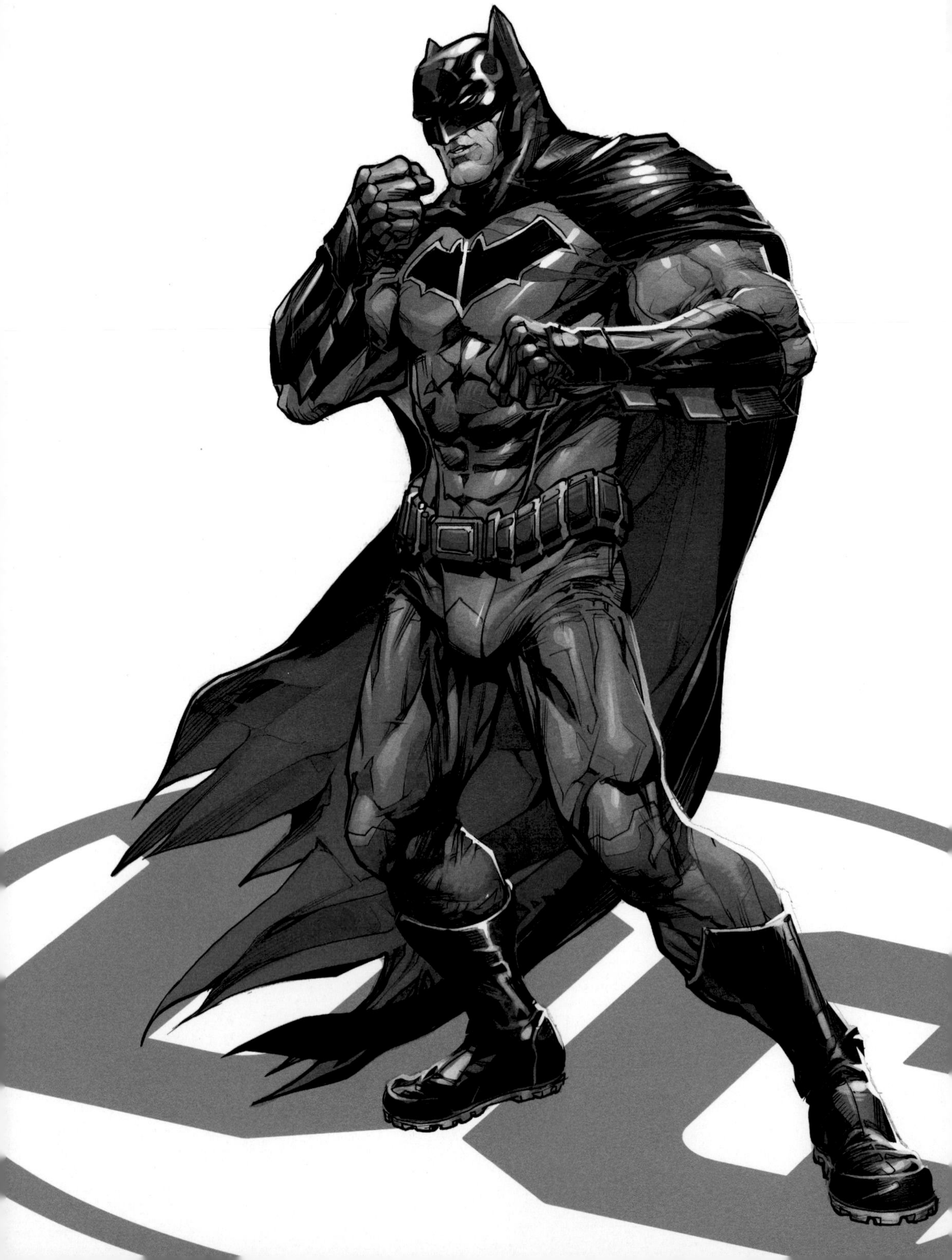

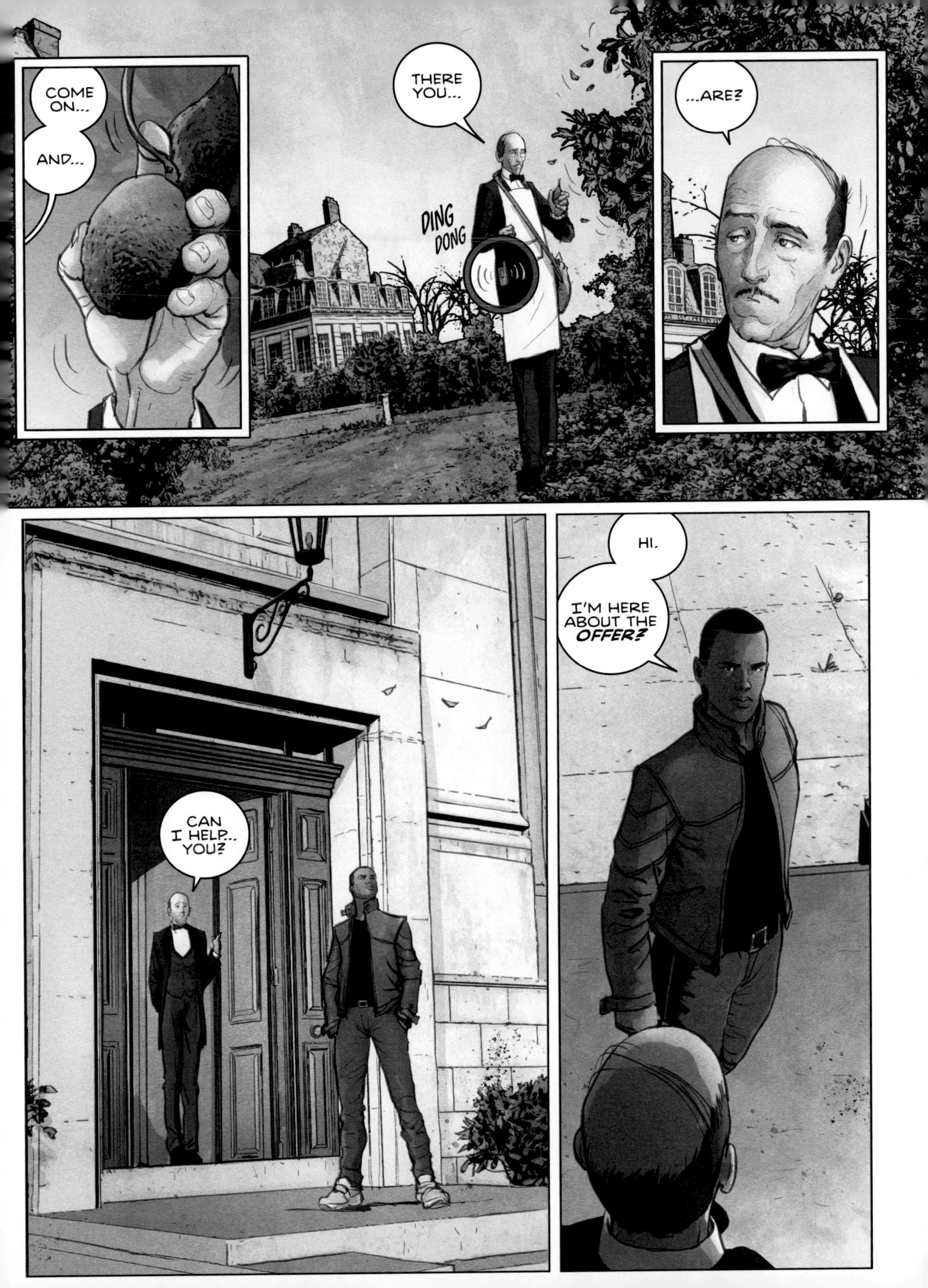
COME ON...
AND...
THERE YOU...
DING DONG
...ARE?
CAN I HELP... YOU?
HI.
I'M HERE ABOUT THE *OFFER?*

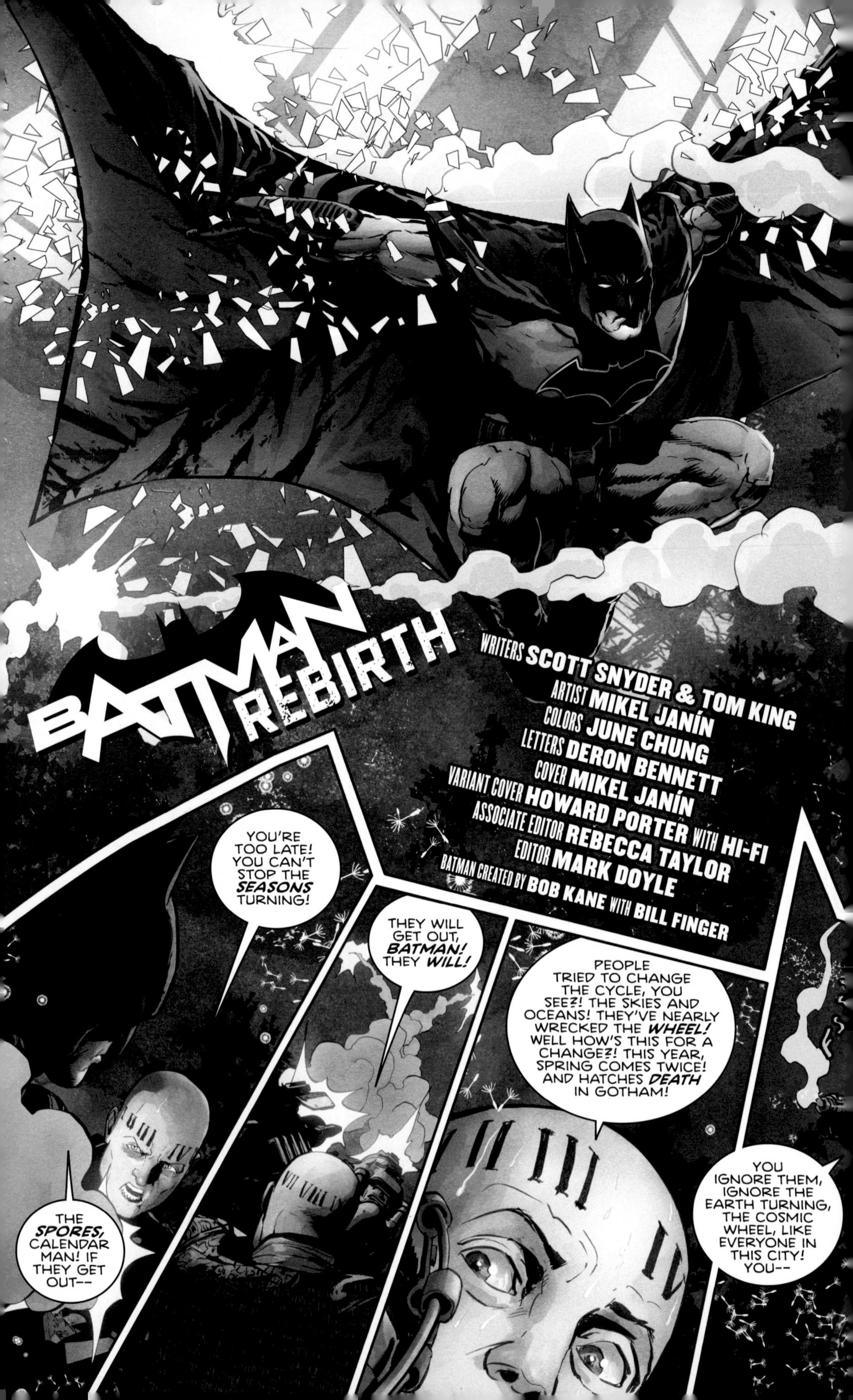
BATMAN REBIRTH
WRITERS SCOTT SNYDER & TOM KING
ARTIST MIKEL JANÍN
COLORS JUNE CHUNG
LETTERS DERON BENNETT
COVER MIKEL JANÍN
VARIANT COVER HOWARD PORTER WITH HI-FI
ASSOCIATE EDITOR REBECCA TAYLOR
EDITOR MARK DOYLE
BATMAN CREATED BY BOB KANE WITH BILL FINGER
YOU'RE TOO LATE! YOU CAN'T STOP THE SEASONS TURNING!
THE SPORES, CALENDAR MAN! IF THEY GET OUT--
THEY WILL GET OUT, BATMAN! THEY WILL!
PEOPLE TRIED TO CHANGE THE CYCLE, YOU SEE?! THE SKIES AND OCEANS! THEY'VE NEARLY WRECKED THE WHEEL! WELL HOW'S THIS FOR A CHANGE?! THIS YEAR, SPRING COMES TWICE! AND HATCHES DEATH IN GOTHAM!
YOU IGNORE THEM, IGNORE THE EARTH TURNING, THE COSMIC WHEEL, LIKE EVERYONE IN THIS CITY! YOU--

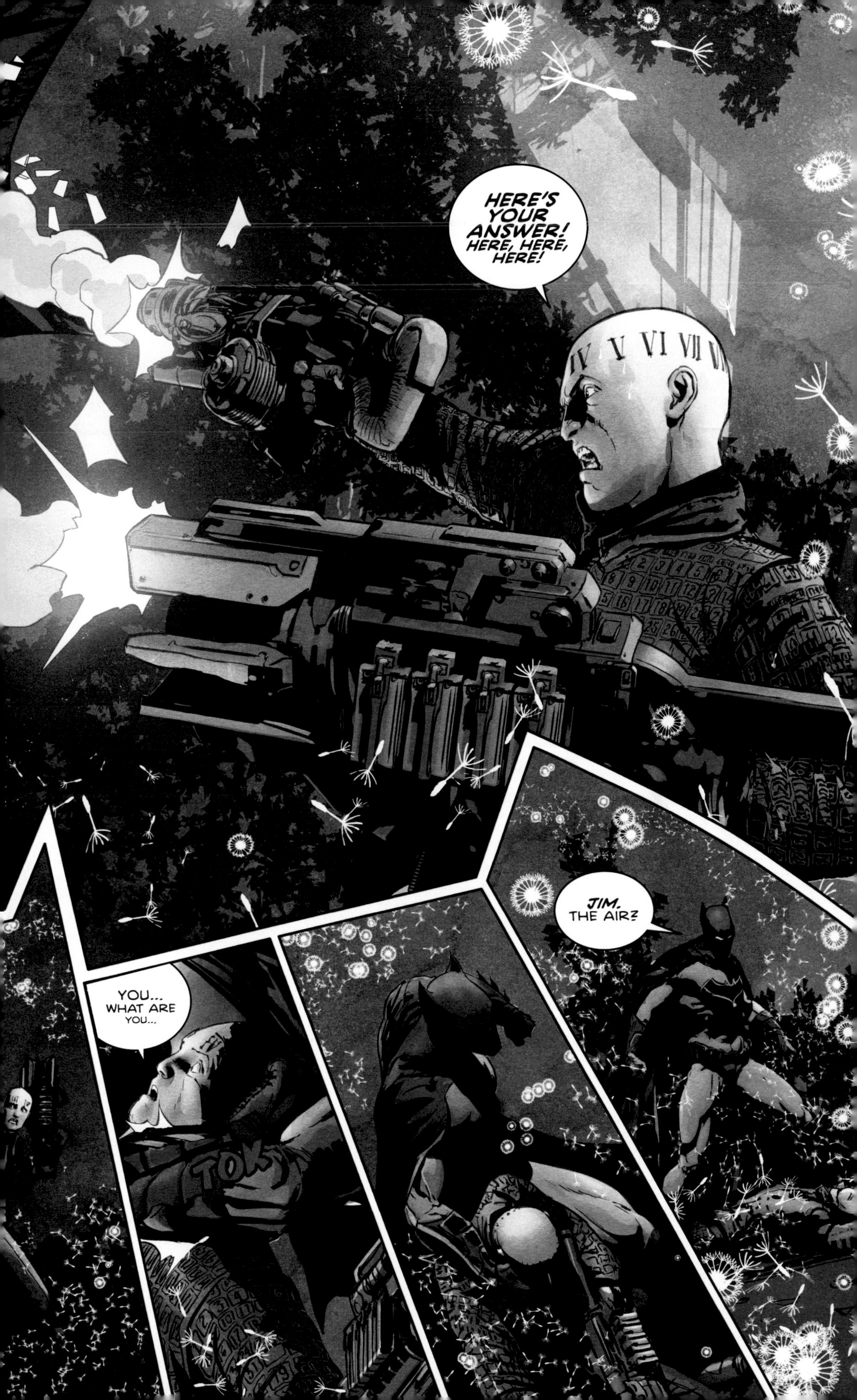
HERE'S YOUR ANSWER! HERE, HERE, HERE!
JIM. THE AIR?
YOU... WHAT ARE YOU...
TOK

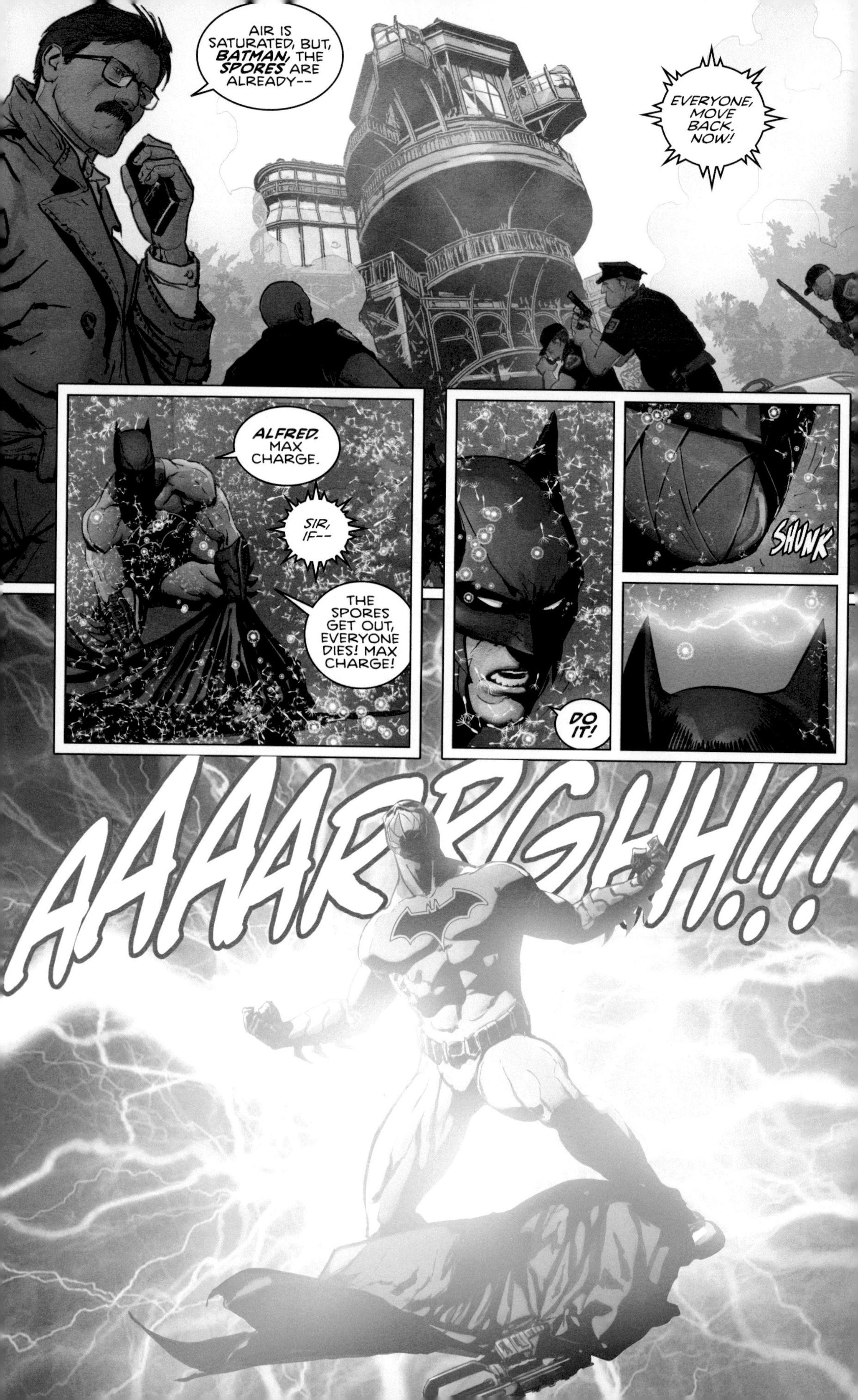
AIR IS SATURATED, BUT, BATMAN, THE SPORES ARE ALREADY--
EVERYONE, MOVE BACK. NOW!
ALFRED. MAX CHARGE.
SIR, IF--
THE SPORES GET OUT, EVERYONE DIES! MAX CHARGE!
DO IT!
SHUNK
AAAARRGHH!!!

TUESDAY. SUMMER.

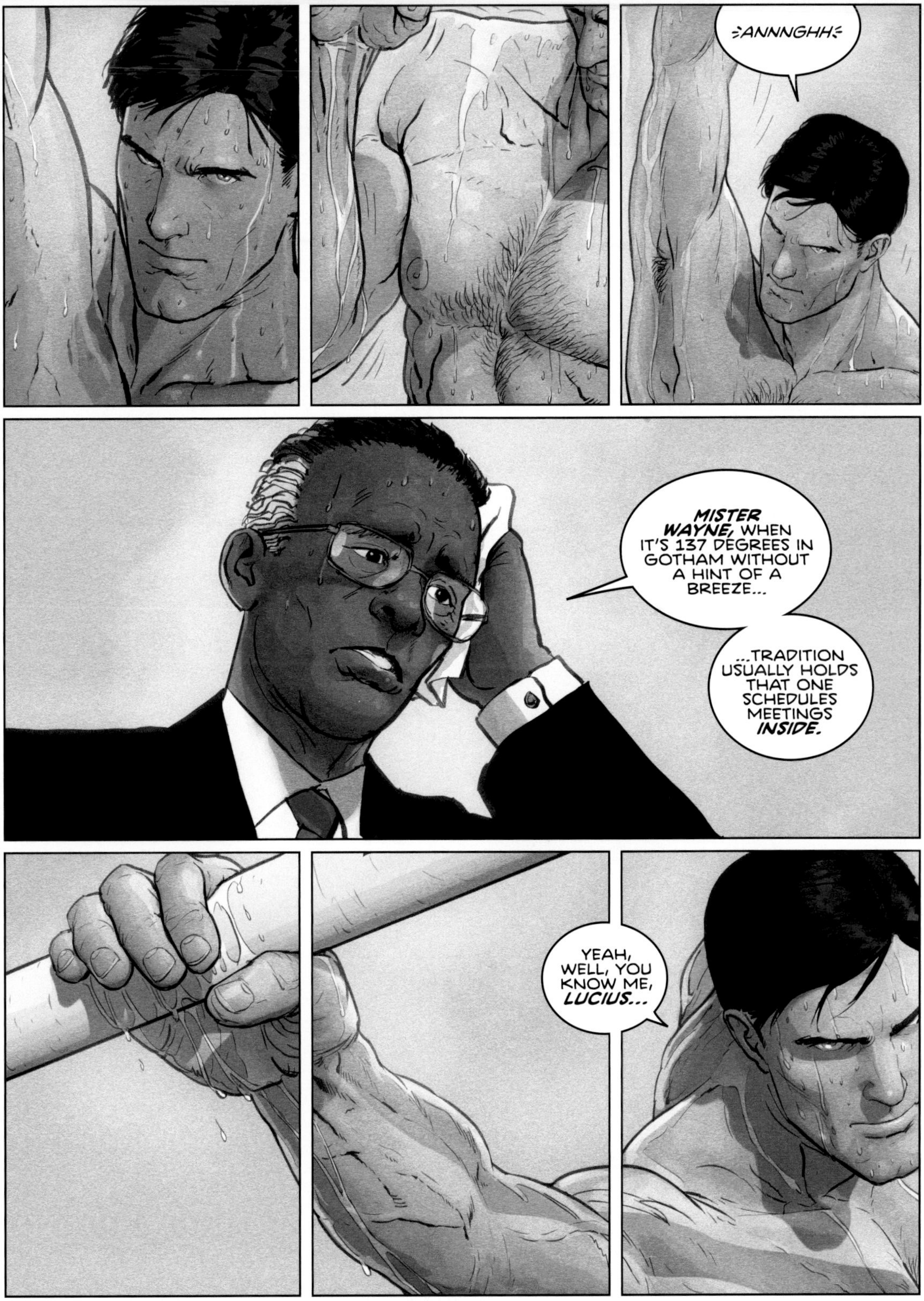

ANNNGHH
MISTER WAYNE, WHEN IT'S 137 DEGREES IN GOTHAM WITHOUT A HINT OF A BREEZE...
...TRADITION USUALLY HOLDS THAT ONE SCHEDULES MEETINGS INSIDE.
YEAH, WELL, YOU KNOW ME, LUCIUS...

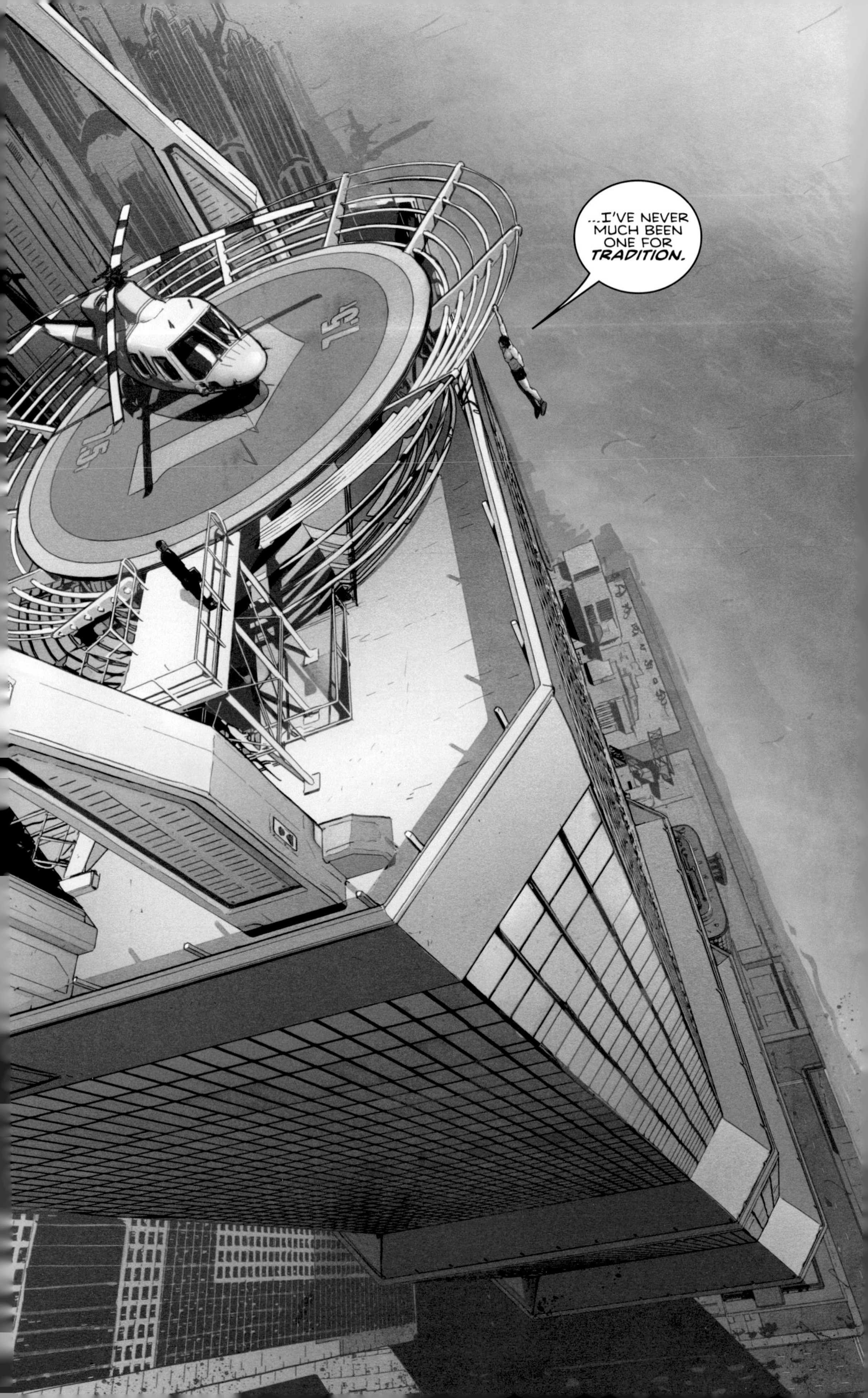
...I'VE NEVER MUCH BEEN ONE FOR *TRADITION.*

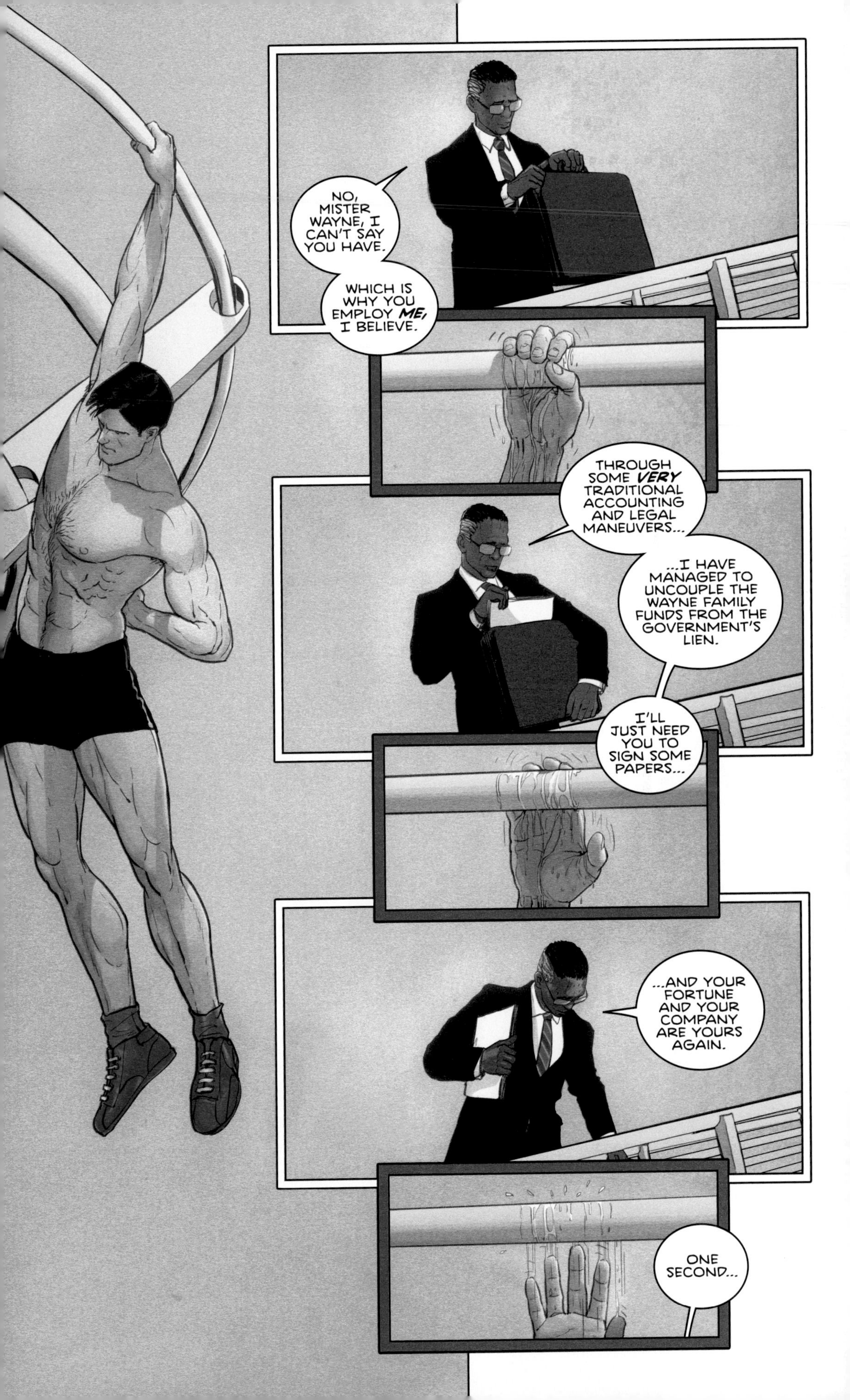
NO, MISTER WAYNE, I CAN'T SAY YOU HAVE.
WHICH IS WHY YOU EMPLOY *ME*, I BELIEVE.
THROUGH SOME *VERY* TRADITIONAL ACCOUNTING AND LEGAL MANEUVERS...
...I HAVE MANAGED TO UNCOUPLE THE WAYNE FAMILY FUNDS FROM THE GOVERNMENT'S LIEN.
I'LL JUST NEED YOU TO SIGN SOME PAPERS...
...AND YOUR FORTUNE AND YOUR COMPANY ARE YOURS AGAIN.
ONE SECOND...

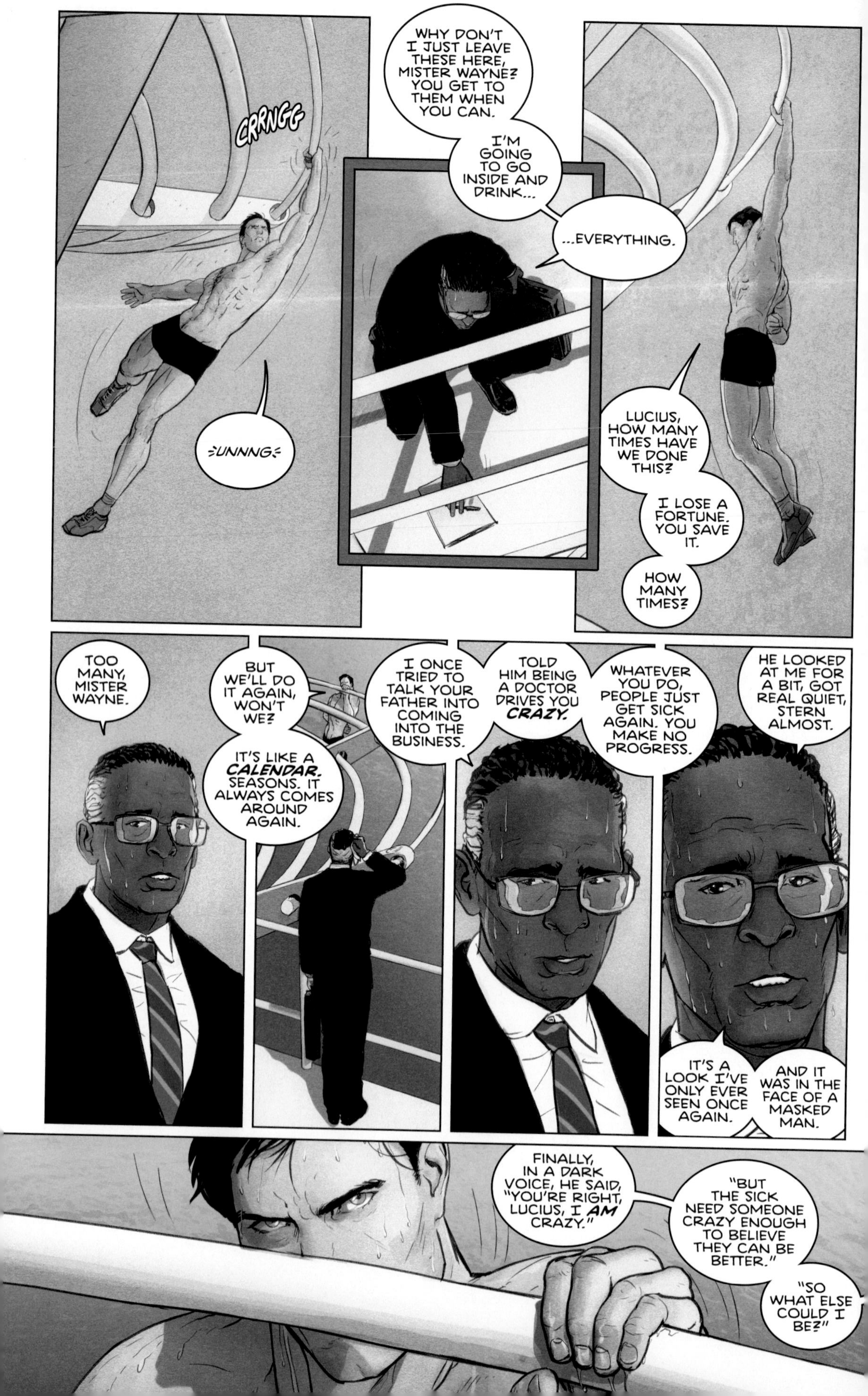
CRRNGG
UNNNG
WHY DON'T I JUST LEAVE THESE HERE, MISTER WAYNE? YOU GET TO THEM WHEN YOU CAN.
I'M GOING TO GO INSIDE AND DRINK...
...EVERYTHING.
LUCIUS, HOW MANY TIMES HAVE WE DONE THIS?
I LOSE A FORTUNE. YOU SAVE IT.
HOW MANY TIMES?
TOO MANY, MISTER WAYNE.
BUT WE'LL DO IT AGAIN, WON'T WE?
IT'S LIKE A CALENDAR. SEASONS. IT ALWAYS COMES AROUND AGAIN.
I ONCE TRIED TO TALK YOUR FATHER INTO COMING INTO THE BUSINESS.
TOLD HIM BEING A DOCTOR DRIVES YOU CRAZY.
WHATEVER YOU DO, PEOPLE JUST GET SICK AGAIN. YOU MAKE NO PROGRESS.
HE LOOKED AT ME FOR A BIT, GOT REAL QUIET, STERN ALMOST.
IT'S A LOOK I'VE ONLY EVER SEEN ONCE AGAIN.
AND IT WAS IN THE FACE OF A MASKED MAN.
FINALLY, IN A DARK VOICE, HE SAID, "YOU'RE RIGHT, LUCIUS, I AM CRAZY."
"BUT THE SICK NEED SOMEONE CRAZY ENOUGH TO BELIEVE THEY CAN BE BETTER."
"SO WHAT ELSE COULD I BE?"

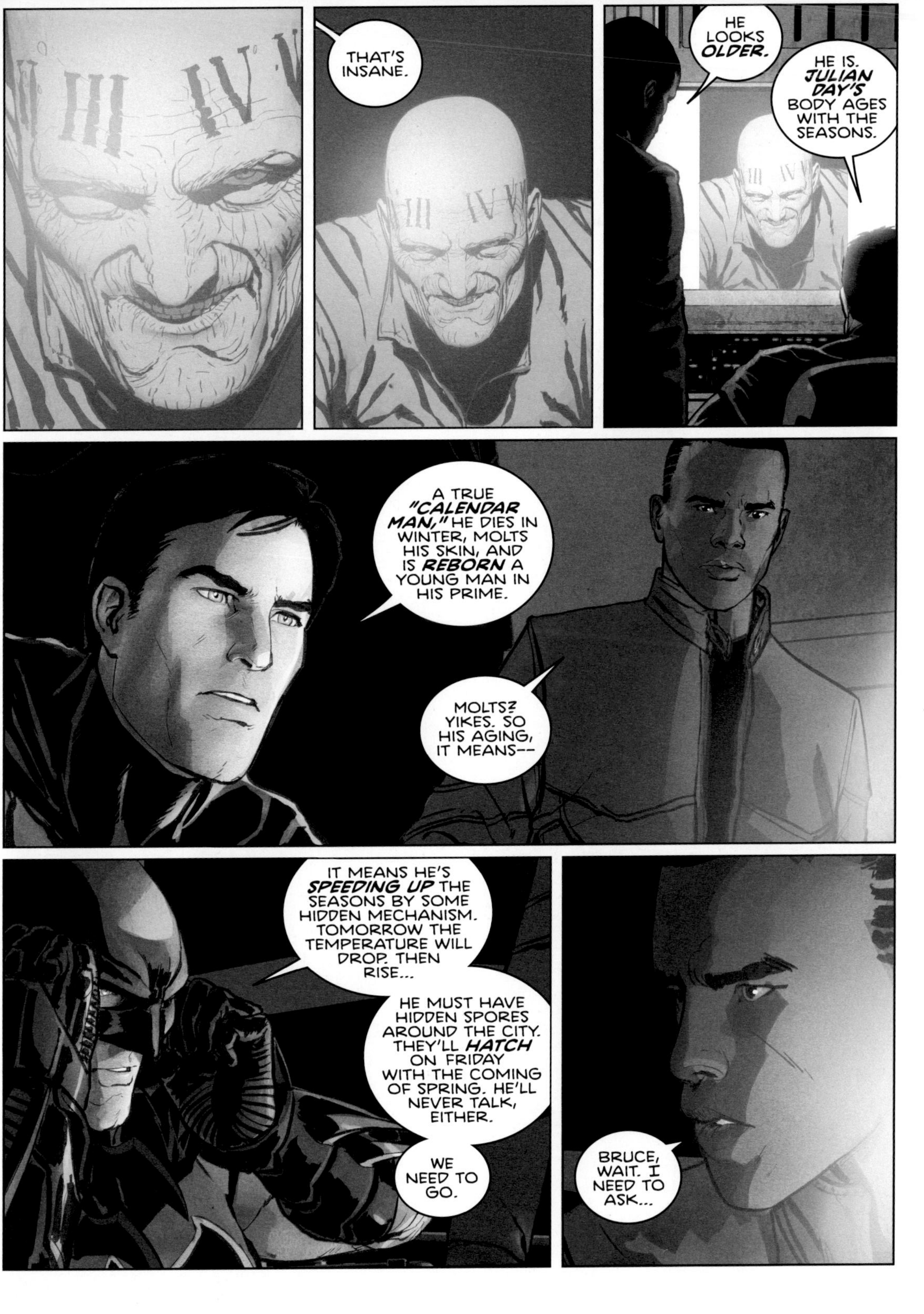
THAT'S INSANE.
HE LOOKS OLDER.
HE IS. JULIAN DAY'S BODY AGES WITH THE SEASONS.
A TRUE "CALENDAR MAN," HE DIES IN WINTER, MOLTS HIS SKIN, AND IS REBORN A YOUNG MAN IN HIS PRIME.
MOLTS? YIKES. SO HIS AGING, IT MEANS--
IT MEANS HE'S SPEEDING UP THE SEASONS BY SOME HIDDEN MECHANISM. TOMORROW THE TEMPERATURE WILL DROP. THEN RISE...
HE MUST HAVE HIDDEN SPORES AROUND THE CITY. THEY'LL HATCH ON FRIDAY WITH THE COMING OF SPRING. HE'LL NEVER TALK, EITHER.
WE NEED TO GO.
BRUCE, WAIT. I NEED TO ASK...

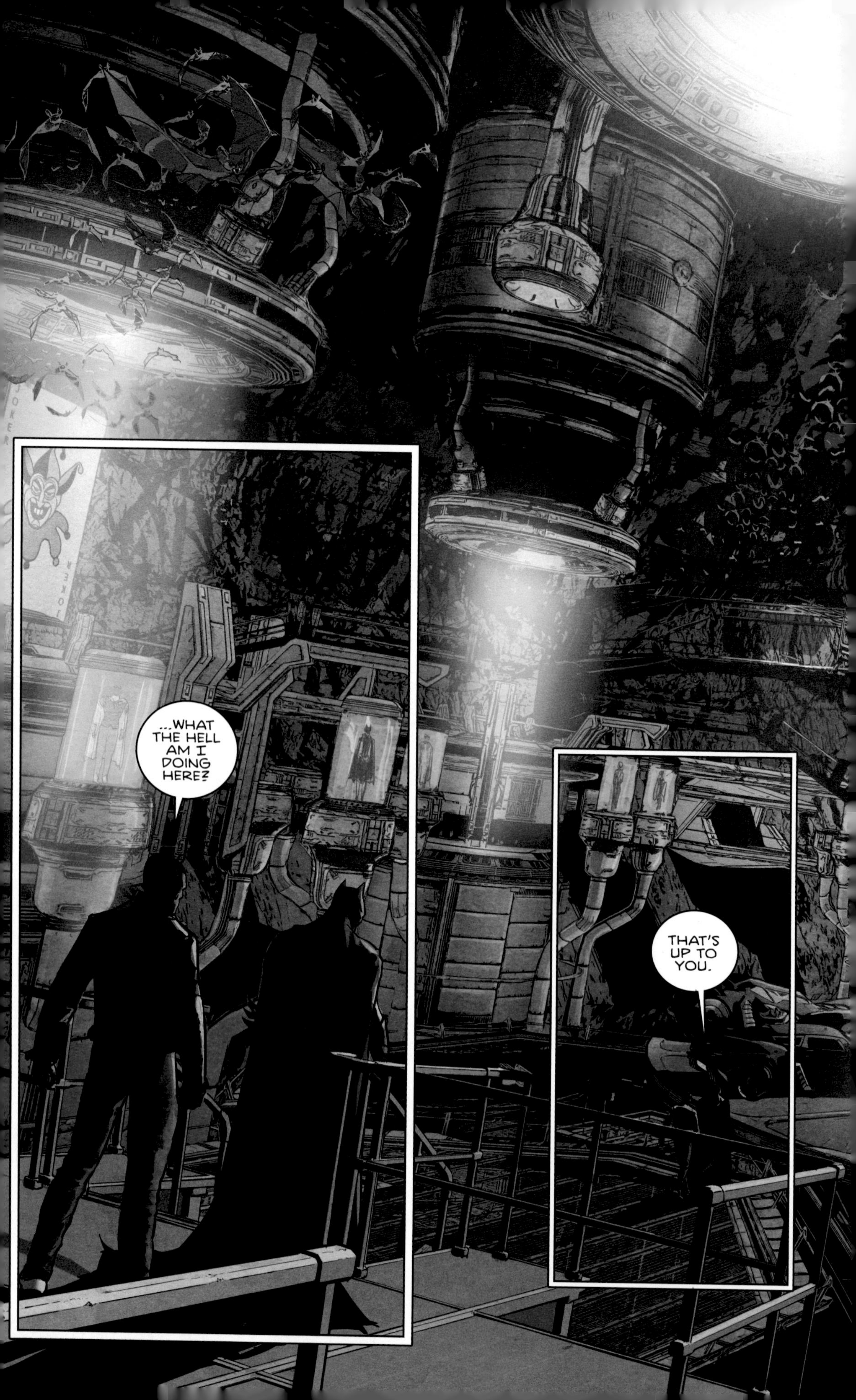
JOKER
...WHAT THE HELL AM I DOING HERE?
THAT'S UP TO YOU.

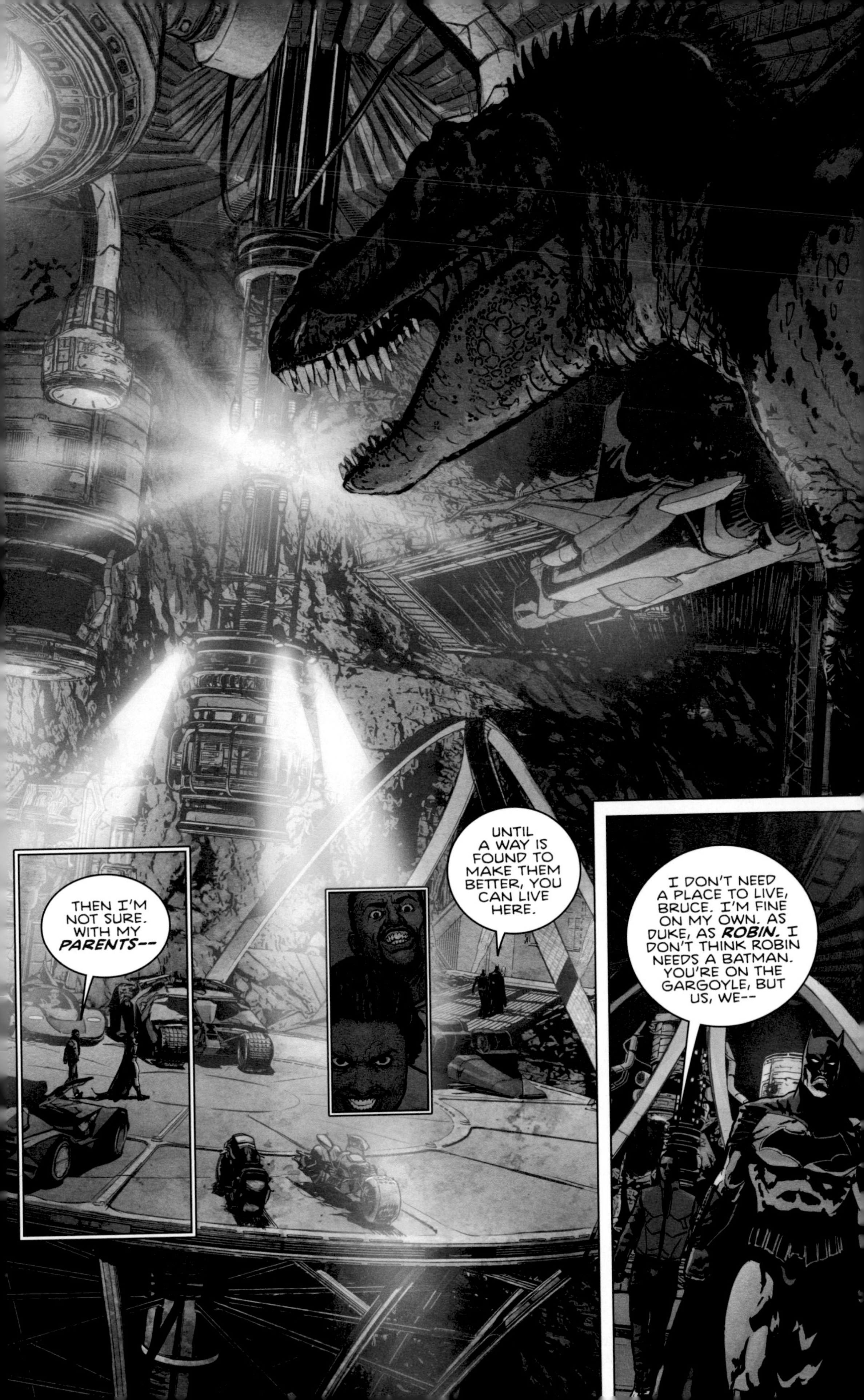
THEN I'M NOT SURE. WITH MY *PARENTS--*
UNTIL A WAY IS FOUND TO MAKE THEM BETTER, YOU CAN LIVE HERE.
I DON'T NEED A PLACE TO LIVE, BRUCE. I'M FINE ON MY OWN. AS DUKE, AS *ROBIN.* I DON'T THINK ROBIN NEEDS A BATMAN. YOU'RE ON THE GARGOYLE, BUT US, WE--

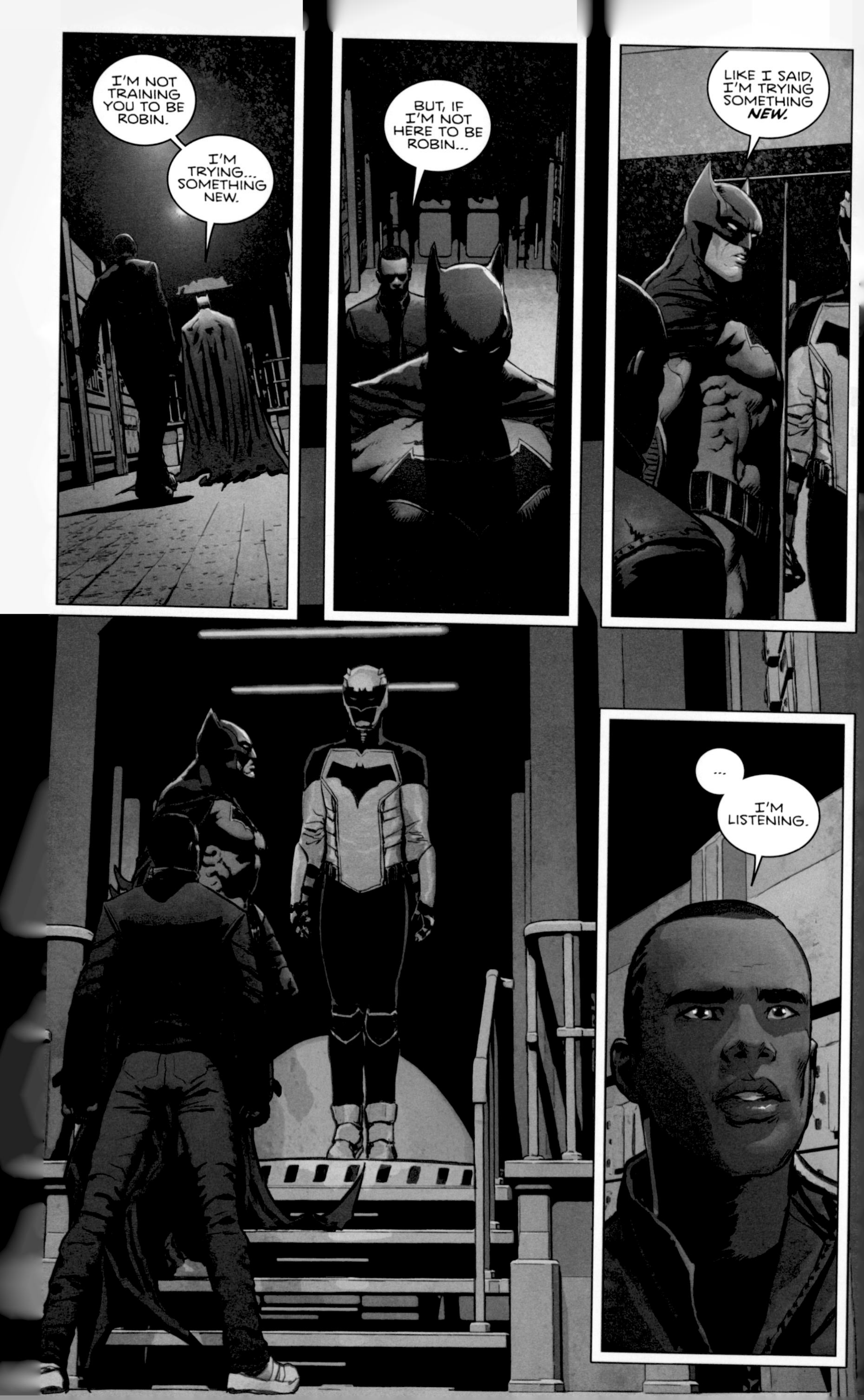

I'M NOT TRAINING YOU TO BE ROBIN.
I'M TRYING... SOMETHING NEW.
BUT, IF I'M NOT HERE TO BE ROBIN...
LIKE I SAID, I'M TRYING SOMETHING NEW.
...
I'M LISTENING.

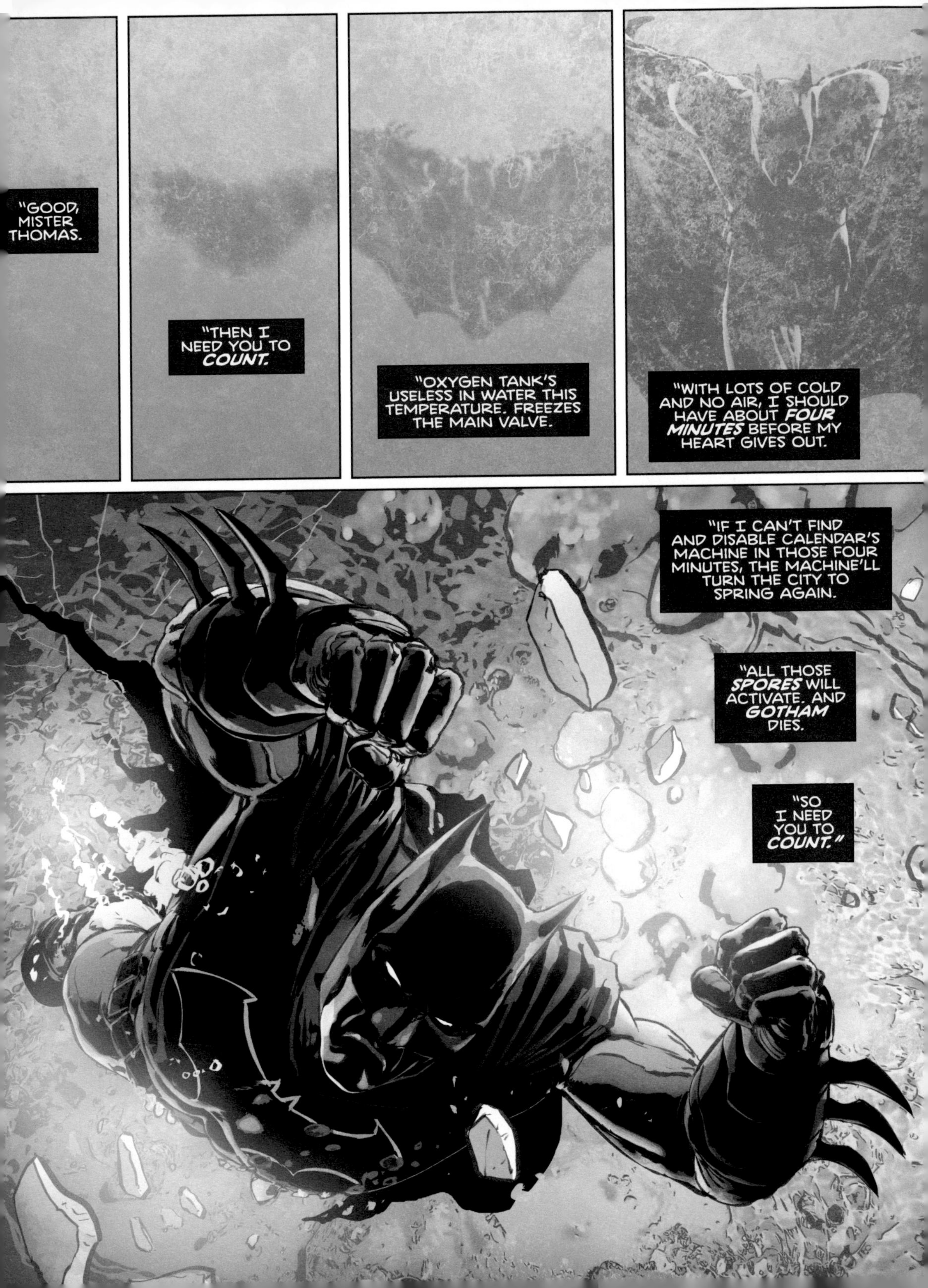
"GOOD, MISTER THOMAS.
"THEN I NEED YOU TO COUNT.
"OXYGEN TANK'S USELESS IN WATER THIS TEMPERATURE. FREEZES THE MAIN VALVE.
"WITH LOTS OF COLD AND NO AIR, I SHOULD HAVE ABOUT FOUR MINUTES BEFORE MY HEART GIVES OUT.
"IF I CAN'T FIND AND DISABLE CALENDAR'S MACHINE IN THOSE FOUR MINUTES, THE MACHINE'LL TURN THE CITY TO SPRING AGAIN.
"ALL THOSE SPORES WILL ACTIVATE. AND GOTHAM DIES.
"SO I NEED YOU TO COUNT."

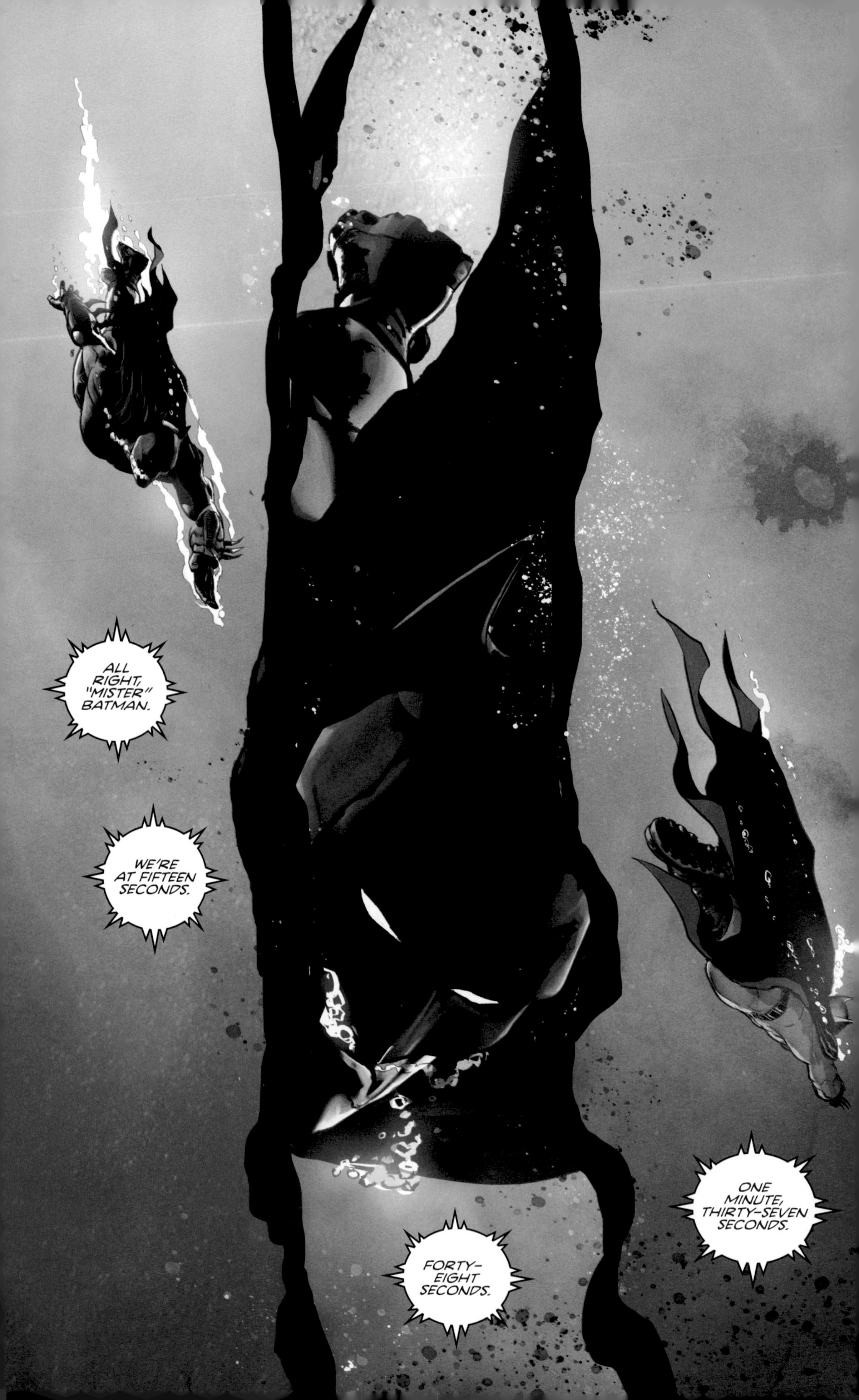
ALL RIGHT, "MISTER" BATMAN.
WE'RE AT FIFTEEN SECONDS.
FORTY-EIGHT SECONDS.
ONE MINUTE, THIRTY-SEVEN SECONDS.

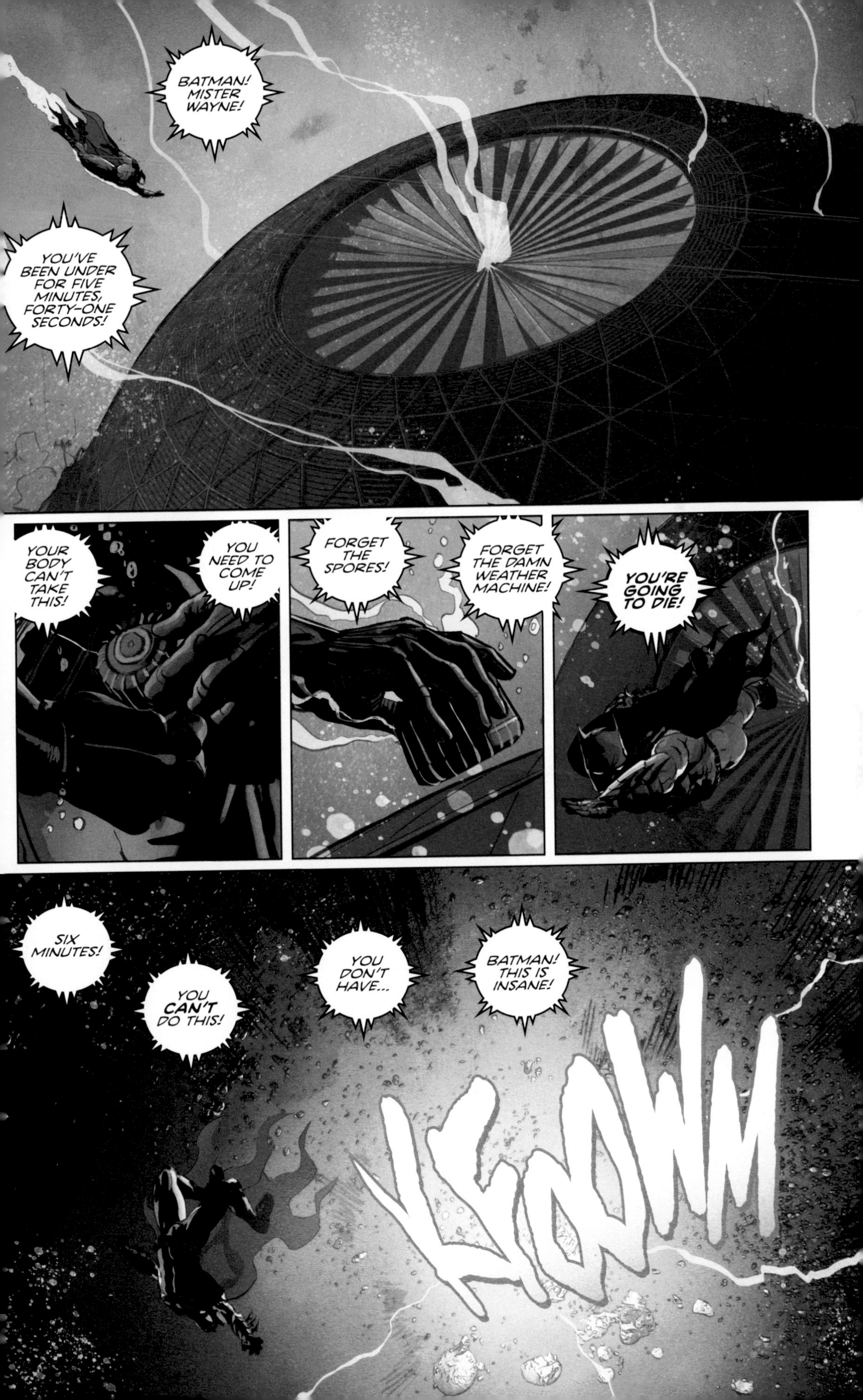
BATMAN! MISTER WAYNE!
YOU'VE BEEN UNDER FOR FIVE MINUTES, FORTY-ONE SECONDS!
YOUR BODY CAN'T TAKE THIS!
YOU NEED TO COME UP!
FORGET THE SPORES!
FORGET THE DAMN WEATHER MACHINE!
YOU'RE GOING TO DIE!
SIX MINUTES!
YOU CAN'T DO THIS!
YOU DON'T HAVE...
BATMAN! THIS IS INSANE!
KGOWM

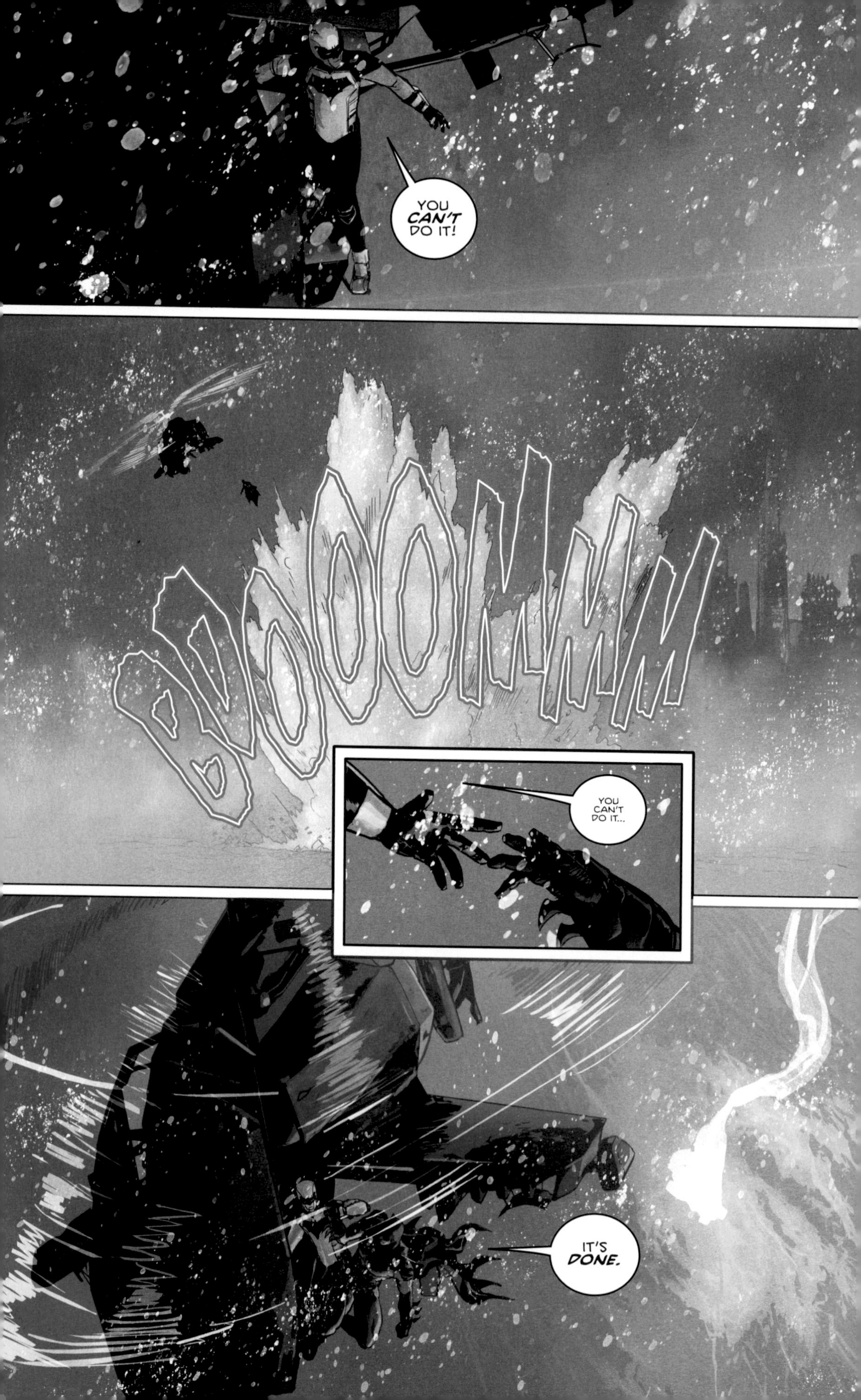
YOU CAN'T DO IT!
BOOOOMMM
YOU CAN'T DO IT...
IT'S DONE.

FRIDAY. SPRING.

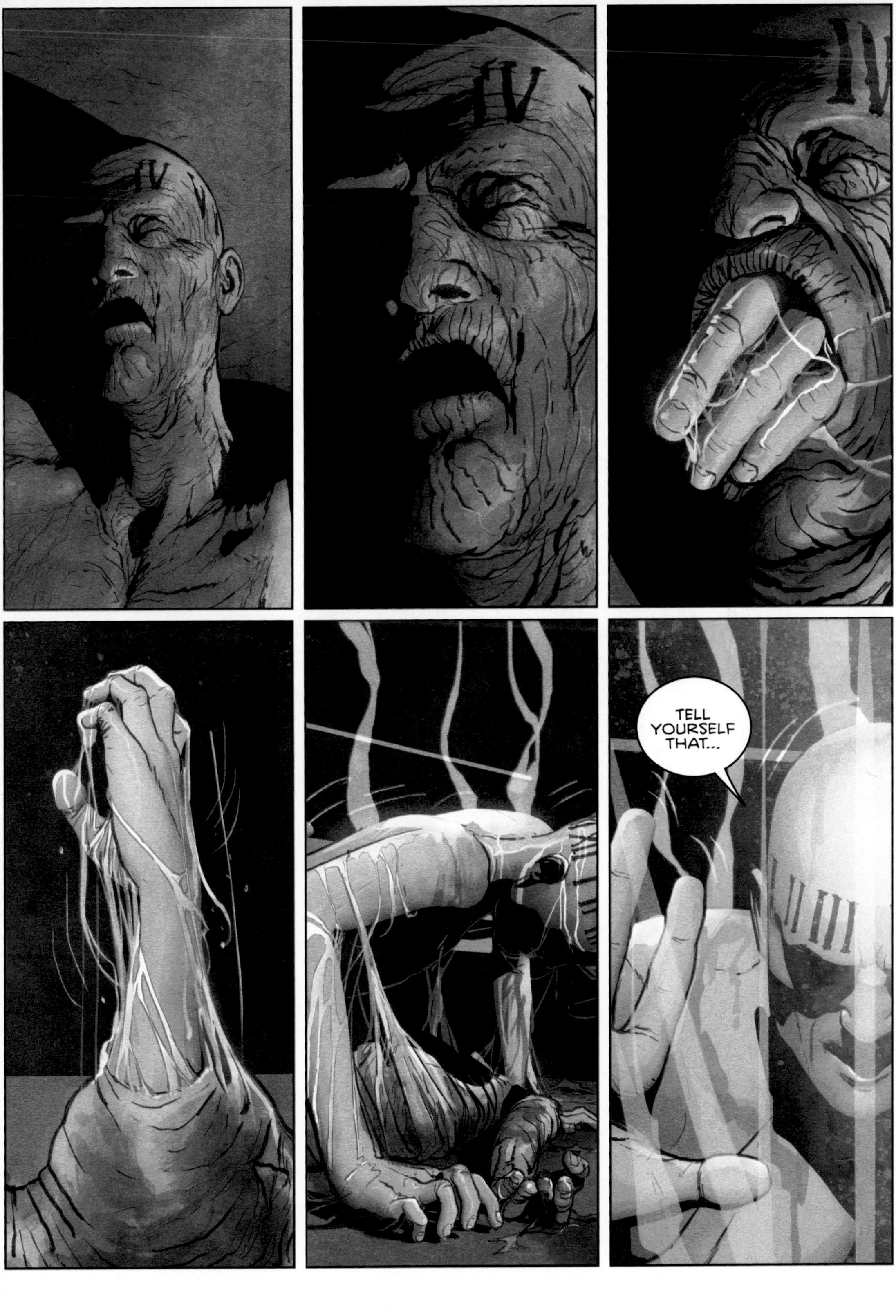

IV
IV
IV
TELL YOURSELF THAT...

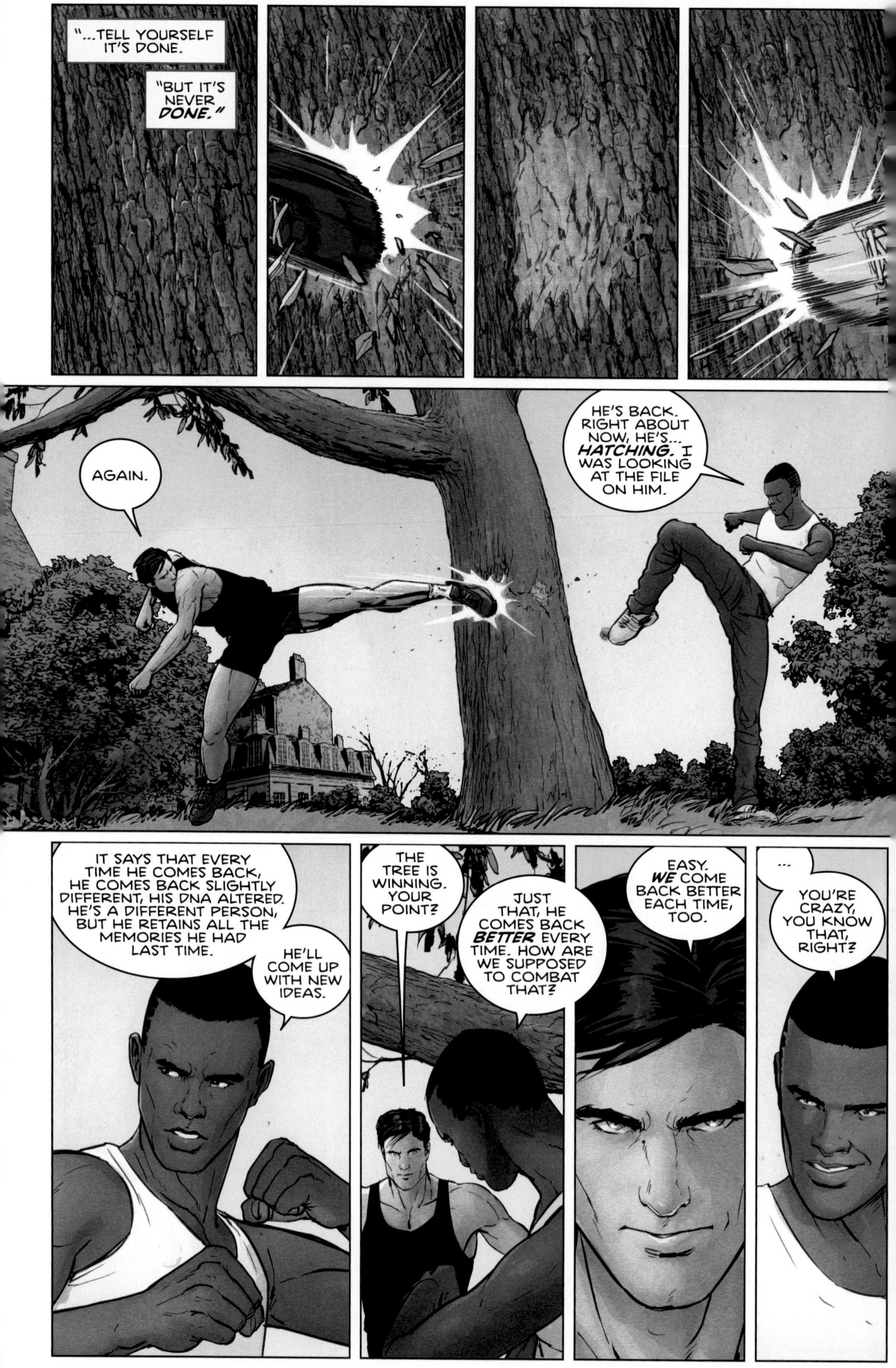
"...TELL YOURSELF IT'S DONE.
"BUT IT'S NEVER DONE."
AGAIN.
HE'S BACK. RIGHT ABOUT NOW, HE'S... HATCHING. I WAS LOOKING AT THE FILE ON HIM.
IT SAYS THAT EVERY TIME HE COMES BACK, HE COMES BACK SLIGHTLY DIFFERENT, HIS DNA ALTERED. HE'S A DIFFERENT PERSON, BUT HE RETAINS ALL THE MEMORIES HE HAD LAST TIME.
HE'LL COME UP WITH NEW IDEAS.
THE TREE IS WINNING. YOUR POINT?
JUST THAT, HE COMES BACK BETTER EVERY TIME. HOW ARE WE SUPPOSED TO COMBAT THAT?
EASY. WE COME BACK BETTER EACH TIME, TOO.
...
YOU'RE CRAZY, YOU KNOW THAT, RIGHT?

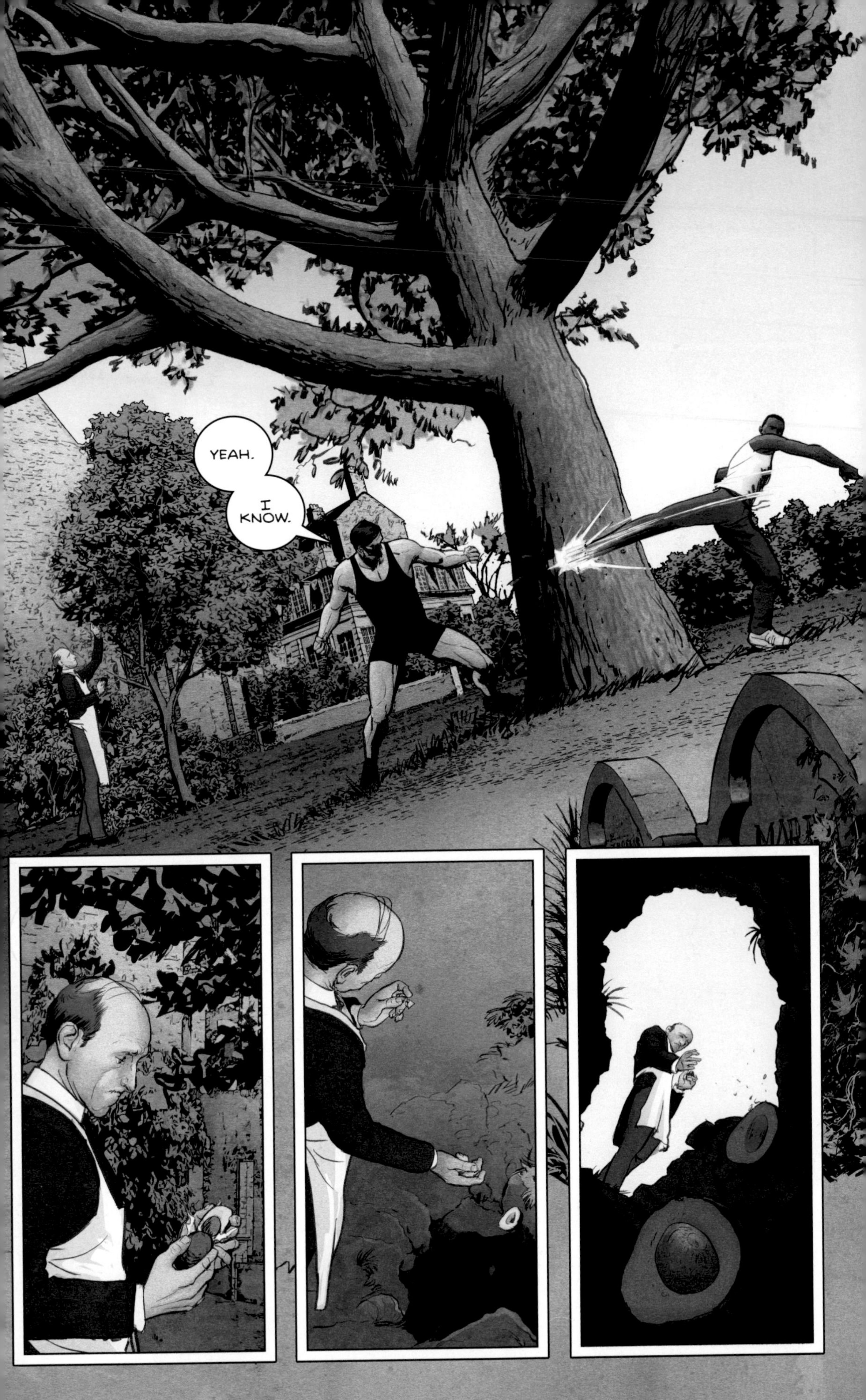
YEAH.
I KNOW.

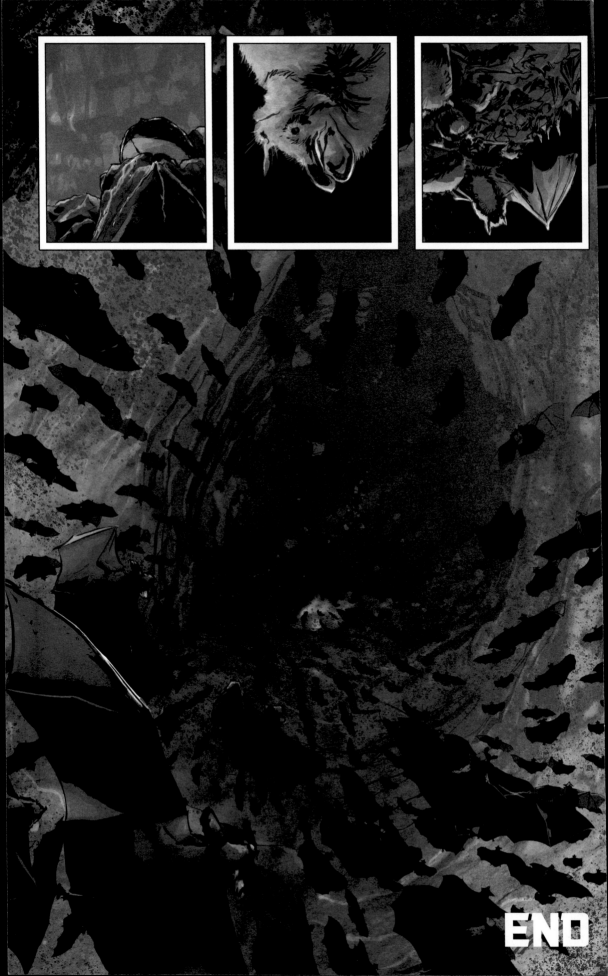

END

START AT THE BEGINNING!

BATMAN VOLUME 1: THE COURT OF OWLS

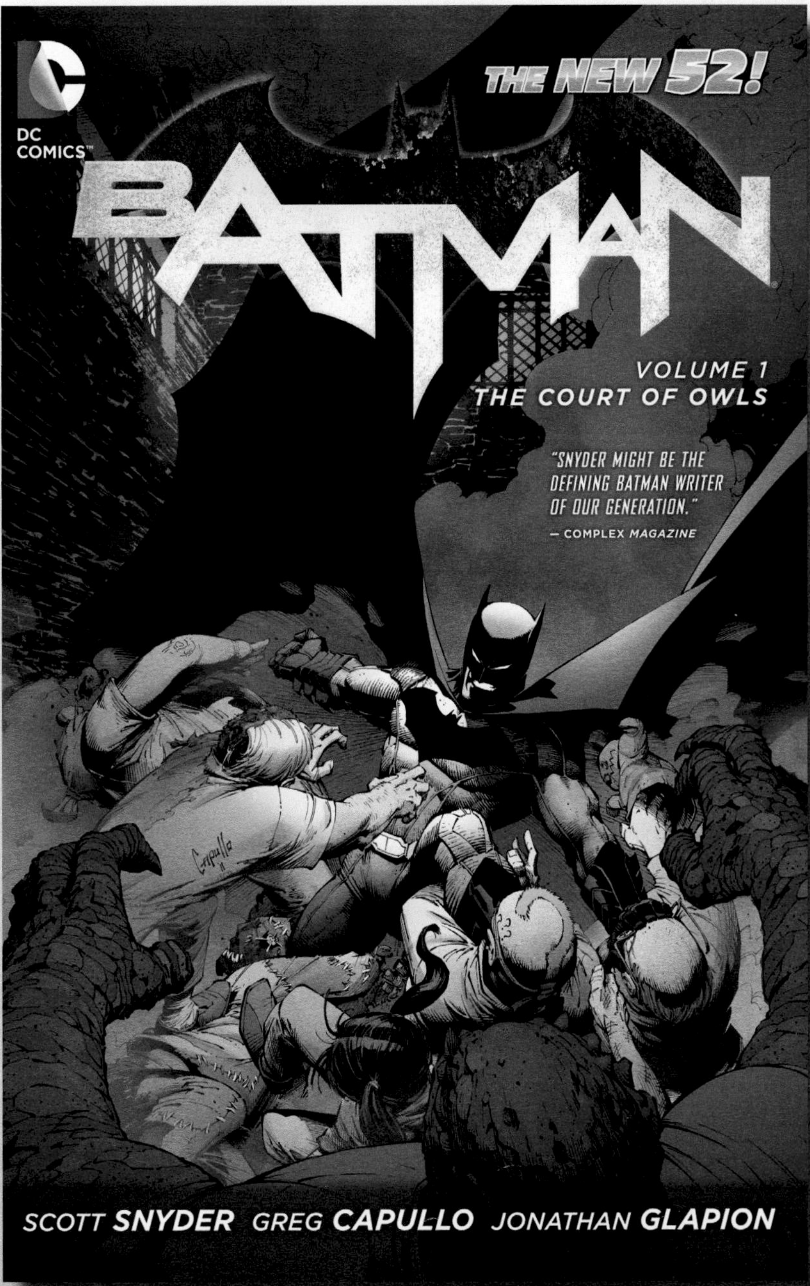

BATMAN & ROBIN VOLUME 1: BORN TO KILL

PETER J. **TOMASI** PATRICK **GLEASON** MICK **GRAY**

BATMAN: DETECTIVE COMICS VOLUME 1: FACES OF DEATH

TONY S. **DANIEL**

BATMAN: THE DARK KNIGHT VOLUME 1: KNIGHT TERRORS

DAVID **FINCH** PAUL **JENKINS** RICHARD **FRIEND**

THE NEW 52!

DC COMICS™

BATMAN

VOLUME 1
THE COURT OF OWLS

"SNYDER MIGHT BE THE DEFINING BATMAN WRITER OF OUR GENERATION."
— COMPLEX MAGAZINE

SCOTT **SNYDER** GREG **CAPULLO** JONATHAN **GLAPION**